misfit

misfit

Growing Up Awkward in the '80s

Gary Gulman

FLATIRON
BOOKS
NEW YORK

AUTHOR'S NOTE: I have done my best to tell these stories as close to how I remember them as possible. I have changed many names and some identifying details, whether or not so noted in the text. All phone numbers have been changed by one digit.

www.flatironbooks.com

Designed by Steven Seighman

The Library of Congress Cataloging-in-Publication Data is available upon request.

ISBN 978-1-250-77706-5 (hardcover)
ISBN 978-1-250-77707-2 (ebook)

Our books may be purchased in bulk for promotional, educational, or business use. Please contact your local bookseller or the Macmillan Corporate and Premium Sales Department at 1-800-221-7945, extension 5442, or by email at MacmillanSpecialMarkets@macmillan.com.

First Edition: 2023

10 9 8 7 6 5 4 3 2 1

For Joan "Joans" Noyes and Sadé

All our lives we rework the things from our childhood, like feeling good about ourselves, managing our angry feelings, being able to say goodbye to people we love.

—Fred Rogers

Contents

misfit

Introduction to the Introduction

Some people skip the intro. I don't trust them. It makes me wonder where else they cut corners, where else they're phoning it in, what other flimflammery they're perpetrating. If you didn't read the intro, you didn't honestly finish the book. Saying you read a book but didn't read the intro is like saying you shoveled my driveway, but you left two feet of snow on the walkway. Or saying you took me out to dinner but let me leave the tip. I've been reading intros, forewords, and preambles since before I knew how to pronounce *preface*. You should *always* read the intro. "But what if I get four paragraphs in and the book seems like a downer?" Friend, you are reading this because either:

A. You're familiar with my stand-up work.

If so, I believe I've generated some goodwill with you, and I promise not to squander it. Over the length of this book, I will entertain you in the way that you have grown accustomed. But first I need to take a couple of pages to let you know how bad things were when I started examining the events I recount herein.

Or,

B. You bought it based on the celebrity endorsements.
   a. Shame on you.
   b. You'll have to trust the fact that the people on the back
     cover wouldn't blurb some slapdash cash grab from a
     virtual unknown.

Now, at the very least you have an idea of the tone of this tome and are impressed by how deftly I deployed the Modern Language Association outlining format that I've retained since ninth-grade English, Mr. Crean. So, I'm going to return behind the fourth wall because this jaunty device, if not used judiciously, can come off cloying.

Introduction

On a white-gray Thursday in March 2017, I was on my way to a 1:00 P.M. appointment with my psychiatrist. I was running late, the only running I could manage anymore. I was sick with worry and contempt for myself. Maybe he had another appointment, a more important one, right after me. Maybe I wouldn't get to see him at all. I didn't think I could survive a postponement. These meetings were the only thing I looked forward to, the only time I felt safe, during weeks of relentless misery. You lazy, pathetic, worthless zombie. It's not like 1:00 P.M. is early. People are halfway done with work. High school kids have one class left. If it were the day before Thanksgiving, first graders would be home by now.

I was forty-six and living in midtown Manhattan with my girlfriend, now wife, Sadé. (Not that Sadé.) We'd been together for two and a half years. The first six months were perfect. Bliss. For the past two years, a sinister third wheel had joined: crippling depression and anxiety. That week, I had been to the emergency room twice within three days because I needed to be separated from spaces that contained anything I could use to harm myself. I felt guilty over how exhausting it was to care about and for me and regularly begged her to leave me. Maybe because I had been so damned delightful for our first 180 days, she had refused. More likely, and this was impossible to believe at the time, she loved me.

My anxiety was relentless. When I was awake, I was in agony, most intensely the moment after I woke and *Oh yeah, my life is in shambles, I'm running out of money, and I hate myself* flooded back into my consciousness. Then I'd walk our two Cavalier King Charles spaniels up Fifty-Sixth Street, to Lexington Avenue, right onto Fifty-Seventh Street, to Second Avenue, and then back to my apartment. A walk around the block; yet my feebleness dragged it out to twenty minutes. I shuffled about, grinding my teeth, chewing my bottom lip bloody, thinking about all the things I needed to do today but would procrastinate, then beat myself up for putting off. Just a couple of years before, I ran thirty miles a week. Now a two-tenths of a mile *crawl* drained me. I'd feed the pups, eat a giant bowl of Ezekiel golden flax cereal covered in maple syrup and almond milk, then go back to sleep until the dogs wanted another walk. When I wasn't asleep, I was catatonic while my brain attacked every weak point in itself, attempting to criticize me into submission.

I was finding it nearly impossible to do stand-up comedy, the only job I'd held since December 24, 1998. A job I'd started dreaming of and practicing in my bedroom in kindergarten. My brain insisted I was inept at it and getting worse. I had saved up enough money to not work for a year while I found a different job, an easier job. Easier than a job I could wear jeans and a Super Grover T-shirt to, make my own schedule, and took up only an hour of my day.

My lease was ending, and I didn't have the energy to hunt for a new apartment. I didn't have the energy to shower standing up. Never mind that my new place would have to be far cheaper and allow two dogs. Never mind that I heard that moving is nearly as stressful as the death of a family member and I prayed all my waking hours that I was that family member.

When I tried to think of reasons to continue, the best I could come up with was my desire to see how season three of AMC's *Better Call Saul,* the ingenious prequel to the ingenious *Breaking Bad,* would end. But even that masterpiece didn't always provide sufficient motivation for me to keep producing my own mordant drama.

Late one night I had pulled a plastic bag from the box a toaster came in over my head in an impulsive attempt at a painless exit. But it occurred to me, as my head emerged from the top, that this was not a plastic bag but a plastic *sleeve.* Funny.

Later that same week, in a furnished apartment on a rare trip out of town to perform in Denver, I removed the carving knife from the kitchen's wooden knife block and held it against my wrists. Then I pictured the person who'd have to clean up on Monday and gave myself an excuse to refrain from ending things that way. I wanted to stop feeling like this, even if I had to die.

Throughout this Bedlam, monthly visits to my psychiatrist, Dr. Richard Friedman, were half-hour capsules of hope. He never gave up, never ran out of ideas, treatments, or offers to admit me into the hospital.

There isn't a subway that goes directly to his office at Sixty-eighth and First-ish, and I didn't have the brain function to figure out the bus combination that would get us there on time. What about Uber? I had resisted Uber for years. I didn't feel safe riding with regulated, licensed, experienced New York cabdrivers. I'm just going to get in the back of a stranger's black Camry? Not yet.

A cab? Out of the question. I was not going to be able to work anymore. Until I found a new job, paying twenty dollars for a ride to a building I could walk to in twenty-six minutes seemed reckless. But we were running late. Depressives, as well as the angels committed to dragging them through life, are late for everything. Just to leave the house we need to overcome standard inertia compounded by the weight of a boulder of resistance in our minds.

Sadé had furthered our delay with a last-minute shoe

change. She decided to put on a sturdier shoe, Doc Martens boots, calf-high, in magenta. I loved that my partner wore combat boots. Made me feel vicariously punk or emo. I'd been too timid to join in the august grunge era, so her bold Docs felt like consolation. This was going to make us even later. Unless . . .

We slid into a cab going across town at East Fifty-Seventh and Second. I never took my eyes off the meter as it soared, eating into my financial parachute at a sickening speed. It was already up to eleven dollars when we cut over around Sixty-Fourth Street and Third. Then the driver stopped short. Gridlock. The meter slowed as the dashboard clock raced.

We had fifteen minutes to get there. We weren't moving. *And* we would still have to wait for the fickle elevator to the eleventh floor. Sometimes there's a gurney or two squeezing the capacity further. Stairs? Eleven floors, dragging my boulder the whole way. Not today.

I started crying. Not gently rolling tears. I was heaving with sorrow. I felt guilty about crying in front of Sadé but more so the cabdriver. If anyone should be crying, it's him. Here I am sobbing and I'm not even working a day job—never mind one that requires navigating the worst traffic on the planet in a seat with such flimsy lumbar support. Hopefully, because of our destination, he thought I was dying. I *was* dying, just not in the way I hoped he thought I was.

We had ten minutes to get there. The Google map said we'd need fifteen minutes to walk. And then the elevator packed with incoming wounded would delay us five minutes more. A thirty-minute session could be cut to ten. What if it took me that long to tell him how dreadful I felt? How sad, desperate, discouraged, unsafe. What if we had to reschedule for next week or further out? People vacation in March.

A decisive Sadé said to the driver, "We need to get out here," and handed him twenty dollars. This exceeded my 30 percent tip policy by dollars, but psychiatrists' meters rise in higher increments. If we were going to salvage a useful portion of the session, we'd have to accelerate our pace.

We got out of the cab and Sadé *sprinted*. For the past two years she'd had to shuffle alongside me to match my geriatric tempo. But in an instant, she was fast, supremely athletic. The sidewalks were crowded. Charging suit-and-tie men and pantsuit women swarmed the block. An elderly woman in a floral-print blouse and black pleated slacks walking a shabby gray schnauzer was walking toward us, just two strides from the galloping Sadé. Oy vey. Either the biddy or the hound would be trampled 'neath Beetle Bailey's hooves. That will warrant a pause in our dash if not a 911 call. I'm screwed.

And then, before you could say Jack Be Nimble, Sadé *hurdled* the schnauzer. I laughed out loud, reflexively at Gail Devers in jackboots. For months I'd been begging her to leave me. "Save yourself," I implored. Then she Super Mario-ed that scraggly pooch and scrubbed my plan. That leap made me so grateful.

We arrived fifteen minutes late. Dr. Friedman waved off my apologies. Such grace.

In a half hour we came up with a plan. We decided that I needed time away from the city and its intrinsic anxiety and landlord's bills. I'd be able to save money while I regrouped and changed careers. I'd move back into my mother's house, the place where I had grown up. The place I liked to visit. For limited stints. Knowing in four hours I could be back in Manhattan. Sadé would stay behind and move in with some New York friends.

On June 26, 2017, Sadé and I packed up the apartment and put it in storage. An act of hope, or possibly, delusion. In 2006 in Los Angeles I put an apartment in storage before a planned six-month experiment in Manhattan. A year later, during a separate episode of depression, I decided to remain in New York City and gave everything away to a friend of a friend. If you stand close enough to one-bedroom-accommodating storage units you can feel the despair through the corrugated garage doors.

Moving is stressful even for the highly functioning; for the acutely depressed it is torture. A harrowing gauntlet of fear, stress, and hard labor. We had loaded our one bedroom into a fifteen-foot U-Haul truck, a behemoth of a freighter I still can't believe they breezily rented to a middle-aged Jew. We brought most of the furniture to the storage unit, then I drove four hours to Massachusetts, carting the four huge boxes that wouldn't fit in storage, to my mom's house. I got to her house after midnight and brought in my suitcases and backpack. I stood in the center of the cubicle I'd occupy until I was well enough to get back to life. I had first slept there in a crib.

During the previous two years, I'd checked myself into the psychiatric ward on two separate occasions about a year apart. For most that would be considered a firm bottom. This felt much lower. I find it easier to tell people that I'd been in the psych ward than to tell them that at forty-six I moved back in with my mother. Still, as I consider my journey *out* of that room, I can't say that my return was inconceivable. The worldview I developed in that house all but ensured the conditions that brought about my return. Now I was counting on it to provide the temporary refuge I needed to fly away, for good this time.

Kindergarten

First day of school. Ever. The transition from not going to school to going to school could not be gentler. I was not afraid. Kindergarten was just a five-minute drive from my house. The sessions only two and a half hours long. The kindergarten teacher, Mrs. Robbins? I'd known her my whole life. I called her Carol. I could see her house from my house. I was over at her house the day before. I swam in her ool over the summer with her three kids who were older than me. I called it the ool because my mother read the sign on the weathered gray fence outside and explained it to me.

Welcome to our ool. Notice there is no p *in it. Please keep it that way.*

I never hesitated to pee in a pool, but I abstained at the Robbinses' out of respect for the wit in their admonition.

We waited for the school bus under a young elm tree directly across the street from my house. I was there with Luke Arcuri (535-0485) who kind of looked like a cartoon mouse, big eyes, big ears, big round head. His mother was there. I was friends with Luke, but our relationship was volatile. He'd promise then withdraw invitations to his birthday party several times each year, once citing my failure to finish a slice of the dry birthday cake his mom made as justification. He had excellent stuff, like a player piano. Our favorite thing was playing the song "Alley Cat" on it and dancing like maniacs. This version of the popular instrumental quickly ramped up its tempo, and we frantically tried to keep pace. Eventually it went too fast, and we collapsed on the carpet breathlessly laughing our little red faces off.

Also waiting under the tree was Suzanne Graff with her mother, Margie. I didn't know her phone number because if I ever wanted to talk with anyone in her house, I walked across the street. I could just walk right in. I didn't even have to knock! She was as tall as me, with short blond hair and blue eyes. If I had to choose a wife that first day of kindergarten, it would be her. She wore a poncho made of an array of different colored yarn. Every girl there and their mothers praised the flashy cloak. It was handknit by Auntie Risa or Ruthie or maybe Auntie Phyllis or Auntie Elaine or Auntie Irene. She had a lot of aunts who were very involved in her life. All very nice to me. I wore a pair of stiff plaid Toughskins, a brand of pants made for boys that had sewn inside the knee what felt like rhino hide. They were not stylish, but they *were* uncomfortable. I wore a Winnie-the-Pooh shirt. It was white and had a full-bodied silhouette of the tenderhearted Pooh stitched over my heart. There were some other kids there who I didn't recognize. They must have lived on a different street.

I carried my Disney World lunch box. It wasn't *from* Disney World nor Land, as we'd been to neither. Like my Pooh shirt and my pants, it was from Sears. It had Mickey Mouse and his friends on the lid. I didn't like Mickey. Never found him or his supporting cast funny. He reminded me of certain grown-ups who talked to kids like we were babies. Nobody in my house talked to me like that.

Luke Arcuri had a Speed Buggy lunch box. He had a lot of excellent things like that. The player piano, bumper pool, a father who lived in the same house with him, and an *in-ground* pool. Notice the *p* in it! Luke leaned his Speed Buggy lunch box on the grass against the trunk of the elm and talked to some other kids.

I gazed covetously at that excellent lunch box sitting on the grass. I wished it were mine. It had Speed Buggy on it *and* a *robot*. My wildest dreams mingling on the lid of this lunch pail. I had these stupid, corny, baby cartoons on mine. Mickey, Goofy, Donald, some dirty-looking bears in a sleazy band.

Without much deliberation I sneakily pressed my new "worker man" boots on Speed Buggy's plastic handle. Snap. *Uh-oh.* I sheepishly looked up from the wreckage and into Mrs. Arcuri's scowl.

Bewildered, she asked, "Gary, why'd you do *that*?"

She really stressed the *that*, drawing it out so that it sounded like *thaaat*.

I considered her question for a second but decided against the truth. I gave the safest answer I could think of: "I d'know."

I did know, but I was ashamed to say. I was jealous. I felt bad, though. And not just because I got caught but mostly because I got caught. Before she could cross-examine me any further, Suzanne rescued me.

She started crying wildly. One second, she's talking with us, graciously accepting compliments on her poncho of many colors and the next she's bawling, heaving sobs, couldn't catch her breath. It was difficult to make out the exact nature of her grievance through the blubbering, but the central theme was that she wanted her mommy.

This affliction seemed to be contagious because just as the cheese box pulled up, a different girl staged an identical protest. I understood their trepidation, I guess, but what could be done at this point? The bus was there.

Neither Suzanne nor the other girl could be coaxed aboard. Their moms comforted them, then patiently led them home.

Ooh, I gotta remember this: Cry. Go home. As undignified and disturbing as these displays were, it was good to know should the need arise, I could escape by pulling a nutty. It's too bad about Suzanne—though I must say, I'm grateful that the tantrum distracted from my vandalism.

The bus arrived. The door opened. To my astonishment the driver was *nowhere near the door*! She sat on a chair high atop *a staircase*. What is this sorcery? And why am I the only one gasping with delight? This was so excellent! Okay. I get it. No witchcraft. There was a handle that she pulled connected to an arm that collapsed and uncollapsed the door. At some point I must either be allowed to open that door over and over or become a school bus driver. Bus driver instantly outranked being the guy who takes change from people driving over the bridge in my list of things I wanted to be when I grew up. Only telling jokes on television outranked it.

The bus driver was a perfectly delightful woman named Ellie. "Hi, Ellie!" is something I can't remember not saying, but I don't remember learning her name. I just knew it. She had dark straight hair down to her shoulders and big glasses. She wore an oversized navy-blue windbreaker. I could tell she liked us. I liked her.

The ride was fun. The first ride I could remember taking where either Auntie Judy or my mom or dad wasn't driving. We drove around picking up other kindergarteners around the area. A lot of excellent lunch boxes and a lot of laughing and yelling. It was loud, but Ellie maintained her poise at every stop, greeting the tots with her warm smile. I waved at some people in cars and a few of them *waved back*! Sometimes, there was a commotion. It seemed wanting your mommy was endemic to the community, not just a Rutledge Road phenomenon.

During the ride, when I wasn't marveling at the hocus pocus of the door, I contemplated the fate of Suzanne. She was the person outside my family I spent the most time with. She was my best friend leading up to and through kindergarten, although I never told anyone because she was a girl. I was over at her house every day. I was surprised by her meltdown because she was strong-willed; whenever we played "house" and she didn't like my suggestions, she'd fold her arms, turn her back to me, and sulk until I gave in. *I'll tell her about the voodoo door later; maybe that will entice her to give school another shot.*

The afternoon bus driver was named Marsha. I don't think anyone ever said, "Hi, Marsha!" She had thick brown curly hair and wore a lot of makeup and a scowl. She never said a word to us unless it was to correct our behavior. I haven't thought about Marsha in over forty years, I almost forgot about her. I think about Ellie all the time.

Carol Robbins was like a version of my mom that was not always on the phone and never watched daytime dramas while I was playing. She sang with us and painted with us and taught us how to print our names. She read to us every day. One book was called *Green Eggs and Ham* about a real pest named Sam. The following week she made us green scrambled eggs using food coloring.

There were people who visited our classroom, too. I looked forward to Wednesdays, when the elderly frosted-hair music teacher, Mrs. McVann, played violin for us and taught us songs. I loved Thursdays—art with Mrs. Phillips, who passed out paint-splattered smocks for us to wear while we flung all varieties of paint at all kinds of canvases.

I loved school.

In December, we started devoting extra time every morning and afternoon to snow boot and winter coat application. My snorkel-style coat required acquisition of a challenging new skill: *zipping.* Aligning the two-piece hardware in my throwing hand with the elongated zipper tine in my baseball glove hand, then pulling up on that slider—*VWOOOT!* It was *electrifying*. It felt great to no longer be one of those kids who had to wait in line to have their coats zipped up for them by Carol. I could now scoff at those kids. Only shoe tying stood between me and complete self-sufficiency.

I was very comfortable, delighting in my newfound freedom. It was fitting that as we neared the bicentennial, 1976, I, too, was exulting in my liberty.

Later in December, while attending an after-school program, we spun an odd-looking top. Amid an aroma reminiscent of sub-shop french fries I found out I was Jewish. I'd heard the term before but usually as a terse dismissal of my desire for a Christmas tree, an Easter basket, or Hickory Farms summer sausage. It didn't change much, though it did shed some light on my auntie Judy's Friday night ritual of placing a paper towel on her head, putting candles on two cans of Libby's-brand corn, and reciting some mumbo jumbo.

My favorite activity throughout the year was show-and-tell. This amateur hour was a reliably compelling spectacle. A few kids reported on their dogs and cats. One kid told us he had a snake! It was mostly tell, but some kids followed the assignment. There was one kid I called "the boy who is only able or only willing to say 'dinosaur.'" I called him that because he was only able or only willing to say "dinosaur." He brought in a plastic *Tyrannosaurus rex* and of course said "dinosaur" and then made some sounds that *could* have been made by a *Tyrannosaurus*. He made those sounds no matter what we were discussing, so it's hard to say whether his lecture was on topic or not.

One especially memorable performance came from Santino Colombo. Santi rose and enthusiastically announced, "I can snap!" Then, before a rapt but understandably skeptical audience, he delivered on this audacious pledge, snapping his fingers not once but *twice*! His nervousness and concentration, indicated by his tongue sticking out, were so endearing. It created quite the hubbub as kids tried snapping themselves. Santi beamed in the limelight. Alas, his star turn was short-lived. Before the group snapping could die down, center stage was seized by the victim of my day-one lunch-box sabotage.

Even though Luke already had a turn—presenting a Batman squirt gun (*loaded*) to much fanfare—he stood up, proclaiming, "I can *whistle*!"

And he did . . . with pizzazz. We were all blown away by the virtuosity. Sadly, this ham erased Santi Colombo's triumph. For in the instrument-less music hierarchy, whistling trumps snapping, as well as clapping and stomping. Poor Santi, he brought a kazoo to a clarinet fight. Hats off to him, though, he handled his fall with quiet dignity and grace, even trying to replicate the whistle, unsuccessfully.

Over time the quality of the weekly production declined. Lying was soon rampant, and when it became clear to everyone that there was no penalty for mendacity, show-and-tell turned farce. I nearly detached both retinas rolling my eyes at some of the fiction. Robin, a raspy-voiced brown-haired pathological claimed to have a container of Play-Doh in her kitchen so large that she used a ladder to climb up into it. Yeah, right! Like it would fit through the front door!

Flustered by the limits my mother put on toys I was allowed to take to school, I succumbed to the stakes and told a whopper one day in service of my comedy aspiration. With a straight face I announced to the entire class: "I can speak French."

The truth was I could pronounce certain words with a French accent owing to the day my mother and I beat the summer heat by sitting in the Danvers Sack 3 Cinema for three consecutive showings of Peter Sellers in *The Return of the Pink Panther*. Rich people of the '70s had air-conditioning; the poor had matinees.

"Pardon me, monsieur, do you have a license for your monkey?"

The rubes bought it. There was much laughter, including from Mrs. Robbins. It was exhilarating. A feeling I was happy to expend all my energy in replicating. I bowed and returned to my seat.

There is a legend about me that my mom liked to repeat and I loved to hear. Supposedly on my first birthday, just about four years prior, while the entire party watched, I took my first steps. Something equally impressive occurred near another milestone at the end of kindergarten, in June. With less than a week left until kindergarten graduation, on a weekend evening, something clicked, generating unprecedented joy within me. Joy surpassing zipping in December and even riding my bike without training wheels in April. This breakthrough was the highlight of my school year, perhaps even my short life. I read.

I had been building to this moment for most of my life, though not consciously. Certainly Mrs. Robbins's tutelage helped, but I'd been spellbound by letters and their idiosyncrasies for years. Usually while basking in the sunny days of my beloved *Sesame Street*. I watched it twice a day. Thanks to *Sesame Street* I had mastered the alphabet long before Carol started parceling it out three letters at a time.

How fitting, then, that the first book I read on my own was a book featuring my favorite *Sesame Street* resident, the furry blue cherub Grover. The book was called *The Monster at the End of This Book*. I'm not sure how the thin hardback landed in my meager home library. It wasn't new; someone had scribbled in red-violet Crayola on the front inside cover page. Must have been dumped there by a family friend looking to unclutter. They must have been unaware of the treasure buried within this Little Golden Book.

Over the years there were a handful of books that had been

read to me. Thank heavens this was not one of them. You see, the first book I was opening blind was a whodunit. What a bonus that no adult had revealed the who. Were it not for this providence, the experience would not have been so divine.

At first, I methodically sounded out every single word, but soon I handled each word seamlessly. I rarely came across words that I had to slow down and sound out, and I noticed that once I sounded out the word one time, it was in me. It was mine. This was excellent. I was learning the shape of words like "afraid" and "scared" and "embarrassed." I'd used them a thousand times, but who knew that they had all been assigned these distinct forms?

Using my new skill was thrilling on its own, but what was lifting this endeavor to the level of sublime was the *story*. *The Monster at the End of This Book* was a riveting thriller from page one. Nay, from the *cover*.

On the opening page, Grover shared his dismay over the implications of the title. He, like the reader, is afraid of monsters. He pleaded with me to protect him by not turning the page, thereby avoiding the end where the monster awaits. I was just sure it was the Count. Count Von Count—the lavender-colored Dracula-like puppet with a widow's peak, goatee, and *fangs*—scared the bejesus out of me. While the Street was teeming with monsters, the Count was the only one who seemed dangerous. Why would a children's show endorse vampirism?

Grover's increasing horror as each page was turned was funny in its melodrama, but I was torn. I felt for him because he was so afraid. I, too, was concerned about the monster but felt safe because my mother and brother Max were nearby to protect me. But poor Grover was all alone. Of course I was dying to find out how the book ended. Also, there were words left to decode, which had quickly become my favorite thing to do. I was giddy. There were these mysteries all over every page. In a book that was *itself* a mystery!

As the potboiler unfolded, Grover kept erecting more elaborate buttresses to prevent the reader from turning the page. A complex web of ropes, a fence of wooden boards, and finally a sturdy brick wall. All demolished by turning pages. But the barrier *Monster* broke that I found *most* enchanting was the *fourth wall*.

Grover was talking to me! After I turned a page, demolishing the brick wall, he said, "Do you know that you are very strong?"

Ha! Thanks, Grover! I am very strong. I do cry sometimes, but my dad said my throws hurt his hand when I play catch with him.

While I felt for Grover—he was a guileless lamb—I couldn't stop reading. I had to know how it ended! Ignoring Grover's most desperate pleas, I gingerly turned the final page. I found out who the monster was and was spun silly by the O. Henry twist. The monster at the end of *The Monster at the End of This Book* was:

Grover.

My word. I did not see that coming. I sat with this revelation for a spell, letting the ending sink in, relieved that Grover and I were safe. The monster was just Grover. I caught my breath and got right back to chasing that high. I took every book in the house and tested my new trick, *reading,* on them. There wasn't a book in our house whose secrets this technique couldn't unlock. I was delirious. And it was just the beginning.

Last day of kindergarten. It was warm enough that I didn't have to wear a jacket. I wore the tie-dye shirt I made in art class earlier that spring, a pair of dark blue dungarees, and a brown belt that had excellent little plastic jewels screwed on. At a morning assembly we honored the marketing gimmick that was the bicentennial by singing "You're a Grand Old Flag," an upbeat, phony marching song. It reminded me of *Donny & Marie,* a show that my mom and brothers and I gathered to ridicule every Friday night.

Auntie Judy came with my mother. Judy Siegel was my mom's best friend and my godmother. She was very pretty, with blond hair and a very small, straight nose and blue eyes. I always kissed her when I went to her house, which was every day before I started going to school. I love her. She treated me like I was one of her kids.

The best thing about the last day of school was that Ellie had descended from her throne and joined us for the celebration. Seeing Ellie out of her bus driver's seat was disorienting, like the episode of *Sesame Street* when Bert danced the Pigeon and you could see his whole body. Where did his legs come from? She talked with Auntie Judy and my mother like they were friends. I knew they would like Ellie. Everyone liked Ellie. And there Ellie was, just drinking Hawaiian Punch and eating the Black

Forest cake, made by the father of the boy who was only able to or only willing to say "dinosaur." Ellie was so regular.

Everyone with a summer birthday—I'm July 17—got a cupcake with their name on it. Throughout the year, kids with birthdays would get to wear a construction paper crown all day and their moms would bring in cake and they'd get spanked five or six times by Carol and then pinched to guarantee they'd grow an inch. I never bought in. I recognized the value of not going to school on your birthday. Keep your crown; I'll be watching *The Price Is Right* and eating cereal on the couch.

I waited in a hug-Ellie line and then hugged Mrs. Robbins, who I slyly told I'd see at the ool. I went home in Auntie Judy's Chevy Caprice. She and my mother were still raving about the Black Forest cake. I was looking forward to this summer and not at all dreading next school year. I loved school. Also, I had known my first-grade teacher even longer than I had known Carol.

I learned a lot that year: how to zip a jacket, ride a bike, write my name, read, and that the monster at the end of your book is probably you.

June 2017

For most of my life summer brought certain bliss. All obligations, grudges, and concerns deferred until September. And I always loved celebrating my birthday. Through two previous summers of acute depression, I yearned for that feeling. Though I recognized it as irrational, I indulged a recurring daydream about a portal I could enter where I would be a child again when every morning the sense and scents of heat and sunlight in the air would spring me out of bed to see what was doing on my street.

There is no bliss on June 27, 2017. I want to stay in this full-sized bed in the corner of my old room and milk the relief, the abridged oblivion sleep provides. I surrender.

The one thing preventing me from sleeping the day away are my two brown-and-white male Cavalier King Charles spaniels: Sandy, aged nine, and Igor, eleven. I've had them since they were puppies and brought them with me from New York. Sandy was named after the left hand of G-d, Sandy Koufax, and Igor (pronounced *eye-gor*), after the assistant in *Young Frankenstein*. Igor was the more insistent of the two. Sandy was athletic and trim, but Igor was aggressive, dominant. When we played ball at the beach, Sandy would get to the ball first every single time, then immediately drop it once Igor caught up and barked for it. Igor dictates the length and locus of our walks. During regular visits to my mom's, he's discovered his favorite neighborhood spots for his interests.

This first day he is determined to reacquaint himself

with Willowbrae Park. A two-minute walk from our house, Willowbrae contains a playground as well as the bisecting asphalt path kids have used for fifty years to walk from my neighborhood to our designated elementary school, West Memorial. On this "day one" of my convalescence, we find the playground a total disaster. I take some comfort in the notion that, unlike Madonna, I'll never have to bemoan the decline of my playground. It was never good. It is in the exact same condition it was forty years earlier when I first walked the battered path to first grade with my then best friend, Wally Mitler.

First

I was kneeling on the living room sofa, looking out our front window. Our house was white with black trim and black fake shutters. It was a one-floor, ranch-style home with a garage, three bedrooms, one bath/shower, and three toilets. The front and back lawns could be mowed in less than an hour. It was part of a dense middle-class development built in the 1960s by the prolific suburban contractor Alfred Campanelli.

I waited in front of the windows every Sunday for my dad to arrive for his visits. He usually got there around noon to pick up my brothers and me and take us out to eat or do fun things. This was the second year my oldest brother, Rick, wasn't living with us. He was a sophomore at the University of Massachusetts, in Amherst. My fifteen-year-old middle brother, Max, pointed out the window and said: "Here he isn't!"

He got me every time. My mother told him to stop antagonizing me. Dad arrived eleven cars later. My brother had guessed nine, I had three.

It was September 1976, a week before I'd start first grade at a new school. Until that year, I dreaded Sundays with my father. Too often they were spent making excruciating visits to packs of old Jews. He would pick us up, and we would traipse around

Greater Boston, calling on more than a dozen shriveled members of his vast extended family. The kissing was out of hand. Everyone got a kiss. I had to hug and kiss these half strangers who didn't even remember my name. It wasn't like I had anything else to do—I basically had one friend, who I never saw on Sunday because I liked to keep my neighborhood life separate from Dad visits because my dad was gruff.

There was never anything for kids to eat or drink on these sojourns. The best they offered was coffee-flavored hard candies. Confectioners asked, "What can we put in candy to keep kids from eating it?" then commissioned this atrocity.

Ten minutes into every visit I'd think, *I'm dying of thirst; I can't choke down another glass of soda water. I want to go home, duck behind the refrigerator door, and drink Sprite right out of the glass bottle. Why can't old people get good television reception? This is torture.*

But something had changed recently, and mysteriously we didn't call on the ancient Ashkenazim anymore. It may have been a result of my dad's recent remarriage. He married a woman named Jan, who was always happy to see my brothers and me. We loved her but tried not to mention her around my mother. It was similar to our policy on J-sus: we recognized his existence but felt it was best not to bring Him up.

Whatever the reason for curtailing the family visits, I was grateful that Sunday had become a day for light recreation. We'd go candlepin bowling or to the Stone Zoo or the miniature golf course or watch people fly remote-control airplanes in the Sylvania Electric Light Factory parking lot. Divorced dad is a far less demanding position than single mother. His weekly time commitment was that of an NFL play-by-play announcer, whereas my mom's job was the equivalent of running CNN.

That Sunday we were at what we call the House-a-Pancakes in Danvers, Massachusetts. It's probably called the *International*

House of Pancakes, but we either hadn't noticed or hadn't yet surrendered to their global domination. This was a special treat. My only complaint was that when we dined upscale like this, my father insisted that I put a napkin on my lap, which made me feel like a little girl. What if a kid I knew saw me with a napkin on my lap? I'd never seen a boy with a napkin on his lap. I put it on my lap but when it fell off on its own, I made no effort to retrieve it. As long as I didn't brush it off intentionally, I wouldn't get in trouble.

My dad, Phil Gulman, was fifty with gray and black and white hair. It looked like it would be dry and prickly, but it was surprisingly soft. He was considered quite handsome with his dark eyes, square jaw, and straight nose, but I just saw a super-old man. I called him Dad or Daddio. He called me Gar or Gar-ino or sometimes Genius.

When we were out to eat or went for long drives, my father always shared stories of his dismal upbringing. My dad's stories were all exciting and told with great enthusiasm and detail. My mother said that this is what she fell in love with.

He had about a dozen or so of these stories in rotation. From the stories I'm permitted to hear plus what I've overheard, I knew that his mother was "not well" and institutionalized when he was born. He was raised in foster homes until he was four, when her Russian immigrant parents brought him to live with them and their *eleven* children in Chelsea, Massachusetts, an early-twentieth-century haven for Jews pogromed out of Russia. The youngest of my father's aunts and uncles was only nine months older than him.

My father said that he heard I'd become a voracious reader. Then he explained to me how it's good to be smart but it's important not to be precocious. He didn't say "smart" and "precocious," however. His Boston accent was super thick, so it sounded like "smaht" and "puhcocious."

Then he said, "Lemme see your nails." He scrutinized my nails every Sunday to make sure they were clean. This necessitated a Saturday night bath, during which I vigorously scoured my fingers with a scrub brush. The brush was a yellow plastic replica of a bathtub, with white bristles on the bottom. My mom got it as a gift for hosting the Avon lady. It came with a cute pink pig carved out of soap that tragically dissolved long ago. I did love baths, though, thanks to my Fisher-Price houseboat with retractable diving board. But as much as I loved commanding this spectacular vessel, I resented the weekly hygiene exams its cruises portended.

There was too much riding on the inspections. I believed that my father was playing Clouseau, determining whether my mother was capable of raising me, based on the amount of dirt under my fingernails. Let me save you the trouble, Daddio. She's not. She got a lot of help from her friends and people in our neighborhood and from my brothers; plus, there was the fact that I was an angel.

My father ordered black coffee with every meal and always called the waitress "dear." He was absurdly polite: "Please, dear" and "Thank you, dear" and "May I trouble you, dear?" He ordered eggs sunny-side up and his toast burnt. He expected me to order for myself, which I hated but was preferable to a lecture on assertiveness. I always ordered pancakes and bacon and a hot chocolate. I read that there was a bottomless cup of coffee, and so I asked my father what that was. He told me it was a "figure-a-speech." It turns out this bottomless cup of coffee was bottomed. A broken promise.

The waitress poured Dad's coffee into a beige mug. He immediately brought it to his lips. No blowing, no cool-off, no delay at all. He may have liked cream in his coffee, but he would never permit his coffee to lose a fragment of a fraction of heat. Most times he told us the coffee wasn't hot enough. One time my oldest brother, Rick, suggested, "Maybe they can brew it in your throat, Phil."

He called my father Phil, which was ballsy. I wouldn't dare. Too precocious. We had all gone recently to drop Rick off in his UMass fraternity house, which he called a frat. It was a run-down building where boys with bad skin ate pizza, drank beer, and vomited. It smelled like a sweaty sub shop. It was just me and Max that day at House-a-Pancakes.

My hot chocolate came a little while later. Max tested it. He wouldn't let my dad check it because one time my dad tested it and said it was fine and I drank it and it was not fine; it was fire. I howled in pain and cried. He felt terrible, and my brothers were furious with him. Rick said Phil's sip was not reliable because "his mouth is coated with asbestos." I had no recollection of this story, but I liked hearing it. It made me feel protected by my brothers.

Max went to high school, and until recently also went to Hebrew school a few nights a week. He once got in trouble at temple for sneaking out with the rabbi's son and walking to Fun Time at the mall, where they had pinball machines and one video game. A lot of girls thought Max was cute, but he was too shy to talk to them.

We left the pancake house, and Max and my dad held my hands in the parking lot, and when they counted to three, I jumped, and they pulled me up, so I was flying. *Breathtaking.* This was probably my favorite thing. I could've done it all day. They were willing to do it for around five minutes.

We drove back to our house on our hometown of Peabody's main road, Lowell Street. Lowell Street passed through my entire city for close to seven miles. In 1976 there were about three traffic lights, one large Catholic church, two small synagogues, three grocery stores, three gas stations, a bowling alley, a cemetery, a bank, two sub and pizza shops, one farm, and our high school. There was not a single Dunkin' Donuts on Lowell Street back then. There are two now. The rest of Lowell Street was residential, as was most of my city, other than the Northshore Shopping Center and a small section of downtown stores.

We were all sitting in the front seat of Dad's 1970 hunter-green Cutlass because his shambolic supply of drapery sample books was spilling over the back seat. The seat belts were stuck within the seats somewhere, but it was okay because my dad would reflexively thrust his arm across my chest whenever he stopped short, which was every time he stopped.

My dad sold curtains for his uncles' interior decorating company. I'd admit this to no one. I told everyone he was a salesman, or sometimes I'd fib and say he was a carpenter, but never that he was an interior decorator.

About a mile from home, we were stopped at a red light behind a faux-wood-paneled Chevy Vega station wagon with a dinged-up rear bumper. There was a little boy sitting cross-legged on the floor of the way back. The wagon was slow to move on the green light near Muntsy's Pizza and Subs. I was praying my father wouldn't honk. G-d wasn't listening. Dad honked, *loud*. Then, before the honk faded, the little boy extended his middle finger toward us. He held it there for longer than the honk lasted so there could be no misunderstanding the message he wished to convey. Oh no. This was bad. I was sick to my stomach.

I'd never seen this sign language live, but I recognized the gesture from a story my mother told people about a man who gave her "the fingah" in the parking lot of the Warren Five Cents Savings Bank, also on Lowell Street. I surmised from the frequency with which my mom retold the anecdote that giving the finger was an unusual and hostile act. Nevertheless, it wasn't until this boy extended his middle digit that I deduced *which* finger was *the* finger. Even without that background I could have gathered from Dad's fury that this was unacceptable. There would be consequences for this R-rated mime.

The little boy's parents were probably not aware that he flipped off the honker. He was in the way back, which is a separate reality from the front seat. I'm certain they wouldn't care anyway. How am I so sure? Because the ill-mannered little boy in the hatchback was my best friend Wally Mitler, a foul-mouthed lout with a knack for vandalism, theft, and disrespect for authority. He was only a year older than me but a complete terror. Wally was about a head taller than me, with brown curly hair, big brown eyes, and an olive complexion. Neighborhood legend had it that the rear bumper damage came when Wally, six years young at the time, backed the wagon out of the Mitlers' driveway and into a telephone pole.

My father was determined to make the boy's parents aware of their son's transgression. He had decided to forego our usual path home so that he could deliver justice to this hooligan. I didn't dare tell him he wouldn't have to alter our usual route; Wally lived a hundred feet from us.

My father was angry. He was capable of great rage. My brother Rick told me a story of Phil pulling a man out of a car for driving recklessly in a parking lot. I once saw him run after a driver who tossed a Coke can out his window on our street. He was like a cop. He wouldn't hesitate to discipline strangers. He wouldn't hit a kid, but he might yell at them and make them cry, and one time he threatened a teenager for saying "asshole" near us at the beach. I was distraught. There was something wrong here. I could feel it in my stomach. My stomach was always an accurate compass for right and wrong, and it was telling me I should tell my dad that this scoundrel was my best friend.

We followed the ragged Vega, and it signaled to make a right onto my street, then pulled into the oil-sotted driveway across the street from my house, diagonally to the left.

I raced into the house and held my breath. My father was over at the Mitlers' house. I was going to play dumb, but I didn't feel good about it. I would not admit that I recognized Wally. This was a fib. On top of that fib, I also fibbed by not letting my father know that Wally was my best friend. These were not official fibs, more fibs of omission, half fibs. My stomach didn't know the difference. I felt very nervous. I believed I'd get away with the deceit, but it would be tacked onto my list of shameful secrets. These included peeing behind the shed, showing Wally the magazine from under Max's bed, and the time I was trying to come up with rhymes for truck and I said "f—" *out loud* in my room. And now fibbing to my dad.

My father didn't know about Wally because when he came on Sunday, I only did things with him and my brothers. He said I could bring friends around with us, but I was afraid that a friend might irritate one of my brothers. Also, I was worried what would happen if a friend stepped out of line around my dad.

My dad had no friends and was weird—or had none because he was weird. His best friend was my mother. My mother was constantly expressing gratitude for her friends. We didn't have the money to do fancy things, but we could go to Auntie Judy and Uncle Bob's, or Margie and Warren's across the street to the right or Rich and Windy's directly across the street or Joanne and Ron's to our left. Or we could go to her friend Inga's, and I could swim while they drank Tab.

It would probably be difficult to be friends with my dad. He's what my mom called "puritanical." The fingernails, the napkin on my lap, drilling of table manners. Also, he doesn't swear, *ever.* The worst thing he would say when he was *fuming* was GD. Not G-ddamn. He literally said "GD." He absolutely never said any ethnic slurs, nor did he permit us or any stranger to say them in his presence. He never used the Lord's name in vain, and he wouldn't allow or say the word many Jewish people casually call gentiles, which is "goyim."

He didn't allow the varsity expletives for sure, but he didn't even allow me to use the word "lie." He insisted I use the word "fib." He believed "lie" was too harsh a word for children. I couldn't say "shut up," "jerk," "stupid," "idiot," or even "fart." Somehow "damn" escaped his censorship. I could say "damn" with impunity.

My dad returned from the Mitlers', and my mother and I acted shocked, *shocked* to find out there was an outlaw living so close. He was satisfied that the Mitlers "will punish him."

No, they won't.

I was relieved that my father didn't seem to know my secret, but I had a feeling I was living too many fibs and it was compromising my character as well as my relationship with my dad. I couldn't tell him that I yawned because I was up until 1:00 A.M. watching *Saturday Night Live* or that I took baths only Saturday nights and that frequently I got scared of sleeping in my own bed and I slept in my mom's and I still slept with my blanky. Also, my dad thought fighting was important, and I was afraid to fight. I'd already let several boys and one feral girl push me around without fighting back.

We watched some of the Jerry Lewis telethon. I didn't know who this guy was, but he had the same name as the run-down cinema near our house. He was oily and exhausted, the walking, talking, sweating, cigarette-smoking version of that shabby cinema where every movie would at some point be stopped while the projectionist fixed the film reel. My mother called him a phony creep.

Around dusk my dad wrote out a check for my mother and then I followed him to the door. He picked me up, groaned from his sore joints, and gave me a hug, and I kissed his stubbly cheek. He smelled of Parliaments and Old Spice. He kissed me on top of the head. He told me he loved me and that he'd see me next Sunday. I loved him, but secretly I thought I was the only child of divorced parents who would be disappointed if they got back together. I was glad he didn't live with us because I wouldn't be able to stay up as late as I wanted on Friday and Saturday. I'd have to bathe more, and I wouldn't be allowed to watch adult shows like *Soap* and *Maude*.

My dad drove away, and I watched from my roost, relieved over the resolution to the Wally crisis. When the coast was clear, I headed over to Wally's to undo any residual damage, and as I predicted, there was none.

I think my mother allowed me to play with Wally because of her friendship with and deep admiration for Wally's mother, Sharon, an intelligent, eloquent, chain-smoking administrator at a prestigious law firm in Boston. Whenever we left the Mitlers' house, which smelled like cigarettes, burnt ketchup, and dry cat food, my mom raved about Sharon's intelligence and said the same thing: "She speaks so beautifully." My mother also pointed out how Sharon "tells it like it is. She's no phony." She said this *every* time—then always denigrated herself, saying, "I'm a deez, demz, and doze girl."

Wally also had a way with words—swear words. He had remarkable ease with all the coarsest components of our language. He said "ass," "asshole," "bastard," "bitch," "dick," "hell," "piss," "shit," and "tits." Naturally. But what set him apart in his field was his fluency in the felony-level profanity. Your various versions of *f,* your *c*'s and your *p*'s. And shockingly, he was allowed to say them right in front of his parents without reaction, reproach, or rebuke. In the '70s, in my neighborhood, when kids were considered bad for saying "butt" instead of "bum" or "piss" instead of "pee," Wally swore like a college kid on spring break and paid no price at home. Maybe they were reluctant to stifle his gift.

It was jarring to hear those words coming from another child. I cringed when he swore. I knew I wasn't allowed to say those words under any circumstances, but also, I didn't think my father or G-d would approve of me being around this gutter mouth, either.

Another aspect of Wally that I found appealing was that because of his mouth, along with a propensity to steal and deface and/or destroy private and public property, most of the mothers had forbidden their kids from playing with him. He was a neighborhood pariah. So he needed a friend. He needed me. Though I couldn't have put it in words, I was always drawn to underdogs, like the library, PBS, and sherbet.

While I played with a few kids in the neighborhood, those kids had other friends or brothers around their age. Wally just had me. And all in all, Wally was *lovable*. Yes, he gave my dad the finger, but he also called my brother Rick—eighteen at the time—Mr. Gulman. He wasn't being a wiseass, either, I think he was afraid of Rick. Or maybe he thought that because Rick was a lot older than me—thirteen years—that he was my father.

But the sweetest thing about Wally was that whenever he wronged me in any way, he apologized by asking plaintively "Be my friend?" It was heartbreaking. Especially given that he was a year older than me. It floored me every time. How do you reject that? It made me think he understood the value of friendship the way my mom did.

On the Wednesday morning after Telethon Day, I heard the Wally noise. While everyone in our life rang the doorbell or opened the screen door to bang on the front door, Wally slammed the side of his fist aggressively on the screen door. It was startling and grating, but it was his leitmotif. There were times when we would be talking about him and then *SCHLANG, SCHLANG, SCHLANG*, he doth appear. And we laughed.

My mother came outside with us and brought her camera. I *loved* getting my picture taken. I put my right arm around Wally and stuck my left arm out and opened my mouth wide like I was

Kermit the Frog milking a laugh. I was puffed up and mugging. I was excited about going to school. Wally was clearly put off by my showboating and hurried us through the shoot. He rarely found me funny.

We were walking together to my new school. He was starting second grade there, so he knew the route. West Memorial School was a little over a mile away. We walked about a thousand yards from my house and entered a narrow asphalt path through the dilapidated, graffiti-soaked playground we called "the pahk." Teenagers had ruined every single fixture in the playground. They did unspeakable things here. I'd seen a cast-off bra and a pair of panties there as well as a million cigarette butts and illegal fireworks casings. G-d, I couldn't stand those jerks.

Everything that went wrong in my neighborhood could be attributed to teenagers. They had different faces but wore nearly identical costumes. Leather or denim jackets, untied work boots, and faded blue jeans with holes in the knees and sometimes below a buttock. When they walked, they bent their knees way deeper than necessary, a kind of incendiary strut. They all smoked cigarettes, and when they weren't puffing on them, they stood around with their thumbs hooked into the top of their front pants pockets. Let me tell you something, anyone who hooks their thumbs into their front pants pockets is *no damn good*.

We walked up the path, past a swing set on our left with two sets of chains but zero seats. On our right was a cracked-asphalt, broken-glass-drenched basketball court. There were two fan-shaped steel-backboarded hoops. The one closest to the path was a foot lower than the hoop farthest from the path. They had metal-chain nets. The backboards were Gorton's of Gloucester yellow. The poles and the rims, boiled-lobster red, the nets were rust-colored.

Near the path's end we entered a ten-yard section surrounded by a dense area of mature trees. This finally led to the steep paved incline used to exit the park onto Bow Street, the street my school was on. There was a beat-up steel pole buried there to keep cars from driving down into the park. The thirty-degree angle it was bent at indicated that the pole had done its job at least once.

We walked the next mile down the one-way Bow Street. It ran parallel to Lowell Street for over a mile, and even though it was less than a quarter of a mile from my house, I'd never walked on it. I'd never walked that far from home until that day.

Bow Street had a few long-ago abandoned and crumbling barns and houses with all their windows either broken or boarded up. Wally threw some chunks of asphalt at them but didn't break anything, thank goodness. He also failed to shatter any streetlight bulbs during our trek.

How he loved to break things. He had great toys at his house, but they were all cracked, bent, scribbled on, painted on, burned, melted, or chewed up by pets. I hated it when kids had good toys and let them go like that. If I had the LEGO collection Wally had, I'd have built a replica of Sesame Street in the family room. I made do with my meager supplies, but what I wouldn't give for his LEGO inventory. It was a damned shame.

About halfway to school there was an enormous electrical transformer substation that was surrounded by a chain-link fence with threatening barbed wire on top. The eerie sounds of late-summer insect buzz, and the ominous industrial hum of the transformer were blending with my unfamiliarity, which caused me to race-walk past the monstrosity. Wally started throwing rocks at the gray metal blight. I plugged my ears and braced myself for an explosion. The rock just bounced off, thank G-d. This kid was going to give me a heart attack.

About fifteen minutes after we left my driveway, we walked down a steep patchily grassed hill and into the schoolyard of West Memorial School. The school was older and not nearly as well maintained as the McCarthy, my kindergarten school. It was located in only a marginally poorer section of the city and not *much* older than the McCarthy, but the school was a wreck. It was built out of yellowish and light orange bricks as opposed to the more refined reddish and reddish-brown brick. All the bricks near the furnace-exhaust chimney on the roof were covered in black soot. Also, some creep had spray-painted graffiti associated with the godless musical group Black Sabbath on the sides of the school. There were a bunch of cracked or boarded-up windows. All this havoc despite a sign warning NO TRESPASSING. POLICE TAKE NOTICE.

While the school was a stark demotion aesthetically, the trade-off was that once again I'd be very familiar with my teacher. Mrs. Burns (535-1478) was my first-grade teacher. She was a tall, thin, fair-skinned woman with light reddish hair and big glasses. She was kind and friendly, with an upbeat voice and a bright smile. Like my kindergarten teacher, Mrs. Robbins, I'd known Judy Burns my whole life. If you walked out my back door and through the backyard of my next-door neighbor to the left, you would be at the Burnses' dark brown split-entry house. Her son Finn babysat me and was the most popular boy in the neighborhood. He was in fourth grade.

As I entered our classroom, the first thing that hit me was the familiar scent of pencil shavings. I remembered it from kindergarten, but in first grade, as if to indicate that this was a more intense enterprise, there was no smell of clay. To the right was Mrs. Burns's desk in front of a blackboard. To the right of her desk was a wall with the heater and above that two rows of five rectangular windows. They had seedy old shades that looked like blank treasure maps stained with tobacco juice and coffee. They were riddled with holes that concentrated the sunlight into blinding beams.

To the far left was another blackboard with white placards of the alphabet tacked above it. In case we forgot it. Just after that blackboard, in the very back corner, there was a classroom sink with the world's cruddiest drinking fountain attached to it. It trickled thin streams of warm water, bringing more frustration than hydration.

Mrs. Burns took attendance, calling out names with only a few problems. Brian L., instead of saying "here" when his name was called yelled "pig." He laughed hysterically. Almost everyone laughed. How is that funny? Mrs. Burns didn't react, so a few other kids gave a "joke" response, too, though none as creative as "pig." I guess you could have said whatever you wanted. *Maybe next time I'll say "aaaaay" like Fonzie. Or maybe "Myah, what's up, Doc?" Those fools probably wouldn't get it. But "pig"? Sides split. Schmucks.*

This lowbrow buffoonery would get you the hook in my house. My older brothers were into some quality comedy. Rick knew all the words to *Blazing Saddles* and *Young Frankenstein* from when he worked as an usher at General Cinemas up at the mall. My brothers and my mom *revered* comedy, especially stand-up comedians.

"Gah, come quick!" squawked by my mother from the family room meant a stand-up comedian was performing on an afternoon talk show or sometimes on *Johnny Carson*. I'd sprint down the hallway hoping it would be my favorite, David Brenner. I memorized jokes from Max's Steve Martin album and sketches from *Saturday Night Live* and repeated them to my brothers' friends and older kids in the neighborhood.

When I made my family laugh, they praised me, sometimes bringing it up later with glee. They'd ask me to repeat what I said, and I got that feeling again, a feeling like when I made a hole in one on the eighteenth hole at the mini-golf place and we won a free game, but so much better because it wasn't luck.

"Pig" during roll call was fine for a first-grade class, but my regular audience was more sophisticated. Pig? My family would have told me to grow up, and worse, they wouldn't have laughed.

After she collected the lunch money and dispensed the light-blue full-price lunch tickets to the affluent and the fluorescent-pink free-lunch cards to me and the rest of the runny-nosed paupers, we stood for the Pledge of Allegiance. The class delivered the oath in the same discordant, singsong voice as they did in kindergarten. These were the same exact notes they used when responding to "Good morning, boys and girls" with "Good morning, Mrs. Burns." That sinister harmony sickened me. They sounded like zombies. By the end of kindergarten, I had decided to do the pledge and "Good morning, Mrs. Robbins" as well as the finale, "Good afternoon, Mrs. Robbins," by reciting nonsense words in the exact same key. "Good morning, boys and girls." To which I defiantly responded, "Blah blah blah blah blah blah blaaaaaaaaaaah." Sometimes I said quietly enough to get away with it, "Morning, Jude!"

Most of us put our right hand over our heart, but there were a few boys in Cub Scouts uniforms who were allowed to salute the flag. They removed their jazzy little caps and brought their hand to their forehead like army men.

Upon completion of the nationalist-indoctrination exercise, Judy led us down the hall to the bathrooms and the drinking fountain, which she called "the bubblah." This fountain across from the bathrooms was a satisfying chilly gush.

The boys' bathroom, however, was a catastrophe. The urinals were those old-fashioned floor-to-shoulder relics, taller than me and begging bullies to shove you in and flush. It smelled like a combination of rust, basement, wet brown paper towels, and of course pee and crap. I didn't investigate the stalls, out of fear, but extrapolating from the artifact I had just peed into, I pictured a tinplate milking pail. In all my years in that joint I never once used the stall. Not *once*, honest to goodness, never. I left the bathroom as soon as I was done. Some boys lingered, hung out. Savages.

Later that day we got separated into three reading groups. I was placed in the middle group and given a book called *Janet and Mark*. The best readers got *Sun Up*, and the also-rans received a book that had no title but which Mrs. Burns called *Palo Alto*. I guess the publisher figured why bother with a title, it's not like they'll be able to read it.

When she called for your reading group by the name of your book, you brought your chair and sat in the front of the room in an oval. *Sun Up* kids read smoothly without any assistance. *Janet and Mark* kids sometimes sounded out words or asked, "What's this word again?"—a cunning way to make it seem like they temporarily forgot how to say words no more exotic than "look." The *Palo Alto*s sounded out every word from "a" to "zoo." *Palo Alto* was a *sideshow*. You heard them read, and all you could think was there but for the grace of G-d . . . Judy never explicitly ranked the reading groups, and she mixed up the order in which we assembled, but you'd have to be in *Palo Alto* to misread the pecking order.

The *Sun Up* kids weren't doing anything out of my reach, but I was content in *Janet and Mark*, and other than this academic slight, and the doubling of the daily time commitment, I enjoyed first grade. I sometimes got admonished for talking out of turn, but usually Judy indulged my wit, like one day right before Halloween, she asked, "What is a chick?"

Mary Ann O'Brien, a towheaded ragamuffin with a pink face and a disarming lisp, raised her hand and said, "A baby chicken."

"Yes, Mary Ann, excellent, a chick is a baby chicken."

You're kidding me. No one's going to pick this ripe plum? I had that familiar feeling in my stomach when I recognized my dad's car turning onto our street every Sunday. Though it may lower my conduct and self-discipline grades, it would be criminal to squander this opportunity. I leaned back in my chair, clasped my hands behind my neck, crossed my legs at the ankles, took a deep breath, and on the exhale, confidently blurted: "Or a girl!"

Pandemonium. Unanimous, door-to-rectangular windows, sustained laughter. Even Mrs. Burns guffawed, unable to maintain her professional comportment. Heaven.

"Yes, Gary, or a girl. What am I gonna do with you?"

Upgrade me to *Sun Up*?

The year went by very smoothly. I enjoyed being there. I loved art class, although I felt the art teacher spent far too much time explaining how to hand someone scissors. She went over the procedure every class for, like, ten minutes, which is exactly ten minutes more than I've spent handing over scissors in my entire life. I could have gotten the point across in ten seconds.

"You'll probably never have occasion to hand anyone scissors, but if you do, *don't make a frenzied stabbing motion*."

Several raindrops into April I got home from school and my mom's oldest friend, Joanie, was there. My mom had been friends with Joanie since my brother Rick was an infant. I didn't see her yet but one sniff of the rich potpourri that accompanied all her visits heralded her presence. Pall Malls and lemon Pledge, a scent as exquisite to me as toasted marshmallows. Joanie came over sometimes to help clean the house with my mother because my mother was overwhelmed by housework.

Joanie Noyes was elfin, with short feathery brown hair, a vibrant pink face, and a boisterous laugh. She brought me books and sometimes toys that she got from "yahd sales." I loved the Encyclopedia Brown and joke books she found. Joanie took me to a yard sale with her once, and she bought me a bag of used LEGO bricks for a quarter. They were like new. No teeth marks or anything. I asked my mother to take me to some yard sales, but she said they're for poor people.

"We're poor people," I reminded her.

"Jews don't go to yahd sales, Gah."

My mother did employ some alternative money-saving schemes. She clipped coupons and used food stamps and went to a shoe store called Abbott that was a chaotic firetrap, but if you could find both shoes you got a bargain. When we waited for the pediatrician in the examining room, she stocked up on Band-Aid Brand bandages and cotton balls. In addition to these traditional methods for stretching a buck, she also applied a more unconventional technique—she switched price tags. In the times before barcodes, my mother took deep discounts from a broad array of retailers by slyly replacing price tags for expensive things with price tags for less expensive things. She avoided larceny charges by never getting greedy.

Joanie said "ahem" a lot to clear her throat from all the smoking. She smoked Pall Malls all day long. She told me to never smoke, and to show me why, she once took a drag and blew smoke into a piece of Charmin. She pointed to a yellowed spot on the paper and said, "This is what my lungs look like."

A disgusting but impressive trick. Joanie had enough energy to clean *and* watch my weather report that I gave in front of a large map I tacked onto the closet door in the family room. Joanie took a break from her electric brooming of the burnt orange family room shag to take in my forecast. Using a pointer, I gave the weather report for the day, which involved a frightening catastrophe.

"Greenland, a giant country made of ice, is going to melt and then float right into Massachusetts. There will be no school in Peabody tomorrow."

"You're such a brain, Gary," she said, then cleared her throat for the ninetieth time that day.

Later, I read jokes from the joke books and Joanie laughed at the one about taking a credit card away from an elephant to prevent him from charging. Joanie was such a good audience for my jokes, I got completely amped up from my show, and so I jumped up and down on my mother's bed. My mother was on the other side of the house watching *Ryan's Hope* and unaware of the lawlessness Joanie abided. My mother said that if anything ever happened to her, she would let me live with Joanie. I didn't want anything to happen to my mother, of course, but being adopted by Joanie would be an excellent consolation.

At lunchtime Joanie made me tuna on toast and then spread out a comforter on the grass in the backyard so we could sit and have a picnic. Joanie did this every time she visited on a nice day. My mom had joined us once and I remember it because she threw out her back and was in bed the rest of the summer.

Joanie opened all the windows and shades and curtains when she came over, so it was always lighter in my house when she was there. It was like a brand-new house. Everything was clean, and the beds were made. She was there that day because that night we were having company over for Passover, the Jewish holiday commemorating the events of television's *The Ten Commandments*. At the end of the afternoon Joanie hugged me, put on her sunglasses, said a final ahem, and sang her signature farewell, a falsetto "bye" but sung Southern so it sounded like "bah."

"Don't ya just love her?" my mother asked.

"Yes! So much."

"You know she's my oldest friend? I've known her longer than Auntie Judy."

My mother had good taste in friends. She said you only need *one* good friend, but she had a lot of good friends. I laid down in the family room on the freshly e-broomed carpet and watched *Sesame Street,* cheerfully sniffing the savory aroma that commemorated every one of Joanie's glorious visits. I wanted to be like my mother and have a lot of friends for a long time.

Around dusk my father arrived, and he kissed my mother on the cheek and said, "Hello, dear." My father was wearing a V-neck sweater with a dress shirt underneath and gray wool slacks with a swollen black leather wallet bulging in his back pocket. My brother Rick was home from college and my brother Max was there with his best friend.

My father explained that it's a tradition to invite people who aren't Jewish to Passover. Excellent strategy. I considered inviting Wally for a moment, but I got anxiety before the idea could take hold. What if he got bored and *swore* to spice things up? Or what if my father wanted to seek retribution for the middle finger incident? I needed someone who was versatile enough to play with me but also possessed some etiquette, someone you don't have to worry will say the f-swear while we're counting down the ten plagues.

We sat at the dining room table. I didn't even know we had a dining room table. It was usually folded up against the wall. But Joanie unfolded and clothed it. That night, it was open and fit all six of us. My father was sitting at the head of the table close to a big window that had a fluorescent light rod across the top. You turned it on by pulling a string and then it flickered to life. Very satisfying. It's bright in this room exclusively on Passover. We put on this many lights only when there's company because of the electric bill. Dad had a pillow under his forearm, which is part of the Passover production. I sewed the pillow last year in art. Each of us had a little booklet that read "Maxwell House" on the cover. Within was the story of Moses and the exodus from Egypt, a tale so implausible that if Maxwell House hadn't lent its venerable imprimatur, I would have thought it was totally made up.

There were small amounts of matzah eaten and Manischewitz grape wine drank at various cues. Matzah is the unleavened bread Jews eat during the holiday to memorialize the haste with which we got out of Dodge. We didn't have time to let the dough rise but packed it anyway.

In typical Jewish fashion there was nothing to interest kids. Except at one point when they sent me around the house to find a ransomed matzah called afikomen. I found it wedged behind the large mirror in the dining room, and my dad gave me a dollar. I was hoping for a five, but really any foldable money was exciting to me.

Later, as the service wound down, we filled a glass for a ghost named Elijah and then opened the front door. According to Maxwell House, Elijah, a dead prophet, will enter the house and drink your glass of wine if you leave the door open for him. It was an exciting abracadabra to the evening and the one case during the year where my mother didn't have an aneurysm over a door being left open. Hopefully the smoke and mirrors would impress Max's friend and his people.

Rick said that Elijah was like Santa but a wino, and everyone laughed except my dad who said, "That's a sacrilege, son."

He said the same thing when I asked how it was possible that not a single Hebrew happened to have baked a loaf on Exodus Eve. I contended that a day-old loaf would be superior to these tasteless crackers.

We finished the service by singing a song called "Dayenu," which was catchy and upbeat but interminable and repetitive to the point of absurdity. I didn't know what it was about because it wasn't in English. There were like sixty verses, and by the fourth I thought, *Genug*, which is a Yiddish word my mother always said when I talked too much. It means "enough."

I was sure there was some trick to learning this other language, like maybe you pronounced only every third letter, or *j*'s were *m*'s, or you read it upside down or backward. Whatever it was I was sure I'd figure it out in time like I did the year before with English.

We went into the family room and watched some baseball. In between one inning I went into the dining room to check on Elijah's glass. It was empty. I gotta tell Wally about this miracle. Although he would probably find a hole in the story. He did that a lot. He was difficult to be friends with. He didn't seem to like the things I liked about myself, mostly that I could run super fast, I could read anything, and I was hilarious. I was dubious about the Elijah business myself. If a ghost really drank wine in my house, I think my dingbat of a mother would have been terrified. I went to the front door to close it with my mother. It smelled so nice outside—warm, dewy grass mixed with moonlight. The house still smelled of Joanie but now there was a thick matzoh ball soup and chicken waft. Tremendous day all around. A visit from my favorite gentile and a holy ghost. *I will remember this.*

Shortly after the last day of Passover, this Jew reached the Promised Land. Mrs. Burns moved me to *Sun Up*, the highest reading group. A well-deserved promotion. *Sun Up* was more like it. This was where I belonged. So glad to be away from the index-finger-beneath-every-word, lip-moving, sound-it-out simpletons in *Janet and Mark*. The book was clean, either because it was new, or maybe the previous users' urbane sensibilities eschewed drawing the boobs, dicks, and poop so rousing to the riffraff.

A week or two into May, on an overcast, drizzly day, my dad took Wally and me to a carnival. My father showed grace by allowing me to invite Wally along on our visiting day after the middle finger fiasco. Wally had either forgotten about it or didn't feel it warranted any shame. Despite there being no tension, there was also no conversation between my father and Wally. We mostly listened to talk radio.

There were a few rides that Wally and I went on together. We went on a race car that was confined to a track, and I sensed Wally was offended by the restrictions. I understood. He'd driven without rails and in reverse in the family station wagon. There were some rides that I was too afraid to go on, such as the Tilt-A-Whirl and the more formidable of two Ferris wheels, the one with spinning cages. My father was a good sport and took Wally on those.

Nothing could get me to go on scary rides. I was ashamed of that and was concerned that my timidity and primness were frustrating to Wally. I walked a tightrope when I was with him. I tried not to disappoint him with my good-boy nature. I couldn't participate in his vandalism and swearing, but I didn't judge him. It made our friendship feel fragile. While there was only about a year that separated us, at this point in our friendship, I was always worried that he was outgrowing me. But I refused to meet him halfway. The feeling in my stomach was too strong of a compass.

What was most vexing was that while comedy was my bread and butter, I could never make him laugh. It wasn't just me; he was a tough audience. One summer night he came over to watch the Kurt Russell masterpiece *The Computer Wore Tennis Shoes* and he hardly laughed. My neck was sore from turning to see if he was laughing, which ruined it for me. He seemed irked. J-sus, I didn't write it, man. I wanted friends, but should it be this much work?

July 2017

I want to start sticking some quotes on the wall next to my bed. Something to give me some inspiration or comfort over the next G-d knows how many months. I sift through the drawers on the other side of the bed for a memo pad. I write the first one on a yellow Post-it memo my mom stole from her job at a publishing company in the 1990s, and stick it on the wall to the left of my bed. It's a quote from the novelist Michael Chabon:

Nothing, not even unbearable sorrow, lasts forever.

The note keeps curling up and falling from the wall, the adhesive no longer adhering, so I rake an adjacent drawer and find a clear plastic box containing clear push-pin style tacks my mom stole from the Hallmark store she worked at in the 1970s. While rifling the drawer that second time I also find an aquamarine-blue note. The note is as old as the tacks. The penmanship is commendable, like the scribe was a reincarnated typewriter. Printed in black felt-tip pen, the message is curt.

Mr. Gulman,
Gary completed all his work this week plus additional work on his reading. He made fewer mistakes because he was concentrating on his work. He still had time for a few jokes but he told them at the appropriate time.

Sincerely, Mrs. Rand

Second First

I was seven. At night, it smelled like the end of summer. My mother was hosting a Rubbermaid party. A bunch of middle-aged ladies were in my house examining plastic containers that a chalk-white, skeletal, straight-brown-haired woman with a pickup truck laid out all over our kitchen. She raved about the items on display in between snide barbs at the leading brand. It was like she was rehearsing for the Dean Martin roast of Tupperware.

Judy Burns, my neighbor and first-grade teacher, was sitting at our kitchen table.

"Gary, this year you're going to have Mrs. Rand. She's new, so I don't really know anything about her."

This was when I learned I was repeating first grade. At a hostess party for some also-ran in the direct-to-consumer plastic-container industry. Under normal circumstances, any gathering at my house included me doing some jokes and some imitations for the crowd, but that night my brain was elsewhere. It's possible that someone had told me before that night that second grade wasn't in my immediate future, but I didn't remember. I can't imagine I would have forgotten such a bombshell. Sure, I got pre-occupied in the summer riding my bike, watching garbage trucks compact their trash, and looking for toads, but it's hard to believe that this jarring information wouldn't have made an impression. I can't imagine I could have compartmentalized something as radical as doubling the amount of time I would spend in first grade. Maybe they didn't want to ruin my summer by telling me?

No matter when the news was relayed to me, the motives behind the decision were explained a few days later by my father and my brother Rick. They teamed up and gloated over what a masterstroke this was. My dad was so convinced of the benefits of his scheme that he boasted about the battle he fought to win them.

"The principal, the assistant principal, the school counselor, all showed me studies and ahticles about the hahm done by holding kids back, but I insisted you weren't ready for second grade. I don't care what their studies say. I know my son."

You do?

Rick told me how he wished Dad had held him back so he could have had a second year on the high school baseball team and so he wouldn't have been the smallest kid in his grade. I'll have an extra year, which will allow me to stand out in sports. They told me how I'd be the biggest kid in the grade and the other boys would be afraid of me. The way they framed it, it sounded like we secured an invaluable advantage. By the end of their pitch, I was grateful to my father for taking this gallant stand on my behalf. I trusted my father and my brother completely. How could these smart, experienced adults be making the wrong decision for me? They had absolutely no doubt that this would turn out great. I felt lucky to have them on my side.

Still, this is *nuts*.

My main concern was how was I going to answer the inevitable inquiries from the nosy snoops at school? Kids were going to notice this. They lived for this type of gossip.

"What am I going to tell the other kids? They're going to ask me why I stayed back."

Dad told me, "You tell them that you didn't *stay* back. You were *held* back. Your father didn't think you were mature enough for second grade."

You're shitting me.

Six- and seven-year-olds were going to understand that? There were only a few kids who knew what the word "mature" meant and none who could spell it. Was there one child on earth, some grade-school Buddha who would respond with compassion?

He'd take his telephone off the hook, light a candle, pour me a cup of lemon-ginger tea, and nod with understanding:

"Sure, Gary, I understand. *Held* back, yes. I get it. Children our age develop intellectually, emotionally, and socially at an irregular pace. It's possible that ultimately this decision will prove beneficial. I just pray your parents will be vigilant and immediately address any signs of stress or regression."

My father didn't think there would be anyone to give me a hard time because they'd be afraid of me. He told me that if they teased me, I should "knock 'em out." This was a common theme in discussions with my dad. Most of his childhood stories were about getting into fights.

My dad was seven when he moved from a poor Jewish immigrant section of Boston to a poorer more ethnically diverse section of the Bronx. In the Bronx nearly every day he was in a fight with boys of every nationality and race. Most of these scrapes developed because someone called him a "dirty Jew" or a "f—in' Jew" or sometimes just "Jew" without any incendiary modifier. You didn't even have to include the word "Jew" to provoke an attack from the young Philip Gulman. You could also provoke him by calling him "Boston Baked Beans" or disparaging his beloved Red Sox.

I went to school without the breeziness I had when I started my first first grade. I was starting over from the beginning. Only four other kids were repeating first grade. Two had serious behavioral issues and two couldn't read. I had to be the most well-adjusted, well-read repeater in the history of public school. This was absurd.

I was very interested to see who *didn't* repeat first. Kevin Bartlett? A kid who punched Mrs. Burns in the chest and ran home? He *had* to be repeating. Nope. He was taking his pugilistic artistry to grade two. So was "kid who is only capable of or only willing to say 'dinosaur.'" Post-kindergarten, the budding paleontologist had expanded his interests to include whacking kids in the mouth with his *Land of the Lost* lunch box, but *he* was promoted. Kids who said "take away" instead of "minus" when they saw the subtraction symbol and "equal" instead of "equals" when they saw = were in second grade that day. Kids who said "yabba dabba doo" instead of "here" during attendance were considered mature enough for second.

But the "here"-saying, *Sun Up*–reading, eighteen-*minus*-eleven-*equals*-seven-calculating, "or a girl"-blurting comedic prodigy must endure another year of this facile drivel? Another year of kids puking on the floor, peeing their pants, and counting with their fingers. Another year of ABCs, phonics, drawing turkeys by tracing my hand, and participation in the "hunter has become the hunted" anarchy of Duck Duck Goose, which wasn't even the slightest bit challenging the first go 'round. I've got to sing "*B-I-N-G-O*," again-O? All so I'll be a better athlete? I didn't give a care about sports. This was an outrage.

I met this Rand on the first day of school. Her classroom was located the farthest you could get from Judy Burns's classroom. Her long red hair, red eyebrows, and pointy nose left her just a black cone hat short of *H.R. Pufnstuf*'s Witchiepoo.

Rand's room was decorated with a lot of large cardboard cutouts of different professions: mail carrier, firefighter, doctor, and so on. Her shelves were packed with more than thirty large stuffed animals, like she spent her summers running the ring toss at a carnival. She'd give these toys away for outstanding story writing during the school year. She didn't smile; didn't seem warm.

I looked at all the kids in the classroom and was struck by how little they were. And *young*. Some of them had not yet grown into their head. Some heads were not yet shaped right. If I should ever be insulted by any of them and in need of a quick comeback, at least three of the boys would vie for the nickname "Hammer Head." Two others were in contention for "Frankenstein." You would be hard-pressed to distinguish between a carnival caricature and a photograph of these trolls. I knew only one kid from my neighborhood. The rest were strangers.

The good news was that from day one I was in the yellow group, the highest reading group. Red was for the middle, and the aptly named blue group was for the kids who were in way over their balloon heads.

It was also odd being in a class taught by a teacher whose house I'd never been in. I knew my lucky streak would run out at some point, but why now? Why couldn't they just send me back with Burns? I would have been like her assistant, could've helped her grade papers, clap erasers, authenticate permission slips.

For the first month distress mostly came from dealing with questions and comments from the second graders during recess. It was excruciating.

"Why'd you stay back?"

"My father didn't think I was mature enough."

"Oh."

What do you mean "Oh"? You don't believe me? Do you think I failed first grade? Ha! Do you want me to whip out my report card? All ones and S's, you little shit. I was in Sun Up. *Last time I saw you, you were sounding out "quack quack, said the duh-uck." You still counting on your fingers? I can count to one hundred by ones, twos, fives, and tens. If there was any justice, I'd be double promoted to third and start ripping through the times tables and dominating spelling bees. You want me in a bee? Let's go. Spell "people" and I'll stop screaming.*

There was one girl, named Julie LaRoche, who was less subtle in her undermining. One day at recess she approached me. She was wearing a purple shirt and her big dumb girlie glasses. She chanted, "Gary stayed baaaack. Gary stayed baaaaack," right up in my face.

The nerve on this dimwit in purple. Not only had she been in *Palo Alto*, the group for I-can't-read-ers, but she was also given additional help several times a week by the remedial reading specialist. This beneficiary of social promotion was taunting *me*, a *Sun Up* vet. I needed to hurt her feelings, so I scanned my insult inventory for a strong but proportional rejoinder.

I leaned in and through a satisfied grin spit, "Shut up, Grimace."

She ran and told the recess lady on me. I protested that Julie had started it, but I didn't have the energy to explain about my father's coup to the teacher's aide, so I accepted the punishment of sitting against the school for the remainder of recess. I didn't care; I was worn out.

Soon enough, the promoted kids got tired of their inquests and teasing and just ignored me, even though I had been an active part of their group about two months ago. There were no salacious details for them to savor, so they moved on. No time for me, probably too busy learning cursive.

It was obvious that Rand was not charming and kind like Carol Robbins or Judy Burns. She was very sarcastic, more wiseass than a first-grade teacher. She yelled at me a lot and punished me by holding me after school and/or sometimes having me write things over and over and over on a piece of green lined paper.

For some reason, putting your name on your papers whenever you handed in an assignment was a matter of grave importance to this shrew. Every week or so someone forgot their name. She'd announce that someone forgot their name and then an elimination tournament started. First, she'd return the papers that were properly submitted, summoning each student to her desk one by one. All those papers she graded. If you got a hundred, she drew a five-pointed star in vivid red ink on the top. Sometimes there was also an ink pad rubber stamp that had a smiling boy saying "excellent." While I waited for my name to be called, I'd get a painful pit in my stomach like when I couldn't find my mother at Marshalls. After she determined whose paper it was, by process of elimination, she graded it right in front of you, so you knew what you would have gotten if you had your shit together enough to put your name on it. She then crossed that grade out and marked it with a big red zero. No star, no stamp. She gave you a chance to see your handwriting and the red circled line on top whose emptiness had lowered you to this. Then, she made a show out of throwing it out. In addition to standing in front of her for this public humiliation, you also had to write "I will put my name on my paper" at least twenty-five times on a blank sheet—more if your last offense was recent. I only forgot to put my name on a paper three times that year, but the process turned me inside out every time. It was mean, but she would get markedly crueler.

She was also not above teasing me or any other kid over mistakes and flaws. Early in the school year my lower-case *r* was a source of much scorn from Rand. My penmanship was weak all around, but when I wrote my name at the top of my papers, I was not careful enough with making sure that the horizontal hook attached to the vertical of the *r* was high enough on the *r*'s backbone. I didn't use two strokes. I used one stroke and sometimes in my haste it looked like a *v*: ✓

Whenever my *r* fell short she would call out Gāvy in front of the whole class, which, in 1970s homophobic American culture, drew hoots of laughter. These jackals devoured that type of low-hanging fruit. I was ears-burning, head-hung mortified every single time.

Quickly I realized that despite my seniority in the classroom, none of the kids respected me or had any use for me. Contrary to my father's assurance, the kids weren't afraid of me and had no problem calling me Gāvy or laughing when Mrs. Rand ridiculed me. She liked being funny, but it was mostly a spiteful humor rather than silly or playful. I hated her. When she was absent from school, I hoped it was because she had been hit by a truck. I pictured her in a cast that covered her entire body with a black cone witch hat on the outside.

One day in January we went to the school library in the basement. This school had a large library where the cafeteria once was. Because of the general decay of this school, I never believed the library was there because of any devotion to literature; rather, I bet the kitchen was blown up by a careless chef and they didn't have enough money to fix it. It was a big library, but there were only a handful of books that interested me. The librarian was named Mrs. Martel and she had completely white hair even though she wasn't that old. I told kids her hair probably turned white when she was a kid and first saw her stupid face in the mirror. I never once saw her smile at a child. She did smile at Mrs. Rand. They seemed to really hit it off, probably bonded while snickering at the short-bus kids. There was a library aide named Mrs. Exum. She was nicer though vapid. She was having a conversation about a book she was reading and how she only counted one typographical error, which was a kind of game she and her husband played when they read books. From that day on I secretly called her Mrs. *Excitement*.

I looked through the stacks, one section in particular, the

Seuss shelf. As usual, all the good Dr. Seuss books had either been taken out or stolen. No *Cat in the Hat,* no *Green Eggs and Ham,* no *Horton Hears a Who!* No *Lorax.* The *How the Grinch Stole Christmas!* was in, but I wasn't so sure I'd be able to groove on it off-season. *One Fish Two Fish* was there, but I'd read it, and to be honest . . . it was insulting. Also available was *If I Ran the Zoo,* another appalling volume. I checked out the only Dr. Seuss book that looked interesting. I paid no attention to the name. What mattered was that it had the good doctor's name in his distinct font that I do so love. I took it home.

Then I didn't read it. I didn't open it, didn't even glance at it. Whatever the title was it didn't grab me or even register, and the cover made no lasting impression. I just didn't want to come back from the library empty-handed. Poor kids are loath to squander any opportunity for free stuff.

I barely remembered bringing the book home.

Books were loaned for two-week periods. Two weeks was a long time to me. *One* week was a long time. I had sent away for only one thing in my life because the idea of allowing four to six weeks, the standard delivery time for anything kids liked, seemed ludicrous. No, I will not "allow four to six weeks" for my X-ray Specs. I'll be an old man by then.

With two whole weeks to read this book and then return it I felt no need to keep track of it. Two weeks is a lifetime at seven. Yet they passed.

We made a class visit to the library the day the book was due, and I asked if I could renew it. I had no intention of reading it; I just wasn't certain of where it was. Martel said sure, bring in the book and I'll renew it. Catch-22. Which was not the name of the book. They never even told me what the name of the book was, always referring to it as "the book" or "the overdue book."

Ooooh, maybe it's in my desk. The desks had a hinged composite wood cover with a large groove carved out near the top big enough to rest your pencil and the pencils of everyone sitting around you. You could lift the "hood" on your desk and in the metal basin keep all of your books and school supplies. The desks had a similar capacity to the trash can Oscar (the Grouch) lived in. In my desk I looked for the Seuss book, rifling through textbooks, torn-out phonics book pages, mimeographed worksheets, a *Weekly Reader*, a crumpled Scholastic Book Club order sheet, a watercolor-paint set, a few drawings on construction paper, an empty flattened generic crayons carton, a bunch of nude (no wrapping) crayon nubs, a broken red graphite pencil, a scrap of scrap paper with dried paste on it, a gray mitten, a navy-blue knit hat, a purple Hot Wheels El Camino, and a lot of crumbs. No Dr. Seuss book. An *El Camino* but no Seuss.

Shit. What do they do to you if you don't return a library book? They probably make you buy them a new one. I don't own any Seuss books, so they must be too pricey for poor people.

What if we can't pay? Will they call the cops? I imagine they'd send me to jail, directly to jail, until we paid up. Do they directly to jail your parents until you're old enough to serve the sentence? Could they take our house? I heard my mother tell Auntie Judy that the IRS was going to put a lien on our house if she didn't pay up. Is it like that with library books? My mother would never forgive me.

I must have brought it home. That's not good. In between occasional visits from my mom's oldest friend Joanie, who still helps my mom clean our house, the rooms get Vesuvian. For people with nothing we had a lot of stuff. Every drawer in our home was bursting. Every closet overflowing, pushing the sliding doors off their tracks. The sink was full of dirty dishes. Opening the freezer incautiously led to a Green Giant avalanche. The garage could only be explored safely with a compass and a flare gun.

I was praying the book was in the house and that if it was, I could find it amid the disarray. What if I left it somewhere else? How would I even know? I so frequently walked home from school lost in my head: if it had fallen out of my Snoopy with Woodstock tote bag the day I brought it back, I wouldn't have noticed. It could be anywhere. It could be in that godforsaken playground, torn to shreds or used to light cherry bombs, Roman candles, and M-80s. Damned teenagers.

I told myself I'd look for the book after school. But the hour hand on the class clock weighed a ton. When I was finally out, I just wanted to numb myself with *Sesame Street*, *The Electric Company*, *Mister Rogers' Neighborhood*, and *Zoom*. Kids my age thought those were baby shows, but they soothed me. I loved them. I wouldn't give them up. It would be disloyal.

I knew the search for the book was going to take a long time. I'd also have to do it quietly and alone, so I wouldn't alarm my mother. The daunting operation gave me severe anxiety, which led to more procrastination.

If the hour hand at school was lead, in my house it was a pinwheel. Every day it was GD bedtime before I knew it. It was always time to get up for school. So hard to get out of bed. Then it was the next morning. I didn't look for it that first night. I didn't have the will.

I had no plan. I was beaten. Maybe it would just turn up. Maybe a kid would turn it in at school. Maybe the school would burn down, and all records and files would be destroyed. They'll have to amnesty all the late-book returners and forgive all the fines. Everybody would get a do-over. Maybe in the confusion I'd be sent to second grade. Doubtful. My life obeyed the parameters of seventies sitcoms. The protagonist strives, stretches his arms out, fails . . . the suffering resets.

I found myself longing for when all I had to worry about was my conflict with Mrs. Rand. Hating school without this warrant hanging over me was torture but at least there was only one layer to it. When I reviewed my index of problems it was just Rand. Now it's Rand, the librarian, and my mother's uh-oh when she inevitably finds out about the missing book. Then there will be the search. But I can't say for sure the book ever made it into the house. It could be somewhere on Bow Street.

Rand asked about it every morning. I'd been disenfranchised, allowed only to browse but not borrow at the library. I visited the Seuss section. Maybe it magically reappeared? Honestly, I wouldn't know it if I saw it.

A couple of weeks went by and the missing book became a quagmire. I'd looked for it along the walk to school and in my room. Checked under the bed, looked in the tiny bookshelf in the family room. I couldn't find it. I started to think of it as a symbol of my weakness. My immaturity. My lack of intelligence. I was so smart, now I'm not to be trusted with a library book.

It got worse. The librarian enlisted Rand's help in securing the book's return. What the hell? This was a Dr. Seuss book, not *Superman* number 1! If it was so valuable, why are you lending it to six- and seven-year-olds?

They started a pressure campaign. Rand enacted a singular policy: I would have to stay after school every day until I returned it. This was too embarrassing. No other kids had forgotten a book long enough for the administration to resort to extortion. Not one. Just me.

Staying after school was a penalty that was cruelly oppressive because it both lengthened the school day and abridged the length of my reprieve. I spent most of every school day staring at the clock on the wall and calculating how much time was left. The agony I felt when I was told at the beginning of the day that I would not be leaving with the rest of the kids, that I would have to walk home alone, filled me with despair. I needed to find this book. I stayed two straight days after school, then realized that I would have to confess to my mother.

I'd never been called a mama's boy but I cringed whenever

I heard the term because it so clearly applied to me. I knew my mother was unhappy with a lot of things in her life: that my dad left, that we were always short on money, that our car was so unreliable, that her own mother, Nana Lil, was a "bitch on wheels." I felt like my good behavior and being smart and funny was her salve. I always told her I was going to get rich and send her on the Love Boat so she could find someone. It was painful for me to bring her grief.

I was drowning. The gray winter days saddened me. The sunny days were a confusing tease. The sun was there, but I was shivering. The day that I vowed to tell my mother about my criminal negligence we sang "You Are My Sunshine" in music class and all I could think of was my mom. She was my sunshine. I thought about how much I missed her when I was at school. I had to stop singing because when I got to "You make me happy . . ." my lip quivered and my eyes filled. "When skies are gray." So gray. Why did I take out that book?

I told my mother. My mother was angry because if we didn't find it, we'd have to pay for it, and we couldn't afford that.

She yelled, "Why didn't you tell me sooner? Why are you taking out books from the *school* libry and not the Lynnfield libry? You're never to take out another book from that libry again. You hear me? Why didn't you tell me sooner? Why? Why did you wait until now?"

Well, Ma, a few reasons. I am familiar with your management of crises; you yell and then you dwell. Like at five years old, when I played in Luke Arcuri's sandbox while wearing brand-new sneakers you yelled at me and then came the dwelling. Every time she'd see them, she'd comment on my misdeed, restating my delinquency again and again. And again. Then frequently she would not talk to me for hours or until the next day, and then when she did resume interaction, she'd have to make clear "I'm still not happy about . . ." The statute of limitations on her "still not happy about" was infinity. The silence was tough to endure. She was all I had.

My mother made a phone call to Judy Burns (535-1478), my original first-grade teacher, from the wheat-colored kitchen phone mounted to the cabinet above and to the right of the tower of crusty dishes in the sink. When Mrs. Burns called back later, she was able to provide the name of the book and how much it would cost to replace it.

My mom put me on the phone with Mrs. Burns, who sounded very calm. She must have been in the middle of a sentence because I was confused by what she said. The sentence fragment I heard was "and to think that I saw it on Mulberry Street."

I was bewildered. I thought, *Why in the hell didn't you pick it up and return it to me? Now I have to find Mulberry Street? I've never heard of it, so it must be far away. I just hope the book is still there.*

As it turns out, the book's name was *And to Think That I Saw It on Mulberry Street.* It was the first book Seuss ever wrote and the last I'd ever take from that library. I can't believe I had ruined my life over a book with such an uninspired name.

They wanted six dollars for a new one. It could have been a million and it wouldn't have been any worse. Anything over one dollar was going to bring me hardship. Maybe a lien on my birthday presents. I must find this book.

Finances were a constant concern in my house. My parents talked about fiscal issues in front of me all the time. I was seven but I understood the tax implications of the alimony versus child support apportionment in my parents' divorce settlement. Every Sunday when my father wrote out a check for one hundred and ten dollars, he recited a litany of slogans associated with the dire monetary situation we were in.

"Money's tight . . ."

"G-d forbid I die . . ."

"Every month it's Peter to pay Paul."

Whenever I was mad at him, I'd retire to my room and sing this catalog of strife to myself in a blues tone. My mother was careful about not bad-mouthing my dad in front of me, but I'd overheard her say to Auntie Judy that "Every Sunday, he cries poor."

My mother expressed her fears of poverty by passionately extolling the virtues of wealth. She always got laughs from her routines that I'm sure she stole from Mae West or Joan Rivers or some other forty-niner.

"Money buys a softer pillow to cry on."

"They say money can't buy happiness, but I'm happy to give it a try."

And the people laugh and say, "Oh, Barb." I can't imagine they'd be as tickled if they'd heard it nearly every day of their conscious life.

My mother and I looked for the book as hard as we could but lost hope. I continued to be forced to stay after school for several more days but then G-d smiled on me in the form of my mom's friend and domestic savior, the irrepressible Joanie. She came over early in the morning, and my mother gave her the lowdown on the missing book and the stakes.

"We'll find it," Joanie announced. I believed her. It didn't turn up right away, but Joanie, undeterred, turned to her Catholic upbringing, reciting a special prayer: "Something is lost that can't be found. Please, St. Anthony, look around."

I'd never condoned witchcraft, but I'd never been this desperate. I closed my eyes and repeated Joanie's magical prayer, beseeching this overburdened saint for a miracle. Sure enough, Joanie found the book wedged between my bed and the bureau. I pledged eternal reverence for St. Anthony. Monday, I would march up to Frosty the Librarian and clear my name.

Sunday night there was less of a stomachache than usual. On Monday morning I tied my light brown "worker man" boots, slid on my mittens, my maroon UMass ski hat, zipped up my bright yellow winter coat, grabbed my Snoopy with Woodstock canvas tote bag and headed off to school. I was even early! We were lined up outside the door, waiting for the teachers to open for business. It was cold, a little misty. I could see my breath. Good Sherlock Holmes weather.

A boy who had been following my book drama closely asked, "Didja re—"

I opened the tote, but without looking inside, I could instantly sense: 'twas nuttin' but a Fluffernutter within. I'd left the book at home.

It got around quick. A lot of "uh-oooohs" and snickers. The kids were thrilled. I was horrified. I wanted to cry. I wanted to just run home, but I was afraid of truant officers. How could I forget it? It's the only thing I had to remember. *I am such an idiot. So stupid.*

This was a problem. My mother had warned me that she needed to take Max to a new job he had and so she'd be picking me up after school.

"Don't dillydally!" she said.

"Did you remember the book?" Rand asked.

"I forgot it in my room." I thought maybe if I was specific, she'd know I'd found it and give me a break. I was a fool.

"See you at two thirty."

I meekly approached the bench.

"I can't stay after today. My mother is picking me up from school . . . ," I softly spoke.

"She'll have to *wait*," she snapped.

Chr-st. Even meeker now I asked, "Can I stay after tomorrow instead?"

"No."

"Please . . ."

Now I was begging. I was standing, but I felt like I was on my knees. My lip was quivering. Where was the tough guy? The biggest kid in the class?

"Well, why don't we have the class vote on it?" offered Rand.

In that moment, I should have just said *never mind*.

AND THEN IT HIT ME: This was *diabolical*. Deliberately cruel. She had to know the default ethos of six-year-olds is schadenfreude-infused sadism. They're all rats and snitches. Firing-squad cheerleaders. You should see these beach ball–headed vultures circle when there's even a whiff of a fight after school.

To make the situation even more brutal she waited until two fifteen to hold the vote. I had five hours and fifteen minutes to brood, to fret, to contemplate the voters' mindsets, emotions, and leanings.

I was looking around the room. Would anyone from yellow group vote for me? No, those smug prigs are law-and-order voters. Sure, I was one of them, but they'd give me the electric chair if it was on the menu. The red group kids were going to side with the teacher, try to curry favor, maybe get moved up to yellow. Blue? Unpredictable. You'd think maybe they'd go against authority. But then again, they have an anti-intellectual bent, so why would they side with a yellow? Plus, there were some total incorrigibles in the blue group who would probably be glad to see someone else get punished for a change. Kids have very little power, so they crave it, reveling in every opportunity to wield it. Choosing teams in gym class, having the kickball at recess, being left in charge when the teacher leaves the room. And if you can wield power, why would you use it to *not* punish someone? They probably also knew that Rand wanted to win this. If she won, she'd be more likely to call on her judicial branch in the future and they'd get to play judge again.

I knew I was going to lose because I knew this monster well enough to know this about her: she wouldn't have held a vote if she didn't *know* she would win. For months she had seen how the kids treated me, how they laughed when she called me Gāvy, how solitary I was at recess. My word, she's the devil.

At recess I thought about soliciting some votes, campaigning, maybe telling some of them my situation. Maybe I could "pretty please with sugar on top" a couple of votes. Maybe I could "be your best friend" a faction. But then I made a decision. No way am I going to beg these Beelzebubs for leniency. Give them *more* power over me? I couldn't live with myself if I asked one of these Damiens for a favor.

At two fifteen Rand sent me into the hallway to give the tribunal a secret ballot. In the hallway, I thought that maybe I'd be acquitted. These kids weren't heartless. They colored and painted, and on Mondays they reveled in a new version of show-and-tell that eliminated the show and was basically just a doody/peepee open mic. Maybe it will even be unanimous. If they all voted for me to be set free, I'd thank them all individually.

"You won't be sorry. I'll make you proud. You won't regret this generous show of compassion for one second." I'll be like Scrooge after the Ghost of Christmas Yet to Come showed him his tombstone.

"I've learned my lesson, sir. I'll return all my library books days before they are due."

Who are you kidding, Gāvy?

You're finished.

A few minutes later a girl named Marlene came out in the

hallway. It all went down as I had expected. Rand delivered the verdict: I would be staying.

It hurt. As the kids filed out to line up for dismissal, I did an informal exit poll. I didn't find a single kid who voted Gāvy. Small sample but statistically relevant. Even that one kid I knew from my neighborhood, whose house I sledded at, slept over at once, and ate dinner in—he voted against me. I was too disheartened to get angry at them or lash out. Who knows how I would have voted? I forgot the book. I didn't deserve forgiveness. I was asking for something as evolved as *grace* from kids who still tied their shoes using the bunny-ears technique.

Of course this wasn't a vote on whether to pardon my offense and release me from the torture of staying after: it was simply a vote for a stay of execution, a twenty-four-hour clemency. They wouldn't even grant me that. Bastards. *I'll remember the book tomorrow. And so help me G-d, I'll remember every last one of these weasels for the rest of my days.*

I stayed after. Out of the window, I could see my mother's 1973 blue Chevy Bel Air on Bow Street.

"You should put the book by the door when you get home," Rand said.

"I will." The deference I feigned was excruciating for me to witness from inside my head.

What I wanted to say was: "Is that how you remember your Vroom Broom Witchiepoo?"

At two forty-five, Rand let me go. I raced out of the door to the waiting Bel Air.

My mother was apoplectic.

"We were waiting and waiting and waiting. Did you tell her your mother was picking you up?"

"Uh-huh. I'm sorry."

"What did she say?"

"She said no." *What the hell do you think she said? She said okay, but then we got to gabbing, you know how girls can be.*

"We waited and waited, and I'm thinking did he walk home? Did we miss him? I told him to be out there. I know I told him. We waited and waited. Now Max is gonna be late. We were waiting and waiting. You're never to take another libry book from that school."

I never wanted to *read* again.

I didn't tell my mother about the vote. I couldn't be sure about how she would react. I'm almost certain she would be appalled at Rand's kangaroo court. But she was so angry about my lateness that I couldn't be sure that she would express the compassion and outrage that this wickedness merited. In fact, she might have even sided with Rand. Also, what boy wants his mother to know that he's not liked? And I'd have to tell her right in front of my brother. He'd think I was a loser. I could punch myself in the face for forgetting that GD book.

I got home and put the book in my Snoopy tote and put the tote by the front door. My mother reminded me that I should have done that the day before. She had always been an expert at the game of "Shoulda," a spinoff of her other favorite: "if only." "You shoulda left earlier. You shoulda told me. You shoulda stuffed your hat in the sleeves of your coat." She never let anything go. I remembered to bring it the next day. I gave it to Rand as I entered the room.

"Was that so hard?"

Despicable.

After that, nothing was the same. Now I hated school. Any joy I squeezed out was gone. I no longer even looked forward to show-and-tell or gym or recess or art. . . . I was holding my breath every day from eight thirty to two thirty. Every week I was angst-ridden until Friday. All weekend I was anxious because I knew how soon Monday becomes today.

I practiced several weekend-conservation techniques. The main one was to stay awake as much as possible. Any time spent sleeping Friday through Sunday was frittering away my furlough. I stayed up as late as anyone in the house on Friday, often being carried into bed in the middle of the night by my brother after I'd fallen asleep watching *Quincy, M.E.* on the family room shag. Saturday mornings I woke up early and watched cartoons until they switched to sports in the afternoon. I always made sure I was aware of the clock. I spent time with Wally but stayed conscious of the time, at any moment able to tell you exactly how much weekend remained before my eight thirty bedtime Sunday night.

The main thing I longed for when I was at school was my house and my mom, so I tried not to spend too much time away from my house, especially on my favorite day, Saturday. I loved the feeling of the rest of the weekend ahead of me and the one-day relief from my nervous stomach. Doing anything distracted me; I simply wanted to stay indoors immersing myself in freedom.

As the year progressed, I prayed for snowstorms, and on February 5, I manifested an unprecedented thirty-three-hour nor'easter that dumped twenty-seven inches of snow on Massachusetts and the surrounding New England states. There were drifts as high as fifteen feet. A state of emergency was declared, and schools were closed for an entire week. Thank heaven.

But returning to school after that unscheduled vacation was harder than after any previous break. My adversarial position with Rand was deepening. She was my archnemesis, my Joker, my The Spellbinder, my Mr. McGee (that one reporter who followed the Incredible Hulk around. Why weren't there more journalists interested in covering that juicy story?).

My Sundays were ruined by the looming anguish that resumed every Monday. As the sun set and my father said his goodbyes, there was a canopy of gloom over the house. I felt the hours and then the minutes of my freedom dwindling. It occasionally occurred to me to blame my dad for my predicament. He was the one who came up with the plan to hold me back. It was his fault. If it hadn't been for his arrogance, his ignorance, there would be no Rand in my life.

But most of the time I didn't blame him. I blamed myself for not being tougher and not doing what he told me to do: beat up the kids who teased me. I blamed myself for being so thin-skinned about Rand's insults and not being able to formulate the right comeback.

I blamed myself for not being the smartest in the class.

After my dad left on Sunday evenings I was tortured. Misery overcame me as the grating stopwatch *ntz, ntz, ntz, ntz, ntz,* of *60 Minutes* gave way to Rhoda Morgenstern, my beloved Jewish princess, of CBS's *Rhoda*. It started at 8:00 P.M. Her instrumental opening theme was my taps. I was allowed to stay up until eight thirty, which meant that I had to go to sleep at the end of Rhoda's *own* weekly tilt at despair. I marched to the gallows right after the iconic MTM orange kitten's "meow" that signaled the end of the show. I knew how that kitty felt. It was hard to sleep knowing that when I opened my eyes again, I would be the furthest from Friday two thirty as I could get.

On March 8, 1978, a Wednesday morning, I had an excellent idea. What if I warn of impending sickness? Do they send you home for a credible vomit threat?

I thought back to first first grade. Miles Zellen threw up on the floor around his desk. The choreographed response that followed was unforgettable. Mrs. Burns quickly isolated Miles from the biohazard, dragging him toward the front of the classroom while whisking the desks and their occupants away from ground zero. She then picked up the black phone by the door and made a brief call. I couldn't hear what she said. I always imagined that it happened so frequently that there was a code. "Dottie, this is Burnsie, I got a four-oh-nine here in room 2B, B as in 'Balloon Head.' I'm gonna need a butler with sprinkles, over. . . . Ten minutes? Woman, are you drunk? In ten minutes we'll be swimming in upchucked SpaghettiOs."

The custodian, Mr. Dropo, arrived moments later with his equipment.

He brought a dustpan, a broom, and a pail full of sawdust. Elementary custodians are magicians, the mop their wand. He tackled that puke without any gagging, retching, or hesitance. How? That stink, my word, as Nicolas Cage once said, "Some things you can't un-smell."

But that custodian didn't blink or clothespin his nostrils. He put his Brylcreem-covered head down and lickety-split, we were back to phonics. And all he got was a thank-you from Mrs. Burns. He deserved a standing ovation and an accent-lighted portrait in the lobby. In oil! Without the combination of a poised teacher and a deft custodian, we could have had a catastrophe.

The Zellen puke incident was all as clear in my mind as if it happened yesterday. What I remembered most vividly, though, from the incident was that Zellen was sent home before the (saw) dust settled. He didn't even get to witness the dynamic cleanup. I'll bet a teacher, especially a new one like Rand, would send a kid to the nurse's office to get sick rather than risk presiding over calamity.

"I think I'm gonna throw up," I told Rand that Wednesday morning. "Can I go to the nurse?"

Thus began a phase of second first that would culminate in a reckoning for Rand and me. It would change our relationship as well as some in my family.

I was granted permission and walked to the nurse's office, which was conveniently only three doors down from our room.

It was kind of nice, clean, and smelled like rubbing alcohol and Curad adhesive bandages. There were Disney characters painted on the walls. They were well done, I have to say, though clearly unlicensed. I'm surprised that greedy rodent hadn't brought a suit against the trademark-infringing infirmary.

I told the nurse I was sick, and within twenty minutes I was home watching the Showcase Showdown. I was so relieved. My mother took care of me, convinced I truly was sick. I sat on the floor on my blanky and she brought me Ore-Ida crinkle fries on the toaster-oven tray and a bowl of Campbell's alphabet soup as I watched the *ABC Afterschool Special,* the weekly maudlin-thology schmaltz fest. True to form, that day's episode, titled "It Isn't Easy Being a Teenage Millionaire," jerked a thousand tears. I'm susceptible to blatant sentimentality even on my best days, but my current state had made me especially vulnerable to this weepy melodrama about a cute fourteen-year-old girl who won the lottery. The poor thing, she thought her troubles were all behind her. But this is the *ABC Afterschool Special,* so we knew that the real trouble lay ahead. By this time in my relationship with the *Afterschool Special,* the opening theme song was enough to send me on a crying jag.

I milked a second day out of my "illness" and then a third, which happened to coincide with a Friday Joanie visit. I had conned my way into a miniature March vacation.

I returned to school on Monday, but the clock was moving unusually slowly. At 9:50 I still had that same pit in my stomach that I always had on Sundays and through the entire school week, along with the familiar sense of doom. How could I make it through another four and a half hours with this angst racing through me?

I am not supposed to be here. That was the unspeakable mantra in my brain. It was on a loop. *I want to go home. I want my mommy. I hate my school. I hate my teacher. I hate my classmates. I hate my life.* Though I'd never say it out loud, I wanted to die. I asked to go to the nurse again.

I went but it didn't go as smoothly as it had the previous week. The nurse, Mrs. Libby, a forty-something brunette with wavy black hair and a blue cardigan sweater, who wasn't especially nurturing on my first visit, was skeptical of my condition this time. She took my temperature and let me lie down on a leather analyst's chaise. Then she sent me back to class. I had tears in my eyes. If I cried, this situation would get worse. I wanted to cry. Would they send me home for crying? I felt frail, shaky. My mind had been ravaged by worry, shame, and embarrassment.

The next day, I had a realization: *Once I leave my house, I'm dependent on decisions by the nurse. At home, I only had to convince my mother that I needed to stay home.* So I decided to start every morning saying I had a stomachache. This was not a lie. I did. I had that "the world is ending" pain in my stomach. I couldn't think about anything except school. All my time away from school was spent paying attention to how long I had until I went back. I became increasingly clingy with my mother. Following her around, kissing her, sitting next to her. I was always late to school because my mother had to plead with me to go every morning.

One morning my mother didn't have time for my intransigence.

I complained about my stomach and cried, "I can't go to school. I have a stomachache. It hurts," I said through tears.

She lost her cool and shrieked, "Because you won't make a doody!!!"

I was shaken by her volume but more by her insensitivity. *You daft bimbo. I have a stomachache because I am being bullied by the woman who was supposed to educate me and foster my well-being. I'm surrounded by fatheaded devils who cheerlead Medusa, and there's no*

*one there to save me. I can't put this into words but how could you be
so dense as to not pick up on any of this? Did you notice that last year*
none of this *was going on?*

My mother dropped me off at school. I went to the front office and checked in, but I never knew what you were supposed to say. I was never late once the previous year.

"I'm late. I'm here," I told the secretaries.

This made them all laugh and applaud. *Dingos.* This whole school year felt like I was in one of those diners where the waitresses are deliberately mean. I went to the classroom. I asked to go to the bathroom but instead went to the nurse. She told me to return to my classroom. I had a feeling my mother told them not to send me home. It was a conspiracy! I returned to Rand and told a lie.

"I'm being sent home by the nurse."

I didn't know what I was going to do if Rand let me go nor why I thought Rand wouldn't confirm this with the nurse. She made a call to the nurse to corroborate. I knew my fate. She was incensed. She took me out into the hall. Again, my weak bottom lip was quivering. She dressed me down, made me admit that I lied. I returned to class. I wanted to die.

I have no memory of how my father came to meet with Mrs. Rand on the following Monday after school. I may have told him that Sunday that I needed him to save me. She may have insisted he meet with her to tell him what a problem I was.

He came back to the house after the meeting. I was afraid I would get in trouble. My father told me about the meeting. At one point she told him about the vote. He described to me what happened next.

"I *blasted* her," he said. "I said to her, 'You *WHAT*?'"

He told me that he really laid into her and she was shaken! Ha! *How does it feel, you wicked witch of the West School?* They came to an agreement. I would go to school and not talk out of turn or make any clever asides. She would be careful about how she treated me. She would write a note home to him every Friday describing my behavior.

In that moment, I didn't think about how I wouldn't be in this nightmare if it hadn't been for him. He was my hero for protecting me from Rand. He stood up for me and put her in her place. I wish I could have seen her face when he yelled "You *WHAT*?" My dad had saved me.

For the rest of the year I kept my mouth shut and did my time. Eventually, the school year was almost over. I had one day to go. I'd survived.

I went to school on time that last day. Got my report card—1's and S's; I even got a satisfactory in self-discipline.

At closing time, Rand had a final announcement. It concerned the bedraggled stuffed animals that she had been giving away as prizes for the best stories written about the cardboard cutout professionals on the wall. I hadn't won one all year. As it happened, there were a few left and she was giving them away that last day. I took a pink pig. It was old and dusty, with asymmetrically glued eyes. I loved stuffed animals, but this one was tainted. I threw it into the woods on my way home.

August 2017

I wake up and check my iPhone 7. It's turning on and off and won't hold a charge. I'm distraught. Phone trouble, computer crashes, tax returns, and insurance claims are all features of a gauntlet of quotidian stressors that, in my fragile state, can sabotage the momentum of being awake and send me back for more of that sweet, sweet oblivion. I owe thousands of dollars in taxes that are months overdue, I have tens of thousands of dollars in denied insurance claims from my psych ward stay, and now the phone is dead. I'll need to spend more money that I can't afford to get a new one.

I have to make a trip to the Northshore Mall. When I'm sick, it's painful to interact with people at stores. I feel dumb and dependent and meek. I'm also afraid of running into people I know. They'll ask me how I'm doing or what I've "been up to," and I'll either have to lie or tell them "Better, I feel safe around shoelaces again and you should see all the kitchen knives they leave out! I'm sleeping in a twin bed at my mommy's house, but things are lookin' up."

I park on the same side where my mom used to park when she worked at Murray's, a Hallmark greeting card and stationery store. I enter through the same entrance Wally's mother, Sharon Mitler, dropped me off one time. There were no phone stores at the mall when I was a kid because when I was a kid, you had to rent your phone from "the Phone Company."

I'm anxious and self-conscious about my disheveled appearance, shorts with holes in them, wrinkled, ragged

Bob Dylan T-shirt. But I'm also thinking back wistfully about how at one time when I was only eight, I was a star here, the prince of what was then called the North-shore Shopping Center.

Second

Wally Mitler was the first friend I ever lost to cancer. But I was losing him long before he was diagnosed.

By the beginning of second grade I wasn't spending as much time with Wally as I used to. We didn't walk to school together anymore, and we rarely hung out after school. I didn't like how I felt about myself around him. He had become more of an antagonist than a best friend.

Wally was only about a year older than me but that's a large gap at age eight, amplified by his parents' laissez-faire approach to raising him. He lived more of an adult life than me. He was allowed to watch all the shows and movies that began with the "viewer discretion is advised" warning. My mother didn't even need to forbid me from seeing those; I ran screaming from the TV the instant they flashed the warning. For Wally I imagined the advisories were a cue to mix himself a highball and light a pipe.

I wasn't envious. I wanted no part of that world. I knew that kids who watched those programs were doomed to a life of depravity and vice.

It was no matter that I didn't see the shows because Wally reenacted them in detail, always sure to emphasize the most unsettling aspects. I would've had no idea what the devil in *The Exorcist* sounded like if it weren't for him. He loved *The Exorcist*. Saw it *in the theater. Quoted* it. Told me about the spinning head, pea soup vomit, and what the priest's mother dined on in hell. He would often hide behind my mother's car, and when I came outside, he would jump out, doing a pitch-perfect impression of that ghastly voice, "Gary, it's the devil."

Every time, I sprung backward with a shriek. And every time, he doubled over laughing with his hands on his stomach. It wasn't funny. It was abusive. It's why at night I *sprinted* from the family room to my bedroom through the dark kitchen and dining room. It's why I insisted my mother leave my bedroom door open and the hall light on. Only after I heard the clamorous *snap* of the hall light switch could I relax.

Wally reinforced his terrorism by giving me the dramatic backstory of hell and Satan. I had become terrified of the devil. Wally told me he was real and I believed him.

Over the years, Wally had seen all the things considered too upsetting, scary, or emotionally sophisticated for children. He had watched *Roots,* the Charles Manson biopic *Helter Skelter,* and *The Exorcist* again when it aired on TV.

But it was his *Holocaust* miniseries recap back when I was in Rand's class that caused me the most pain. It had a permanent effect on our friendship and my self-image.

He had told me about the miniseries the day after it started airing in April 1978. We were playing catch on the side of my house. Wally was not good at baseball, but, like every other boy, he had a glove and played Little League. Playing Little League was basically compulsory in 1970s Massachusetts. He threw wrong and seldom caught the ball. He claimed he needed a new glove. No, he needed new hands.

I had been sent out of the family room and its door was

shut when *Holocaust* premiered on NBC the night before. It was the talk of the town, especially among the town's Jews. Our *Roots*.

I am not sure if I had even heard the word "Holocaust" before the series began to air, and I definitely knew none of the particulars. I had a fear of Hitler identical to my fear of the devil, but I'm not sure of its origin. If it was discussed around me, it was done quietly; my mother forbade the discussion of anything solemn or emotionally challenging in her presence. Wally, now an expert after having seen the program, filled me in on what happened to Jews during the Holocaust, sharing with me the unspeakable specifics. He said that Jews were burned alive in ovens and starved in camps. My people were also gassed with poison. I was horrified, hoping he would stop talking about it. But much like with his devil voice, I think he enjoyed unnerving me.

When his précis ended, I asked the unanswerable question. Why? Why did they do that to the Jews? What could we have done to deserve this? I was asking out of genuine curiosity, the same way when I was five, I had asked him what G-d looked like. But I also asked him because I knew that whatever he said would let me know what he thought about Jews. I understood, as early as kindergarten, that my people were the object of pervasive hatred.

"Why?" I asked.

Without any hesitation Wally gave me his analysis.

"The Jews were rich snobs . . . walking around with their noses in the air."

He said this with certainty, like it was an indisputable fact and, what's more disturbing, a valid explanation for Hitler's atrocities.

There is no way Wally generated this explanation on his own. This was an idea an adult in his life must have expressed. Until that moment I'd never thought about how close Mitler is to Hitler. They're one letter apart.

I'd bet that after watching the show he'd had the same question I just asked him. Instead of giving a historically accurate attempt at an answer, someone in his orbit must have said to him, "Well, kid, these kikes got too big for their britches and Uncle Adie had to put them in their place. Also, the numbers are exaggerated."

Wally's next move, and this was particularly sadistic, had been to let his favorite Hēb in on the exigency of the final solution.

No matter the provenance of his despicable "snobs" theory, once again my gut told me how I should respond and hammered me for resisting.

It was my fault. I had appeased Mitler. I should have fought him when he gave my dad the finger that time when we honked at him. And now, he'd gone too far.

I had let my dad down. Phil Gulman would fight you just for saying the word "Jew" in a less than reverent tone; surely, he would have torn the throat out of some Nazi spawn announcing that the Jews were to blame for the Holocaust.

"They were snobs."

A good reason to dislike someone? Maybe. A defensible reason to torture and murder them? J-sus Chr-st.

I had to keep this to myself. If I shared this with anyone, they'd ask why I didn't violently attack him. I did have an answer for that: I'm a coward. As evidenced by the fact that I couldn't even defend the honor of my people. I said nothing and instantly hated myself. And *I stayed friends* with him. Like a schmuck.

Wally was pretty much the only friend I had in second grade. There just weren't many worthy choices for friends on my street. Being friends with him was more habit than harmony.

This was proving to be another tough year in school—not as traumatic as second first, but still unpleasant, more of a chronic emotional malaise. It probably had the same number of sunny days as any other, but that year felt gray. Ever since a month into my second stretch in first grade, school had become a place I went to watch a clock, and I hated every second of it.

For second grade I had a teacher named Mrs. Eve Turner. She was a tall pale woman with short curly gray hair and beady gray eyes behind big gray glasses. She looked like a bird that I saw in the Stone Zoo aviary called a gray crowned crane, but with enormous glasses.

She was humorless. I heard her laugh only *one time*. At lunch one day I didn't finish a baloney sandwich. She asked why I didn't finish it, and I said I'd had enough.

She said, "You mean you're full of baloney?"

Then she laughed *out loud* at this *dud*. I faked a laugh. Out of compassion. But I was ashamed of myself for betraying my comedic ethos. Full of baloney. Oh, Eve, you dreary crone.

There was really nothing in second grade that I wasn't aware of or able to do two years before, other than cursive handwriting. We learned each letter's capital and lowercase form individually and then practiced them for longer than I could tolerate but not long enough for me to develop any skill. It was tedious. All the lowercase and most of the capitals are lifeless. I did like making the *F*. Just a gorgeous letter. Majestic. And when occasionally lowercase *t*'s would mate, exulted over crossing them with a flourish. Other than that, the time spent studying cursive would be much better spent on a foreign language or typing. Anything but this shortsighted calligraphy class.

Mrs. Turner didn't yell as much as Rand and rarely kept anyone after school, so that was helpful. But I continued to resent being away from my house and my mom for such long stretches of time.

I was still unable to make friends with any of the little brats in my class, so I came to cherish my hours out of school more and more. It's not that I got actual pleasure out of my free time. None. But my deep unhappiness in school was suspended and that transient relief substituted for pleasure. I spent most of my time watching Channel 2's (local PBS affiliate) lineup, reading Encyclopedia Brown and Lewis Barnavelt books that Joanie brought me, drawing Peanuts characters, and organizing my growing stuffed animal collection that included a seal named Sammy, a hippopotamus named Salvy, and an elephant named Hannibal. Always in my room, always by myself, always feeling the next school day looming.

There was one fortuitous change that year. My mother got a part-time job. It was a godsend. Three days a week she drove fifteen minutes to the Northshore Shopping Center to work at Murray's, a stationery store / gift shop. I went with her to the mall at least two of her work days after school. It was a function of my clinginess, my reattachment that started during my second stretch in first grade. I had this recurring dream that there was a nuclear bomb and I was at school away from my mother when it mushroomed over the horizon. To hedge against that outcome, I was neurotically attached to her, which meant spending more and more time at the mall.

The Northshore Shopping Center was a grand, high-ceilinged, composite-tiled retail palace that had recently completed construction that made it fully enclosed for indoor shopping.

There were about thirty small stores and a three-story Sears, as well as two large upscale clothing stores called Jordan Marsh and Filene's. There was also a Toys"Я"Us that was the same size as the Purity Supreme supermarket it had replaced. Across from Toys"Я"Us was a moribund department store called J. J. Newberry. It was the only store that hadn't been refurbished to conform to the mall's new image. It had been neglected so long that it better resembled a museum *exhibit* of a department store than an actual department store. It did offer one intriguing feature, an iron-on T-shirt kiosk called T's 'n Things. T's 'n Things had counters full of binders with iron-on transfers of all kinds of slogans and pop culture images mostly related to doing drugs.

I think the "Things" in T's 'n Things was aspirational. The business never expanded beyond T's. I often teased Hercules Metatakis, the sixteen-year-old entrepreneur who owned T's, by asking, "When will the Things be arriving?"

"Any word on the Things?"

Or when a package was delivered, I'd say, "Quick! Open it! It could be *Things.*"

Northshore Shopping Center had an eclectic collection of retailers, food stands, and a few dine-in eateries.

There was a Windsor Button Shop, a Piercing Pagoda, an Earring Tree, and a men's salon called the Golden Shears, whose talc and Vitalis you could sniff from the Baskin-Robbins two hundred yards away.

Next to Windsor Button was a Brigham's, a diner that sold excellent ice cream but had roughly twenty-one-derful fewer flavors than Baskin-Robbins. There was His Place, Florsheim Shoes, Kinney Shoes, and Thom McAn shoes, which I insisted was misspelled.

Across from Brigham's was Herman's sporting goods, where they devoted too much space to archery. It had a pleasant aroma of sneaker rubber. There was a records and tapes store called Musicland and a C.B. Perkins Tobacconist that had a delightful, masculine scent. There was a Fanny Farmer shop, which my mother called "stale candy sold by old bags." I didn't need any candy because Murray's had a vast selection of Russell Stovers that my mother frequently pocket(book)-ed at closing. Whatever holiday was nearing, there were related milk chocolate icons, usually stuffed with marshmallow. Across from Murray's was Kennedy's, which sold men's suits, including some of the same finery worn by television *game show hosts*!

There was a pizza parlor called Papa Gino's. I called it Papa Gynecologist's except in front of my dad, who would not truck such risqué humor. The tables were excellent because they looked like a red-checked tablecloth but there was no cloth, it was *painted onto the table*! Whenever we ate there, I got a slice of cheese pizza and a medium Sprite. It came with a cool straw that accordioned to facilitate sipping. Papa Gino's was one of only two spots that were doing anything daring with straws; 7-Eleven with its straw/ spoon—stroon? spraw?—being the other bold innovator.

There was a bookstore called Bookends, where my mother refused to buy me any books. She told me we can get whatever I want at the libry. Drove me crazy, because of my lost-book incident, but mostly because I hated how she pronounced it *lie-bree*.

There were two toy stores. One was called Kay-Bee Toys, a boutique with inventory as limited as its future in the toy biz. The other was that colossal Toys"Я"Us. They were new on the scene. I believed they came from California, but I tended to think that about all cool new things—Jack in the Box, go-karts, Aquafresh.

Toys"Я"Us's arrival spelled ruin for all the other toy retailers in the area. That backward *R*? Gimmicky. Sell toys at significantly lower prices than your competitors? I'm sold. No need to pander.

I walked the aisles of Toys"Я"Us for hours, fixating mainly on a talking-robot learning toy called 2-XL (*to excel!* brilliant!). 2-XL was $54.87. That figure became a melody for me. I had figured out what that would look like in various denominations of coins and currency. When people mentioned large salaries on TV shows, I figured out how many 2-XLs they could buy. I asked friends and family to loan me $54.87. They thought I was kidding. I wasn't. I'd counted all my pennies and put them in rose-colored paper wrappers. I was about four thousand pennies short.

My other preoccupation there was a Matchbox cars parking garage with a working *car elevator* and *two gas pumps*! It was sold by Matchbox but there was nothing in the nomenclature to suggest that Hot Wheels cars weren't compatible as well! There were *three* levels! And it was made of plastic with a *vinyl placemat*! $10.95.

I wasn't allowed to be in the store where my mother worked while the owner was there—only after he left, around 6:00 P.M. Then I came in and hung out in those evening hours. I became friends with all the girls and empty nesters who worked at Murray's. Sometimes the cashiers let me ring things up. But mostly I walked around the mall by myself, going into stores, browsing and talking to the employees, checking back in with my mom by and by.

I spent much of my mall time talking with the teenagers who worked at Orange Julius. They gave me free hot dogs and Pineapple *Juli-i*. Sometimes they mixed different flavors together and had me test them. One time I tasted it and said, "What the f— was that?!" And everyone laughed. Despite Orange Julius's devil-with-a-pitchfork logo, I felt safe there thanks to my friends.

I was very outgoing at the mall in a way I wasn't at school. Maybe because the mall people didn't know me as the crybaby, first-grade repeater. I could make them laugh with my memorized Steve Martin albums and *Saturday Night Live* routines and with some of my more eccentric interests, like my ongoing search for a floppy hat with a feather in it that I called a "pimp hat." I didn't know what pimps did, but I coveted their garish haberdashery.

I asked salespeople at the various men's clothing stores, "Do you guys sell hats for pimps?"

They laughed. I wasn't joking.

I shone bright under the mall's harsh commercial lighting.

I was a star. The mall provided thrice-weekly five-hour respites from my loneliness and an outlet for my flair, but one afternoon it triggered the demise of my friendship with Wally.

One warm fall afternoon around 4:00 P.M., my mother was leaving for work. I was playing with Wally and another boy in front of my house on the street. It was a rare occasion where it was not just Wally and me—we had been joined by a neighbor kid. My mom asked if I wanted to come, and I said no. Five minutes later the other kid got called home for dinner and then it was just Wally and me.

I immediately regretted not going with my mom. Hanging out with Wally would not be stimulating and, as always, it was fraught. We went over to his house, but I quickly found myself in emotional distress. I simply missed my mommy. In tears, I asked Wally's mother, Sharon, if she'd drop me off at the mall. They were both noticeably exasperated by my request, but they gave in and drove me.

The three of us got into her red AMC Spirit. I was on edge the entire drive. All I could think was that if they got into an accident, they'd blame the Jews. I'm the mama's boy who couldn't bear to be separated from his mother while she went to work, and now, if they crashed, I will have wrecked their Spirit. I didn't care. I didn't want to be away from my mother and my mall friends hanging out with the Mitlers the whole night. As we approached the mall Sharon said something to Wally I found truly shocking.

"We should pick you up some new jammies."

Mrs. Mitler parked the car near the Toys"Я"Us side of the mall. I thanked her profusely, and she seemed over the initial irritation. Wally seemed aloof. They went left toward Sears, embarking on their jammies safari, and I continued on to Murray's and checked in with my mom. She was happy to see me. Then I made my rounds.

As I roamed the vivid confines, I saw that the Peabody Electric Light Commission was giving out free yellow helium balloons with precious smiley-faced light bulbs on them across from Scotty's piano and organ store. I was able to get two balloons, but when I went for a third, they told me it's one per person.

At first, I was disappointed and more than a bit perturbed. I'd have to outsmart the Electric Light Commission. I was confident that I would. If hours of Sunday Monopoly games with my dad had taught me anything, it was that utilities, especially the Electric Company, are feckless. Soon, a light bulb appeared over my head, but this one was not painted on a balloon. I noticed tens of orphaned balloons on the ceiling and devised a brilliant idea.

I asked T's 'n Things Hercules to tie the end of the string of my first balloon to the top of the string on my second balloon. I then went to Murray's stationery store and borrowed a roll of masking tape. I made a large loop of masking tape with the adhesive side facing out and then stuck it to the top of my first balloon. I had the reach I needed.

It was like fishing but with certainty and without the gag-inducing stench of drunken fishermen. With this contraption I deftly liberated fourteen balloons from their ceiling graveyard. It was incredibly satisfying. The best part was that a lot of mallers watched me perpetrate my caper. I swaggered with my bouquet of balloons. People were looking at me with great respect and admiration. The same way I looked at the mustachioed studs who won giant bears for the painted tarts they squired 'round Six Flags.

Had I stayed at Wally's I wouldn't be getting all this attention. It was absolutely worth blitzkrieging my friendship with him to pull off this heist. I was glad I insisted on being taken to the mall. I wish I hadn't cried in front of Wally and his mother—I'm sure that diminished my standing in his eyes—but this was one of the greatest nights of my life!

At the end of the night a teenaged girl who worked with my mother sucked in some balloon helium and made her voice sound like a small child. Everyone laughed, and then I did it. More laughs. Even my mother did it. How delightful to hear a child's voice come out of my mother's weary visage. Once her shift was over, my mom drove us home with a carload of balloons. She was very proud of my ingenuity. I felt brilliant.

After that night, I noticed Wally becoming colder. It seemed that he had indeed lost respect for me after I *literally cried for my mommy.* A few weeks after my display of tears and spectacular balloon heist, things became even more strained with Wally.

I was in his family room on his new burgundy plush carpet. The date: October 14, 1978. A historic night for Americans as we eagerly anticipated the conclusion to one of our nation's most vexing ongoing tragedies. That evening, in prime time, on NBC was the premiere of *Rescue from Gilligan's Island.*

I had gotten into *Gilligan's Island* reruns for a brief time earlier that year. Although, after about nine episodes I had become frustrated by the castaways' Sisyphean condition. The only way they were getting off that island would require Gilligan's murder. The title of this TV movie held promise, but I was still concerned that Gilligan would bungle the rescue. I'd have been more optimistic if the movie were called *A Death on What We Once Called Gilligan's Island.*

I had to watch it. If they escaped and I missed it, I would feel like I had missed out on one of those Oswald shoots JFK, man walks on moon, Fonzie jumps shark "Where were you when . . . ?" moments, so precious among my elders. Wally seemed equally enthusiastic. We ate homemade, overbuttered, oversalted popcorn out of a big steel mixing bowl.

As the night went on, I noticed that he was increasingly distant. Not really laughing at some objectively funny parts. I found myself laughing and then turning to see if he was laughing. He wasn't. Here we go. I hate having to be aware of whether someone else finds something funny. Friends laugh at the same stuff. Why else would they be friends? Shared values? *Please.* I had to keep turning to him to see if we were still friends.

Clearly, he no longer liked being with me. I could sense it. It must have been that drive to the mall. *Why are you still upset about that? I'm a mama's boy. I'll probably grow out of it.*

Finally, I asked him, "What's wrong? *Are you mad at me?*"

I'm asking this of a kid who less than two years ago was up my ass, *be my friend*–ing me left and right. *I didn't even want to be friends with you! I had to choose you over every other kid in the neighborhood because they weren't allowed to play at your Addams Family house. Now I'm trying to win* you *over?*

Despite knowing I wouldn't like the answer, I pressed him. Then he wrote something in the carpet. It was new enough that the fibers allowed you to spell in them. He slowly printed *S.I.* in the carpet. I knew where he was going even before he finished the capital *I.* I had wondered about it myself: I hung around with my mother a lot. I was sensitive and had a lot of stuffed animals and a blanky. I was most comfortable around teenaged girls and middle-aged women. I could have written the last three letters without him. Still, when he carved *S.S.Y.* into the plush, my mouth went dry and my stomach relocated to my neck.

I watched the rest of the *Gilligan's Island* segment. When it went to commercial, I told him I had to go home. I went to my room and cried. Into my blanky. With the door open and the hall light on. I never even found out whether the castaways got rescued. The second part aired the following Saturday, but I had as much interest in watching that as I did *The Exorcist.*

At least I have the mall. The kids in school wouldn't recognize me there. I'm special at the mall. I am confident, flamboyant. My mall friends are always happy to see me. I can walk into any store and get a "Gary!" and a 10 percent discount.

I still hated school except for a few writing projects. Those I loved. Early in the year I wrote and gave an oral report on the whale. Do I ever love the whale! When I found out that the whale belonged to the same vertebrate class as humans, the mammals, I was overjoyed. Proud in a similar way to when I found out Fonzie from ABC's *Happy Days* was Jewish. I went deep, covering several whale species and delivering a lengthy condemnation of brutal international whaling policies.

Soon thereafter, about a week before Thanksgiving, I wrote what I believed to be a hilarious short story about an acerbic turkey and the farmer who was going to kill him. The turkey was very insulting to the farmer. I wanted the turkey to come off like a streetwise scamp. I had her use words like "gonna," "ain't," "loser," "putz," and "hick." Mrs. Turner was outraged by my looseness with grammar and vocabulary. She covered the paper in red ink. It stung. I thought she was going to marvel at my facility with humor. She recoiled.

In December I had a chance for redemption. Mrs. Turner gave us a project where we were tasked with creating a real holiday book. We were to write a book and then she would teach us how to make real covers using cardboard and fabric. We would then sew the pages together and glue them into the cover. Having been chastised for my disregard for academic conventions at Thanksgiving, I was meticulous with my Christmas effort.

Following in the illustrious tradition of Jewish contributions to the Christmas canon ("White Christmas," "Santa Baby," "Rudolph the Red-Nosed Reindeer"), I wrote and illustrated an eight-page opus titled *The Lonely Tree.*

Writing the book gave me a stage I hadn't had before. A

forum to express an ineffable sense of melancholy and fatalism that I had never been able to explain. It wasn't that I knew that anything was wrong. I just felt that if you were unpopular, ugly, sensitive, on free lunch, soft, and emotional, you were destined to be sad and nervous your whole life. How could you not be? How could you feel good or optimistic unless you were rich or beautiful or popular at school? You had to hold out for a miracle.

In my book I told the story of a fir tree who was overlooked, underestimated, held back, but then triumphed. I knew no one in that class could write a better story about Christmas. As a Jew, I was an enthusiast and an expert on Christmas with a reverence and enthusiasm only an outsider could summon.

The book opened with a simple sentence: "There once was a tree that no one liked." The tree in question was being teased and bullied by other trees and forest creatures. He was so sad and lonely that he cried all day long. The tears gave him the nourishment to grow big and strong and beautiful. And popular.

So striking was this tree that a lumberjack cut it down and brought it to New York City to be the official Rockefeller Center Christmas Tree. People came from far and wide to adore him. I built suspense by having him dry out and nearly catch fire. Ultimately the tree survived, and Christmas was saved.

The reception for the book was extraordinary. Just what I had hoped. Even stern Mrs. Turner liked it. My father was so impressed that he brought it to a publisher who politely praised it but explained that his company made textbooks.

No one, including the publisher, asked my father, mother, and teacher how they could all be so obtuse about a work that, despite its remarkable artistry and execution, was clearly a cry for help.

Toward the end of second grade my mother took Wally and me to the coastal town of Scituate, Massachusetts, to visit her twin brother, Uncle Norman. Wally had come with us on this trek quite a few times over the years, so there was some nostalgia built in.

We were sitting in the harbor on a bench looking at boats and seagulls and my mother said to Wally, "Wally, what's this on your neck? Come here, honey, let me feel it. Does it hurt? I don't like the looks of it. I'll tell Sharon when we get home."

I really wish my mom hadn't noticed it. My friendship with Wally had withered; I'm certain that this impromptu shoreline excursion only arose because he had nothing better to do. I was happy to be reunited with Wally, and I didn't need my mother killing the mood by initiating a cancer scare. Kids shoot messengers and maybe their timid sons. But in those days pessimists like Barbara Gulman were convinced *everything* was cancer until a doctor and a board-certified second opinion assured you it was not. It was probably nothing.

Upon returning from Uncle Norman's that night, my mother told Wally's mother about the lump. In the days and weeks following, several tests and visits to the hospital resulted in a diagnosis of Hodgkin's disease.

Wally didn't die: radiation wiped out the cancer completely. But I lost him, nonetheless. The outpouring of affection and encouragement he received after his diagnosis from the neighborhood made him a star. Our friendship had been hanging by the slenderest thread, and now I had to share him with the whole community. Kids who avoided him or mocked him were now clamoring for his favor.

Luke Arcuri, the owner of the Speed Buggy lunch box, who had never even been in Wally's house said, "If Wall dies I will cry so hard."

Oh, *come ON!* You avoided him up until two seconds after the cancer was detected and now he's your hero? You shameless fraud. Also, you have to be friends with him awhile before you can call him Wall.

It was no longer just Wally with me and maybe that other kid from the house down the street when we hung out. I wasn't great at playing with more than one kid at a time, two at most. I got jealous and felt ganged up on or undermined by slights and cliquishness, real and imagined. I got no credit for my years of loyalty and patience with this hellion. The ghouls just wanted to be friends with a dying kid. *I was here first! I knew him before he was riddled with disease. I hope he lives, that'll show 'em!*

At one point in the spring, Wally had to go into the hospital for some treatments. I was the only kid who visited him there. His wayward teen sister, Kris, drove me to the children's hospital in her mom's Spirit. I brought him a gift I picked out at Murray's and a carrot cake from the bakery.

Kris was a wild child. She grew marijuana plants in the backyard and smoked its pungent leaves right in their family room with a rogue's gallery of thumb-hooking, ponytailed burnouts. Wally once showed me a hole near his front door that came about after Kris broke up with a guy and the guy drove by in a van and shot at the house. For the first thirty minutes of the ride, we didn't say a single word to each other. What were we going to discuss? Dope? Our only conversational intersection was Wally.

She finally broke the ice, crassly asking: "So . . . whadja-get-fuh Wall?"

Pardoning her churlishness, I replied, "Magic mahkiz . . . and a cake."

I didn't tell her the whole truth, which was that I got him Mr. Sketch *scented* markers. I had a set, and I treasured them but I didn't want her to think I was a sissy, like her brother did. It was the same reason I didn't say it was a carrot cake, which is the second-daintiest cake. Daintiest? Sponge.

That was the end of our discussion. We didn't say another word for the rest of the drive. Which was fine with me. Why should I be the one who makes conversation? I was *eight*. I guess I could have expounded, saying how the orange marker smelled like an orange, and the black smelled like licorice. I could have waxed poetic about how the sublime brown cinnamon was life-affirming and possibly therapeutic. But I didn't have the energy to endure someone being unimpressed by the indisputably impressive. Unless the green smelled like Maui Wowie I'd never spark her interest.

We visited Wally, and he was remarkably strong. He wasn't in a great mood, but he also wasn't wailing and begging for mercy from G-d like I would be. I never heard him complain even though I saw an IV in his hand, which must *kill*. He was like a stoic. What was left of our friendship would not survive the cancer-related celebrity. We'd hang out here and there over the next several months, but our bond was never the same. His popularity shrank along with his tumor, but a kid moved in down the street whose interest in minibikes and go-karts was more in line with Wally's passions. The kid was tough, gritty, grease under his fingernails and cuticles, T-shirts with torn-off sleeves, braided rope wristbands, and an aptitude with ratchets. I watched as Wally and he hit it off and knew I was out for good.

Pathetically, I tried to cling to the friendship, which sickened me. One day I asked what "brand" of fuel the go-kart took.

"Leaded or unleaded?"

They ignored me. I stopped going over to Wally's when that kid was there, which was almost all the time.

My trips to the mall became less frequent, its appeal waning. If I was the Lonely Tree, the mall was my Rockefeller Center. It was fun being the center of attention, but it wasn't the real friendship that I wanted, that everyday-friend situation I longed for. That would take a while.

My mother used to say, "All you need is one good friend."

Until then, I would rather be alone, with a book and some markers that smell like food.

July 2017

Joanie Noyes was the only person other than my mother who I visited every single time I went home. Today I am at Joanie's house with my mom on a Wednesday in July, looking for a way back. I've just turned forty-seven. In all those years she never failed to bring light, as reliable as the sun. Today, as always, she sets a tray of snacks in front of me. Roasted mixed nuts, sliced cucumber spears, ruffled potato chips with an adjacent dip, M&M's, Muddy Buddies Chex Mix, green grapes, cheddar cheese Goldfish crackers. She plays some DVRed 1970s *Match Game* episodes from the Game Show Network for me.

Usually, our conversations are light and easy. I always ask her to play some of the hits, and she repeats the stories I knew all the words to. But my illness has dulled my Joanie receptors. I spend the whole time grinding my teeth, biting my lip, and wishing I could find a way to start over. We stay three hours.

As I walk my mother back to the car, I see Joanie is looking at me with pity. She's never looked at me with anything but glee. As we leave, it's clear she can't pull off another miracle. I go back and hug her and instantly break down in tears.

"I know, honey," she said, "I know."

It's ninety degrees out. I've never felt this bad this long. As long as I've known Joanie there was never a gloom she couldn't lift me from.

Third

To humble a gifted subordinate, King Solomon challenged him to find a ring that could make a weeping man laugh and a laughing man weep. He returned with a ring engraved with the sentence "This too shall pass." It was a parable I first came across in school in 1980, though not at West Memorial. I learned it at Temple Ner Tamid, where I began my religious education that year. Had I been mature enough to apply the ring's power it would have made third grade and probably the rest of my life much easier to navigate.

Third grade began better than second. There was crying but not as frequent or as aggressive. And I spent less time on the verge of tears. As I maneuvered through the school year, overlapping with the end of my first decade, I made some progress. I ventured outside of my narrow orbit, grew closer to my brothers, and in that temple began a dysfunctional relationship with G-d. I was also given permission to say "shit," "ass," and "sucks" in front of my mother and brothers but still *never* in front of my dad. There was no ceremony in which I was given the keys to the misdemeanor swears. It was mostly trial and error, usually through jokes. I saw what I could get away with, and I added them to my palette.

I didn't hate school more in third than I had in second. By third grade an equilibrium of misery had been reached. There were some minor fluctuations, some bullying or teasing could swing things worse, but a snow day, a field trip, or the time we had a free book fair could swing things back.

Like every year, there was anxiety over warnings that the difficulty would increase or that there would be homework, book reports, or other academic bogeymen. Multiplication had been one of the perils promised for third grade, but the threat was overblown, providing minimal challenge. Times tables were actually fun up to the fives. Six through nine took some effort. You had to memorize those and accept on faith that nine times six *is* fifty-four. But then, as if in reward for that effort, ten was a joke. And eleven! Oh, my beloved eleven. Eleven was a slaphappy *romp*. I would love to teach third grade just for the joy of anticipating the day we covered the elevens table. To see the faces on those kids when the pattern becomes clear. I'd been warned that the twelves table would be murder, but in reality, only twelve times twelve required any brainpower. How do you learn the twelves table? You learn the ones through the elevens, then twelve times twelve equals 144. That's how you learn the twelves table, friend.

Then, the only thing that could have made my life substantially worse than it was the year before arose. A week into third, seemingly out of thin air, several more hours in a classroom were added to my schedule.

It's possible my mother had mentioned it over the summer. Perhaps the news had been delivered far enough in advance that I had suppressed it. In order to maintain my flimsy grip on sanity over the years, anything distressing dated more than two weeks hence I marked in my mental calendar as *never*. That self-delusion at least allowed me to limit the duration of my agitation.

On a Monday early in September I began my religious indoctrination. It was time for Hebrew school. I had to go three days a week, every single Monday and Wednesday, 3:30–5:30 P.M., and every Sunday, 8:30–10:30 A.M. *Sunday.*

My already insufficient respite from school was being *short-ened*, my weekend torn in half. My sacred hiatus desecrated. Effectively, I was sentenced to a sixth day of the anguish I had been gritting my teeth through for five.

I pressed my entire family for justification. My mom could offer no more cogent rationale than "Because your brothers went!" declared in an exasperated *wail*. I think she knew it was bullshit, but my father would have raised Cain and/or Abel if she capitulated. I was enraged by the hypocrisy and the injustice. We weren't observant Jews! My dad worked every Sabbath. We ate bacon and cheeseburgers, sometimes in the same *bite*, often on the Sabbath. We didn't go to temple save for the occasional bar mitzvah. We had a couple of Passover seders, but let me tell you, without the detailed instructions provided by our Maxwell House promotional Haggadahs, the Gulmans wouldn't know the four questions from the Four Tops.

My mother who had on numerous occasions boasted herself a "Jew in name only" couldn't have named ten commandments if you spotted her nine plus "Thou shalt not . . ." and fired a pistol.

After my lament she promised me that I would only have to go to Hebrew school until my bar mitzvah when I was thirteen. Thirteen? I'll never be thirteen. That's *four years.* A GD lifetime!

My father's Judaic knowledge consisted of fragments of memories from his youth and a litany of superstitions. In his defense, he was obsessively committed to the superstitions. Any time a person mentioned illness or death he would prevent it with an urgent "G-d forbid!" He ended all sentences describing future plans with "the Good Lord willing."

His other religious avocation was designating a variety of actions as sacrilege. Most of the things he deemed sacrilegious were merely bad etiquette or hygiene. I was once reprimanded for flattening a macaroon with the bottom of a juice glass; my dad deemed it sacrilege. A similar verdict for not washing your hands after you pee.

My brothers offered no assistance. Their support of my enrollment was part of their spiteful policy of insisting my path through childhood be just as painful as theirs. I'm surprised they didn't protest my immunization with the *oral* polio vaccine.

I believed in G-d, but my relationship with Him was fearbased, a result of my parents' distorted faith

Barbara Gulman may have believed in G-d, but the only time she mentioned Him was when I hurt myself while misbehaving. For example, if I started crying after stubbing my toe on a corner of the cabinets while running around.

"See, G-d punished you," she'd snap.

Cry after bouncing on the bed and falling on the floor?

"G-d punished you."

Forge a golden calf and then a hailstorm kills my oxen?

"See, G-d punished you!"

The impact of her demented theology was that even when I sinned in private, I felt guilty and terrified of G-d's imminent wrath. It left me in a compulsive and persistent state of contrition, begging G-d for forgiveness and leniency throughout the day. At some point I became convinced that all prayers needed to be recited out loud for them to be admissible, even at school. Thanks to that, I was often mocked by classmates for talking to myself. I had no explanation. What could I say? "I'm not talking to myself! *I'm repenting.*"

On a Monday in the fall of 5739 (Hebrew calendar), we drove twelve minutes down Lowell Street, toward our synagogue, Temple Ner Tamid (pronounced Nēr Tah mēd). It's a mostly windowless, two-story white building on top of a steep hill less than a mile from the Northshore Shopping Center. My brothers had dubbed it Temple Near *the Mall*. It's comprised of two rectangular structures, one a little taller than the other, with a flat roof on each that slightly juts out over the sections so it looks like two giant shoeboxes with lids. It was a kind of modern take on Middle Eastern architecture although it could also have passed for the world's largest Greek diner.

During the ride I vacillated between outrage and despair. We turned right onto an S-curved hill, past the double-doored main entrance to the 'gogue, and around back to the shabby public entrance of the Hebrew school. Owing to the reverence my father had for G-d and the Jewish religion, I found the building intimidating. Serious business transpired within. Don't act up, for if G-d doesn't smite you, Phil Gulman would.

Inside was a tiny version of a regular school, just two classrooms. Same fluorescent lighting, same kids' desks, teacher's desk, tile floors. Same American flag but alongside it the flag of an ally sporting forty-nine fewer stars. Mysteriously absent from Hebrew school? The laminated "In God We Trust" banner my public school displayed behind Old Glory. Perhaps the temple thought the placard would be gilding the theological lily, a yarmulke on a yarmulke, if you will. Same classroom doors except these doors had slanted mezuzahs hanging in their frames. The only significant difference from my school was the odors. In addition to the familiar public-school scent of commercial solvents and floor wax, this school smelled like a deli platter.

As we approached the Hebrew school entrance at around three fifteen there was a cluster of kids within a small grassy pitch. They were all running around and laughing, squealing with joy, the way kids tend to between stints in lockdown. I was a little unnerved by their intensity and recognized no one from my own school, so I planned to avoid the commotion.

My mother had a different reaction to the exuberance. She shook her head, squinted disapprovingly, and in a conspiratorial tone hissed, "Look at the *Jews*. . . . They're *wild*."

It felt like an admonition or worse, she was so put off by Jews that she found even the merriment of their toy-sized offspring *grating*.

My mother walked me into school that day to explain to the teacher, Beverly Shuman—whom she called Bev—why I had been absent from the first day of Hebrew school the day before, a Sunday. They knew each other from when my brother Max had her five years earlier. Barb explained to Bev that I frequently spent Sundays with my dad. She left out the part where he doesn't arrive until well after Hebrew school lets out. It was disconcerting to see my mom so blithely bear false witness in the house of G-d. Mrs. Shuman's shoulder-length dark hair, light complexion, and the way her eyes squinted and sparkled when she smiled reminded me of Snoopy. She was exceedingly sweet.

My mother started to leave, and I kissed her in front of the whole class. As ashamed as I was by this exhibition of mama's boy–ing, I thought, what if G-d killed her because I didn't kiss her goodbye? I'd never recover.

Everybody had to go by their Hebrew name, so just like that, I was Leibel, pronounced *label*. I hated being called Leibel. It's not a name. Nobody teased me, though, probably because they had equally atrocious names like Gershon and Yishayahu, a name begging to be *yodeled*. There were some pretty girls' names, like Aliya, Shera, and Tamara, but for every harmonic name there was a Malcha or a Bracha. Names that would make effective alternatives to "ahem."

Right away it was clear that this was school. You had to be quiet, and there were lessons and handouts and writing and listening. One of the lessons each day was learning Hebrew. It's read backward from a book that opens backward. And it has its own strange alphabet. At least six letters look identical to another letter. Certain letters made different sounds depending on what letters surrounded it or when and where you learned to speak it. Vowels were used in some texts but appeared beneath the consonants and were made especially tiny and must account for the pervasiveness of nearsightedness within the Jewish community. We were told early on that vowels were training wheels and the truly pious didn't need them.

For the third time in four years I was in first grade, only this time it was called Aleph.

In addition to the language, I learned bizarre laws and customs, many centered on infusing everyday objects with sanctity. Every boy had to wear a yarmulke. We wear them to show that there is something higher than us, G-d. Every day of Hebrew school I'd have to reach in and pull one out from the community yarmulke box on the wall by the entrance, my fear of lice overridden by my fear of being smote for insufficient humility. If it slipped off your head and onto the ground, which happened to each boy sixteen times a day, you had to pick it up and *kiss it* before putting it back on your head. You were also supposed to kiss a fallen prayer book the same way. This is *nuts*. But I did it. Swiftly. Every time. I didn't want to piss off what, according to every lesson, was a petty, temperamental, *vengeful* G-d.

The whole academic charade was taken seriously. There were quizzes and tests and projects, grades, and honor rolls. *What a farce.* But I was so conditioned to following rules and striving that I accepted the ludicrous setup. The whole venture was as meaningless as a kickball game. Nobody would ever care what my Hebrew school marks were. Were colleges going to pass me over because I flunked Leviticus?

Also, the teacher, the principal, and even the rabbi had no real redress for all but the most contemptuous behavior. What could they do, make me repeat Aleph?

Still, I would get nervous about the grades and getting the projects in on time. So much so that I once *cheated* on a test. I had never once cheated in legitimate school. I never had to because I was always prepared, but one day my resistance to this extra schooling overwhelmed my natural tendency to do what was expected, and so I showed up unprepared for a Genesis exam. The question I cheated on was, "Who was Abraham's nephew?"

I had no idea. His nephew?! Who cares about a prophet's extended family? I was desperate, though, because Mrs. Shuman was so understanding of my frequent Sunday absences that I didn't want to disappoint her. Panicking, I asked a girl called Rivka, who sat in front of me.

With a tone implying this was comically obvious, she turned her head and whispered, "Lot."

Yes. Lot. That creep whose wife was turned into a pillar of salt just for looking back when Sodom and Gomorrah disintegrated. One lesson they wanted to inculcate through the Bible lessons was that G-d doesn't hold back. He'll flood the earth if you dishonor him. He'll destroy your cities over kinkiness. He'll salinate you just for being a yenta. What is he going to do to me for cheating on this Genesis test? That was the only question I cheated on. I didn't have the stomach for cheating on any of the others.

We learned prayers in Hebrew and songs in Hebrew and Bible stories and the biblical origins of every holiday as we celebrated them. I was not just celebrating most of these holidays for the first time, I was *discovering their existence* for the first time. I had never heard of Sukkoth, Simhath Torah, Tu Bishvat, Purim, Lag b'Omer, Shavuot, Tishah-b'Ab, or even Shabbat, which is the weekly observance of the Sabbath from sundown Friday to sundown Saturday. With every new holiday it became clearer that my family was not very Jewish.

There was a consistent arc to the stories behind each holiday: centuries of brutal oppression, an uprising, followed by a miraculous victory. G-d was always praised, hymned, and psalmed for the deliverance with no mention of the hundreds of years our lamentations went pending. And as far-fetched and implausible as these tales were, there was no allowance to question or scoff, even in my head. I feared I would be lightning bolted for observations like:

"Boys need to wear a beanie to show deference to G-d? What an ego on this guy! And why doesn't it bother him that the girls in my class, including Mrs. Shuman, think they're better than Him?

It's *H*im with a capital *h*. Even his *pronouns* are sacred? This is shameless vanity. And on the subject of vain, we can't write out *G-O-D* because it's considered using the Lord's name in vain? But that's not even his name. It's an *English* word. We have to put a dash in between the *G* and *D* to keep from angering Him? *That* will get old, *quickly*.

And the subtext to all my skepticism: Does this all sound made up, or am *I* an asshole?

The stories all had the same theme: *It is never safe to be a Jew.* You are not safe from your neighbors, your leaders, nor from your G-d. The only thing you can control is an unwavering faith in Hashem, which must be maintained no matter the penalty. An oft-repeated narrative was of rabbis/prophets being tortured yet refusing to renounce their Judaism. They would die proudly, with a prayer exalting G-d called the Shema "on their lips."

No thank you. If I died under those circumstances, on my lips would be: "Jew? *Me?* I'm no Jew. Ha, that's funny that you thought I was a Jew. Am I pronouncing it right? Jah-oo?"

This realization caused me endless anxiety. I believed in G-d absolutely and knew he would be furious if I disavowed, but in a face-off between my two biggest fears, death slew G-d's wrath.

Every Wednesday, there was a brief visit from the Hebrew school principal, a relic with a tortoise look, named Mr. Linick. He would come into the room to plug Saturday morning services in heavily accented English using the same singsong rhythm.

"*Come . . . to Shab . . . bat . . . services. You learn to read the Toooooo . . . Raaaaah. You get refreeeeeeesh . . . meeeents . . .*"

He would always say "refreshments" in a way that made it seem like there was going to be more to his pitch. It was refreshments, period, but he made it sound like a comma. Like a *there's more* rhythm as if he were going to say "You get refreeeeeshmeeeents, you get a prize not unlike those found in a box of Fruity Pehhh-hhhbles, you get a BMX dirt biiiiike, a dalmatian puuuuuppy, all the orange jelly beans you can eeeeeat."

But no. *You learn to read the Torah* and *you get refreshments,* period.

Every week, I thought: *That's it? Reading Torah and refresh-ments? With all due respect, Your Holiness, I don't think you are aware of what you're programming against. There's an entire* industry *based on Saturday morning children's entertainment. I would be choosing your soporific service over* Super Friends, The Bugs Bunny / Road Runner Hour, The Super Globetrotters, *and* The Scooby-Doo Show. *Plus, I'd be sacrificing my one opportunity to sleep in. It was only my empathy and my fear of G-d's terrible swift sword that kept me from laughing out loud at his* schtick.

The first time Principal Linick addressed us, I did ask around because although *refreshments* evoke 1950s sock hop culture, I found it intriguing. A kid in the know, by the Hebrew name of Tsvi, said the "refreshments" were Hawaiian Punch and Hy-drox. *Hydrox? Please. Are* Vienna Fingers *too posh? Our cupboard currently contains Cookie Crisp Cereal, Frosted Mini Wheats,* and *Sugar Smacks. Once my mom gets up just after Bugs Bunny o'clock, she'll make me pancakes until I'm comatose. No sale, Doc.*

After a week, my mom had arranged a carpool so that she could share the driving duties with other families. I resisted at first because I didn't want to be forced into proximity with strangers, but I relented and found the kids and one mom, Gail Greenberg, fun to be around. It could be a good time going to and from. I got to know what other people's cars smelled like, and, more important, I had a fresh audience for, among other routines, my Principal Linick bit:

"Come to Shabbat services. You learn to read the Torah. You get refreshments. Act now, and we'll throw in a coupon for half off on a single scoop at Baskin-Robbins."

And the Jews *went wild.*

The best thing to happen that year was my oldest brother, Rick, had moved back home after graduating from the University of Massachusetts. I idolized him, even adopting many of his habits and philosophies. I stuck out my tongue when concentrating just like him. I preferred dressing down like him in a look he cultivated and I referred to as "always ready to throw a ball around." He also spent very little time styling his hair, saying his hair looked good only after he had exercised. I allowed my hair to be blow-dried just once and by my mom's friend Joanie.

Rick reclaimed his sagging twin bed in the room he had grown up in with my brother Max, who was starting his senior year of high school. Max was more interested in his appearance than Rick, having not one but two brushes and great skill with a blow-dryer, even owning a second one he brought when traveling.

I loved being around my brothers so much that I took a large piece of foam rubber from the garage, covered it with a fitted brown sheet, and set it between their beds over the long dusty strands of the maroon wall-to-wall carpet. The length and heft of these shag locks were similar to a floor mop. It was a hideous floor covering even for that golden age of hideous carpeting. I set up there so I could listen to them talk and chime in with quips and laugh with them. It was the only time in my life I remember looking forward to bedtime. Rick called this time before we all fell asleep "shooting the breeze," and even as it was happening, I knew it would be both something I'd remember forever and that "this too shall pass." Mostly I listened to them tell stories of our family and neighborhood when they were growing up. I had fun there and also felt safe from burglars and the devil.

That winter a very exciting blessing arrived. Uncle Norman gave me a fifteen-gallon fish tank with a filter, a cover with a light built in, and a heater to keep the water at the right temperature. The setup came with everything. Over the years, my mother's twin brother, Uncle Norman, was able to give us a lot of appliances and electronics and small luxuries thanks to his job. He was a criminal. He was a fence, like another middle-aged Jewish man, Dickens's Fagin. Though none of the aquarium components came in boxes, it appeared that everything worked. It was either stolen or used to repay a debt to Norman or bartered for something else stolen. Initially I was suspicious about its quality, as he had given us a few cars over the years that were unreliable/dangerous and a CB radio that only received static, but Norman insisted that it functioned. My brother Max, the handiest member of our tribe, plugged some things in to confirm. The filter motor spun, and the light lit. He didn't test the heater because he said we probably didn't need it. The tank didn't leak. The project looked promising.

It was now just a matter of convincing my mother to give her approval to filling it with life. I was not hopeful. She normally spurned any activity that required any activity. She was a pessimist. She wasn't just "The glass is half empty," she was "Get a plastic cup. Why are you using a glass? You're going to drop it, the glass will shatter, you'll step on it barefoot, you'll get gangrene, they'll chop your foot off, and we'll lose the house." One of her catchphrases was "Our luck . . ." followed by a prediction of disaster. Like, "Our luck, there's a crossed wire and I'll electrocute myself while I'm sprinkling fish flakes." Fortunately, Max volunteered to set it up, and Rick offered to buy me some fish. I was so excited. This type of bounty in between birthdays was unheard of.

On a weeknight after he got home from a long day at Laventhol and Horwath CPAs, Rick brought me to a pet store in Saugus, Massachusetts. They had cats and dogs and supplies in the brightly lit first two-thirds of the retail space. We speed-walked past that and into the Spencer Gifts lighting of the tropical fish section. I jogged to keep up. The glow was all from the fluorescent lights in the tanks. I loved the atmosphere in there; it felt like sitting at the bar of a Chinese restaurant.

We picked up filter material, charcoal, and pebbles that go on the bottom of the tank, and Rick and I, our tongues out in deliberation, browsed the inventory and eventually picked out four different kinds of tropical fish that were netted and transparent-bagged by a lovable aquarium clerk named Paul. These weren't common goldfish or guppies. Oh no, these were upscale tropical fish, Jack. We got four Indian glassy fish. You could see their skeletons! Four pink kissing gourami fish. I could watch them pucker their mouths for hours. Rick said we needed an algae eater, and so we got a little mottled brown one that looked like a catfish. He would suck all around the glass. Although algae fish wore no clothes, I always imagined him wearing a denim painter's cap and coveralls, carrying a mop, and occasionally sneaking behind the filter for a Marlboro Red. We also got four neon tetras that were the snazziest freshwater fish in the store. It was so exciting. We were in a consumer frenzy and didn't stop until we had spent *twelve dollars*! We drove home in Rick's blue 1977 Oldsmobile Cutlass Supreme. I thanked him over and over for so generously spending his money on me.

I was thrilled that we were sharing this new hobby together! Maybe we could save up and get one of those old-timey deep-sea diver with a treasure chest knickknacks! Maybe we'll expand our scope and set up a separate tank dedicated to the more intelligent saltwater fish. The choices were intoxicating. What a feeling when we poured the fish into the tank and they swam around. Rick staring with glee, his tongue obscuring his top lip in focus. It was like the end of *Born Free*. Jubilant, we executed the celebratory maneuver then sweeping America: the *high five*.

Soon thereafter my dad found out about my hobo-like setup between my brothers' beds and insisted I return to my own room. He was angry and vociferous, insisting that I have a bed and I needed to sleep in it. I didn't have the impertinence to break the Fifth Commandment. I was still afraid of my dad, but also, thanks to Hebrew school, I was terrified of the wrath of G-d for disobeying him. This tag team discipline would get me to comply with any command short of my binding and sacrifice upon Mount Moriah.

I have no idea how he found out. It's possible my mother snitched, or one of my brothers may have told him how much they enjoyed my company on the floor. It seemed arbitrary, like he was looking for something to assert his authority over. Shouldn't he have kvelled from this display of fraternity? Dad made me pull up the foam rubber and return it to the garage. I went back to my room that night, making sure to switch the hall light on. The switch went *blap*, as loud as ever.

The abrupt repatriation was softened by the gentle incandescence of the bulb, the hum of the filter, the burbling of the water, a delightful sensory mélange. Everybody in the house liked the fish, but they lived with *me*. I loved all the fish, but the algae eater/catfish was the only one I named because there were multiples of the others, making them too difficult to distinguish. I named him Penry after the janitor alter-ego of Hong Kong Phooey, a short-lived but memorable Hanna-Barbera Saturday morning offering. Penry was the most fun to watch. He didn't possess any flashy gimmick, he was just a diligent worker, selflessly providing a service to community both aquatic and terrestrial. I described him to Joanie this way: "Penry is like if your cat could vacuum."

About six weeks later I trudged into the house from Hebrew school on a Wednesday evening. I hated Wednesdays. And not just because of Principal Linick's uninspiring Shabbat service promos. Everything bad that ever happened to me happened on a Wednesday. The night I got in trouble for spilling a jar of Vlasic pickles on the family room rug was a Wednesday. The day I got caught peeing behind the shed by Max, a Wednesday. The time Wally and I made a dirty audio cassette and my mother overheard us talking about boners and yelled at me was a Wednesday. I believed that Wednesday was *cursed*. I went into my room to put my books away, feeling a tinge of relief that I wouldn't have to whiff the butchery stink of temple again until Sunday. Also, Joanie would be visiting the next morning, and I was skipping school to hover around her all day.

Once again, I turned to my tank to admire my marine reserve. The only fish in the foreground were the kissing fish. I went right to alarm.

"Oh no, oh no, oh no. Please G-d no. Please . . ."

The glassy fish, the neon tetras, and my devoted custodian were floating at the top. I removed the lighting unit to skim the dead fish with my net and my fingers felt the water. It was *hot*. I ran to the freezer to get ice cubes to offset the heat and maybe save the remaining kissing fish. But the kissing fish were dying, too. Even the entire Rubbermaid ice tray wouldn't save them. By the time I got back from the refrigerator they had passed. I dug holes under the bushes along the front walk and quickly buried them there. I was sobbing, horrified, feeling haunted by guilt and shame.

Earlier that day, before heading off to Hebrew school, in a moment I would rue for the rest of my life, I had turned the dial of the heater up. It was a particularly cold day, and I thought the fish would be more comfortable in warm water is all I can guess at for a motive. Or I just *think* I had turned up the heat. My mother said that maybe she had increased it, too. Maybe it was like that fable that I either saw on *The Electric Company* or completely made up, of the people cooking and each adding salt and then the soup was too salty.

Maybe the heater malfunctioned due to a short circuit caused by chance, or it was biblical retribution for consuming the fruit of sin from the Uncle Norman emporium. The aquarium itself was stolen. Also, I can't imagine catfish is kosher; does the prohibition on bottom-feeders include leisurely ogling their day-to-day exploits? Also, I had considered defying my father's eviction notice, could this be G-d's warning shot? And I had cheated on that Genesis test! I had borne false witness about my knowledge of Lot, a vile heretic in his own right!

Or maybe it was "our luck." Who did we think we were, enjoying luxury while people were suffering elsewhere? According to Mrs. Shuman, there were Russian Jews being persecuted for trying to flee the USSR, righteous gentile Raoul Wallenberg was missing, Israel was so desperate for greenery that they hit up Hebrew school kids for donations. All this misfortune was transpiring, and the youngest Gulman boy has an elaborate freshwater habitat in his room?

"See, G-d punished you."

I was gutted, stricken with excruciating remorse and regret. I was overflowing with sorrow for these innocent lives who must have been suffering and couldn't escape, couldn't even scream out. Oh, my dear, sweet, virtuous, fish siblings. My indefatigable Penry. I am truly sorry.

After the funeral, I unplugged the tank and turned out the light in my room. I closed the door to my room, but the undertaking wasn't over. We had to break the bad news to Rick when he got home from work. We all knew he'd be upset, but I didn't expect what happened.

My mom suggested, "Maybe it can wait till tomorrow."

Oh good. Yes, let's delay further discussion of the tragedy until to-morrow. Why face today what can be put off indefinitely? Let's let it fester till it becomes a disaster.

Then Max pointed out from the bathroom, hairbrush in his palm, "He goes in there to check on them and feed them every morning before work. He's gonna notice."

I hadn't known that. Oh my, I knew he was a fan of the fish, but I wasn't aware that his devotion was as intense as mine. I must have been sleeping when he came in. He left the house each morning long before I woke up to drive to the train out of the Wonderland dog track station in Revere.

"Uh-oh," Mom said.

I imagine some families have a more reassuring response. Not my mom. "Uh-oh" was her go-to interjection during crisis. No solace, no resolve. Pure dread.

Rick got home around seven. It was raining. How I hated rain. It always made me feel lonelier. She inquired from the kitchen while Rick was changing into his exercise clothes, a gray sweatsuit courtesy of the Harvard University equipment room, where Uncle Norman had a friend. His tongue showed as he tied his sneakers, also pilfered from Cambridge.

"Richard?" she asked.

"Yeah?"

"Did you notice anything wrong with the fish this morning?"

Oy. This was my mother's art, a heavy brushstroke of oblique misdirection dotted with what she called white lies, which were *any untruths* large or small deployed to keep her out of trouble. Where did she think this was going? What was he going to say? *Now that ya mention it, one of the skeleton fish had a foreboding look in her eye.*

"No, why?"

"Come out here for a minute?"

Then she broke the news to him and used the "We all must

have turned the heat up" explanation. He was outraged. This, of course, compounded my distress. I felt in my reliable stomach that I had done something wrong, so why wouldn't people be angry? He didn't yell at me. And he didn't seem sad, or maybe it was one of those odd displays of emotion my dad had told me about, some people laugh when nervous or heartbroken. Maybe Rick yells when he's mourning. He was yelling at my mother initially, and then at Max, who interrupted his blow-drying to suggest Rick not make too big of a deal about it.

"Why don't you go and buy a new tank of fish, then, Max!"

That wasn't happening. How was Max going to get twelve dollars? Also, I never wanted to see another fish as long as I lived. Not in a lake, not in the ocean, not on Pepperidge Farm.

Rick and my mother argued some more, and he made a vow to move out, and then he went to the health spa to lift weights. I heard the whole conflagration from my mother's bed, where I was hiding. Hiding and crying. I slept there that night, something I hadn't done in years. I didn't know how I'd ever sleep again on top of the murder scene. I also couldn't go back between the twin beds knowing that not honoring my father could beget more Old Testament reprisal, and maybe next time the good Lord would pursue bigger game than fish.

In the morning I woke up and was still grieving and tormented by my conscience. I heard my mother say about me softly from the living room, "He's so upset."

Moments later Joanie opened my mother's door. She poked her head around the door frame, and blurted, "Heard ya had a fish fry!"

For a split second I thought, *How dare you? How can you be so callous?* Then we both burst into laughter, hers more tubercular thanks to twenty-three years of Pall Malls. That impish giggle saved the day once again. Joanie, my King Solomon, my angel, dispensing the most sacred of elixirs, the punch line.

August 2017

Igor, Sandy, and I are on one of our morning walks. I'm dragging myself up the hill, two hundred yards from my mother's house. My anxiety is always worst during the first four hours after waking. I walk the dogs up the hill, repeating, in a loop, through gritted teeth, "Please, G-d, help me. Please, G-d, help me. . . ."

From behind me I hear a car approaching. Then I hear a shout of "Lew-ayyyyyyyy!"

I know who it is. It's Finn Burns. When I was little I told everyone in the neighborhood that I wanted to be called by my middle name, Lewis. There are still people from then who call me Lew or Lewy, but only one says it with such unbridled joy and still lives in our neighborhood. Jonathan "Finn" Burns and his wife, Tracy, had bought their house from his mother, my first-grade teacher Judy Burns, when she retired from teaching. Usually just hearing Finn's "LEWAYYYYYY" makes me happy. Today nothing can pierce the misery.

"How you doin', Lewy?"

Normally I say "good" no matter how I feel, but for some reason I don't this time. Maybe it's that I figured he had to know something was off; forty-seven-year-old men don't move back in with their moms if they're thriving. Maybe it's that only a moment before I had been praying for relief. Maybe it's because I had opened up to Joanie. Whatever the reason, I decide I am going to start telling people the truth about what I am going through.

"Oh man, I'm so anxious, Finn."

He gets out of the car, and Sandy and Igor jump all over him.

"I'm sorry, Lewy. It's bad, huh, kid?"

"I don't know how much more I can take."

"That sucks. I'm sorry, Lewy."

Telling Joanie and now Finn feels like a step. It doesn't cure me, but at least I won't have to expend the energy and feel the shame all the lying begets. As long as I've known Finn, I idolized him and loved how I felt around him. Hearing him empathize and understand, not give me a trite pep talk, or change the subject was significant. This man, a few years older than me, was the heart and soul of the neighborhood, the most guilelessly charismatic person I've ever known. And just like when I was a child, he genuinely cared about me and I could sense it just from that sentence: "I'm sorry, Lewy."

Fourth

The summer before fourth grade I was spending most of my time sitting with my mother and her friends in various living rooms listening to them yent over Ruffles and Fresca, although one night was spent in the back seat of my mother's Chevy Bel Air while she and her friend Inga spied on a man Inga was having an affair with. The two-timer was a sixty-something nightclub owner named Don who was cheating on his wife with Inga, but Inga suspected there was another other woman. Until that night I thought my brother Rick called her Inga "the Swingah" because it rhymed.

Inga was a blond, boisterous, middle-aged married woman with a German accent best described as Colonel Klink–ian. She wanted to catch the Don Juan Don but didn't want to blow her cover by parking her vanity-plated red Pontiac Bonneville too close to where he was shackin' up, so she called on my mother to drive her. Rick was away, so they brought me along.

A few hours into our stakeout the home-wreckers emerged from their love nest. Inga confronted Don outside the building entrance. I was excited. I thought there'd be a face slap or maybe Inga would pull a petite lady's pistol from her purse and shoot him in the chest. We watched as she had it out with Don. I kept my eyes on her pocketbook/holster. Ten minutes later she came back to the car, thanked us, and sent us on our way. Somehow, the silver-haired gigolo was able to talk himself out of trouble. No slap, no gun.

Epilogue: Don died a few weeks later. I was rooting for foul play, but it turned out he died from a heart attack. Inga was inconsolable.

The fact that I fit in so well with "the girls" (my mom's friends) is probably what landed me in the offices of the Jewish Federation of the North Shore in July 1980. During the visit I sat next to my mother and talked across a desk to a young Jewish woman in a glen plaid suit. She had black curly hair past her shoulders, clear ivory skin, and a round face. She asked me questions about my friends, and I quickly realized that this was a child psychologist–type interrogation. I had always imagined that they gave you cookies and LEGO bricks or an Etch A Sketch to play with while they milked you for neuroses, but this lady didn't even offer fig Newtons.

At one point she asked me about my friend Joy. Joy was a high school girl with short red hair and freckles who worked at the jewelry concession next to T's 'n (NO) Things. A couple of times I went to her parents' house in Danvers, and we glued pom-poms together to make animals using felt, pipe cleaners, and *googly eyes*. Googly eyes . . . I find their endurance a genuine blessing. A society that embraces the whimsy intrinsic in those crafting notions is never beyond redemption. Crafting was a hobby I pursued at every opportunity. My mother had limited my own crafting freedom by banning paints, pastes, glues, and clays of all varieties from the house. It was odd because the place was always a wreck. How could some errant finger paint disrupt the aesthetic?

When the social worker asked me about Joy, I cried, probably because it seemed she was confirming my inkling that our friendship was odd. She asked me what it was I liked about these older people in my life like Joy or my neighbor Finn Burns?

"They're smart, and they laugh at my jokes."

"What do you talk about with, say, Joy?" she asked.

"Well, one time, the radio was playing 'The Devil Went Down to Georgia' and I said it scared me, and she told me as long as I believed in G-d the devil couldn't get me, and that made me feel better. It made me like the song, and then I told Joy that it was obvious that the devil outplayed the boy, and even if he hadn't, it was not very devilish for the devil to play by the rules. I always figured the devil for a sore loser. And Joy laughed, and I knew none of the kids in school would find that funny, and my brothers would say, 'It's just a song, Gah.'"

The Jewish Federation of the North Shore was a charitable organization that strove valiantly to fulfill the philanthropic ethos of Judaism, an ethos that viewed providing for the less fortunate as a Jew's chief purpose. It's a lazy and harmful stereotype that all Jews are wealthy, for several reasons, including the indignity in being a member of a minority group known for possessing a desirable trait who doesn't possess it. Imagine the shame in being, say, a Belgian, who try as they might, cannot make a filling waffle. Everyone comes home from their brunch let down and hungry. It's true that some Jews are rich. We are also poor, middle-class, criminal, musical, handy, smart, dumb, kind, spiteful, hard, soft, strong, weak, athletic, clumsy, religious, atheist, drunk, sober, hardworking, slothful, and various degrees within each of those descriptions. Whatever your strengths, whatever your interests, whatever your background, there are thousands of Jews who understand.

The social worker woman was kind and spoke calmly and softly. I would have wanted to be friends with her like I was with Joy and Joanie, and Auntie Judy's daughter, Brenda, who taught me how to rug hook. The woman didn't say there was anything wrong with my friendship with Joy, but before I was able to confirm my mother's motives, they signed me up for a Jewish day camp called Camp Simchah (pronounced Sim— *throat clear*—ah). Because of our financial shortfalls, the Jewish Federation paid for it. I think my mother wanted me to find some friends my own age but also not have me reading and drawing Muppets inside all summer, a routine she called "moping around the house." Also, I still needed a babysitter at times when there were no family members at home. That day in the federation office I sensed a vibe emanating from my mom conveying "All right, Ms. Master's in Psychology, let's label this kid a freak and get him a free month of Jew camp. I gotta get home to *General Hospital*'s Luke and Laura."

That is how I was introduced to the phenomenon of Jewish summer camp. I like to use the following comic book analogy to acquaint non-Jewish people with this wonder: Kal-El of Krypton was ordinary on his doomed home planet. As an infant, his parents expended great effort and treasure to ship him safely to Earth. Upon arrival, the rays of Earth's sun transformed the Kryptonian babe into a super man we know as Superman. To Jewish kids living in majority gentile communities, Jewish sleepaway camp is Superman's Earth, an alien utopia that massively enhances athletic skills, attractiveness, and general worth. This is accomplished, mostly, by extracting the dominant caste. I would not be surprised to find out that the Jewish creators of Superman, Batman, and the Marvel Universe were Jewish summer camp veterans trying to metaphorically convey the gift of flight that is Hēbs-only summer camp.

Jewish camp is a miracle, every bit as deserving of an eight-day holiday and savory appetizer as Chanukah, an invaluable endowment affluent Jews annually bequeath their kids. Two weeks ago, you had your violin kicked into a soccer net by some gentile brute. At Camp "Your Secret's Safe with Us" your new best friend Marc said there's a girl named Jody who told her bunkmate Jodie who told the counselor-in-training Jodey that she thought you were cute!

No one knew your past. You could issue an abridged bio, omitting the violin story as well as the time you dodged a fight by invoking a bar mitzvah lesson. Jewish summer camp: Making Davids into Goliaths for over fifty years.

Every July my wealthier Jewish neighbors would disappear for eight weeks, then resurface in September with better posture. It made me even more resentful of the rich. It's not enough that they have warmer, better-fitting clothes in the winter, in the summer they get to reinvent themselves, audition for a new audience who didn't know whether they were popular at school or had repeated the first grade or cried over a library book. Their only baggage was the designer suitcases rolled in by their Volvo wagon–driving mothers.

For awkward Gen X Jewish kids, two months at Jewish camp were the guardrails on the perilous bridge between preadolescence and a nose job. It was like Kaplan or Princeton Review but for friendship, and just like those shady schemes, they gave rich kids an advantage they didn't appreciate. I remember asking a friend what Camp "First Kiss" cost to attend. He had no idea. Of course he didn't! Only poor kids know how much things cost.

Camp Simchah was not the type of Jewish summer camp that changed lives. First off, it was a day camp. Second, its clientele was poor to lower-middle-class Jewish kids, many of whom were recent Russian immigrants who were attending for free like me. Volvos weren't dropping off kids for the summer. I got picked up every morning by a yellow bus that picked up Jewish kids on corners throughout my city and drove us fifteen minutes to a suburb called Wenham, Massachusetts. It ran for eight weeks; I was funded for only four.

The Camp Simchah campus offered a few typical summer camp amenities. There was a drab Olympic-sized swimming pool with an adjacent rusty, moldy, slimy locker room. For land sports there was a McDonald's parking lot–sized plot of asphalt with faded paint lines for Wiffle ball, street hockey, and four square. If it rained there was a barn-type structure that we would play in. Across a dirt road from the pavement sports was a patchy softball field.

There was also a utility shed–sized hovel for arts and crafts. This indignity made evident what Camp Simchah, as well as 1980 America, thought of the humanities. That year my school had put art class in an outhouse by safety scissoring it down to once every three weeks.

At Camp Simchah they forced the boys to participate in a variety of sports. It was as if camp was one perpetual gym class. The boys were split into different teams that were coached by five twenty-something gentile men. Four had mustaches. One had no mustache but a tattoo on his shoulder to offset his deficit of trite machismo. They all had swollen hairy forearms, hairy hands, dark wavy hair, and deep tans. Those types of men always made me self-conscious about my lack of grit. Just a whiff of Aqua Velva raised my pulse. They never smiled or laughed, and they learned the names of only the really good athletes. The lazy jerks. They coached about thirty boys; with any effort they could have learned all our names in a week. Half the boys were named Marc.

I'll never understand why adult men suck up to preadolescent athletes. These are the kids who are going to be fawned over, deferred to, and effusively cheered until they graduate high school. They'll receive special attention from teachers and coaches and neighbors and girls and everyone else who intersected with an unearned charisma based on America's unhealthy deification of sports.

It was so clear which kids were comfortable with themselves and which kids were awkward and in need of patience and encouragement. I recognized it, not only in myself but within so many of these camp kids. There were kids even more shy and self-conscious than *me*. How did *they* manage?

What unimaginative minds in these counselors. This wasn't one of those cutthroat Florida tennis camps. It was a day camp for poor Jews, left-outs amid the left-out, and yet these men ignored the nonathletes and coddled the jocks. "Jocks" who, once the non-Jews were reinstalled, would spend the majority of their lives on the bench.

My idol Finn Burns, prince of the neighborhood, was only thirteen, but he'd accepted me since we met when he was probably ten. I thought it was because I was so funny, but with hindsight it's clear that Finn, himself the youngest of three boys, innately understood the need for a young boy to be appreciated by an older boy, preferably a *cool* older boy. That an enthusiastic greeting, embracing of a nickname, an occasional bike ride could give a lonely, timid boy an infusion of confidence that would endure. I liked how I felt around him. These camp counselor guys made me hunch my shoulders and stare at my feet.

To my dismay I failed to demonstrate even a glimmer of talent in any of the Simchah sports. I had played Little League with some competence the spring before but I always found it difficult to carry victories forward. This "only as good as your last game" mentality gave me an outlook that made every tryout, game, scrimmage, or practice a test of my worth. The anxiety accompanying this feedback loop was maddening.

I made no lasting friends. I made one enemy: a boy named Kapler. He may have had a first name, probably Marc, but I always called him Kapler. He was a pale, skinny, sepia-haired boy with swollen pink ears that stuck out like my other enemy, Steamboat Willie. He had narrow, blinky brown eyes behind big glasses that he attached to his stupid head with some kind of stretchable ribbon scheme.

Kapler was not a good athlete, but he made the camp's softball team, and I didn't. An outrage. I was the last kid to sour-grape about camp politics, but I believed the fact that his mom ran the camp's theater program played a part in his selection. Also, his landing the lead in *You're a Good Man, Charlie Brown,* where he brazenly violated the camp's kosher dietary policies with his broad "acting."

This kid irritated me every day but especially on the day we went to a zip line in the woods. I opted out because I was afraid of heights, as well as slopes and velocities. Kapler was chosen to go first, naturally. He came off the zip line, and kids mobbed him. He was flushed, splotchy-faced, bubbling with pride, dying to share the details of his odyssey. In response to numerous queries—"Was it fun?" "Was it scary?" "Would you do it again?"—he announced to his adoring crowd, and friends, I *swear* to you, on my blanky, I am *not* making this up:

"You learn so much about yourself."

You couldn't have typed up and forced this nebbish to recite a more phony, self-aggrandizing, *Ain't I* smart; *ain't I* deep; *ain't I* mature? sentence. He wasn't joking, either. He probably heard someone who just scaled Mount Everest say it to Joan Lunden on *Good Morning America* and then he memorized it and packed it away for an occasion when this type of schmuckery arose. He was probably rehearsing it while they attached his harness.

I *scoffed* and said, "Oh, *come on!*"

"What?" he said, oblivious as to just how big a putz he was.

I yelled, "Kapler, why are you so *preachy? J-sus Chr-st,* you sound like a commercial for Outward Bound."

Then to underscore my indignation I said, "You learn so much about yourself," but in a funny voice.

I couldn't have articulated it at ten years old, but what irritated me about Kapler was that he was not an athlete, a good actor or singer. He wore glasses, which at that time was shorthand for intelligence but, more important, weakness. And these were *glasses*. Thick-framed, dense lenses with that strap that let you know, even from behind, this kid can't see. I needed glasses, but I wouldn't wear them because I was afraid of being made fun of or presumed a nerd. Yet he went out for the softball team and the play and went on the zip line and felt comfortable with the other kids, the macho counselors, the girl counselors. I thought I was as smart and athletic as he was, and I didn't wear glasses, but I didn't feel safe doing any of that. I wanted to feel good about myself the way Kapler did, but I didn't, and I hated him for it. *I don't believe in myself, why does Kapler get to?* He didn't seem to even care what I thought about him.

Why was this kid so self-assured? Or any of these kids. Every Jew should be insecure. For millennia we've run for our lives from every nation we've inhabited. We also worship a G-d who is insecure, a G-d who demands there "be no other G-ds before Him," that His name be hyphenated, that His pronouns be capitalized, and that His followers take the same day off as He does.

I hated just about every minute at camp, but there were two reprieves from the sports obsession that involved activities I liked:

One: arts and crafts, which the boys called "farts and craps." That type of hackneyed word play infuriated me. How dare you? That leaky gray shed was the only thing that made that cesspool of a camp justifiable. While the grittier boys grunted through violent games of a dodgeball sport they called "bumbahdmint" I joyfully designed colorful candles, ceramic-tiled ashtrays, and jazzy bracelets made from the mystical element our forefathers called "gimp." Gimp is a craft system based on taking flexible plastic laces and weaving them into ugly key chains and ugly bracelets. Modern gimp peddlers have expanded their product line to include ugly lanyards and ugly earrings.

I loved to craft, and only girls and nonthreatening boys attended these free periods, which made me feel quite manly there.

To borrow a parallel from *Fiddler on the Roof,* I was a Perchik among Motels. The hour each day after lunch when you could choose among tarmac sports, free swim, and arts and crafts was *my* Jewish summer camp.

Two: the day we went to Wingaersheek Beach in Gloucester, Massachusetts. I didn't go in the water because of my limited selection of swimwear. In my family's tax bracket, you could have either jeans that fit or a proper bathing suit, not both. In a robbing Peter to pay Paul wardrobe trade-off, my mother would take the jeans I outgrew in the spring and with a midthigh scissoring, turn them into a bathing suit. These swim trunks, with no similarity to the expertly trimmed and tailored Daisy Dukes of popular culture, were not only ragged and grotesque on land but, when pickled by the Atlantic, the source of violent chafing.

I've never understood the expression to describe something difficult as "no day at the beach." To me "a day at the beach" was a living hell. On a typical "day at the beach" with my family, my dad would park on the side of the road no less than a mile from the beach so that we could save three dollars for parking. We would carry a twenty-pound chaise longue chair under each arm and take turns carrying a steel cooler filled with ice and two-liter bottles of Diet Pepsi (the first Diet Coke wouldn't be sipped till over two years later).

By the time we arrived at the beach we were bruised, scraped, and lacerated from ankle to thigh, and our fingers and wrists were cramped from clawing fifty pounds of equipment for an hour in the sun. Four hours later we'd limp back to the car, dehydrated, peeling from sunburn, and seething at the people looking out of their summer homes at the wandering Jews.

I was never given sunscreen. There's no explanation for this negligence. The July 1980 sun shone with the same intensity as today's version. It's not like they didn't sell sunscreen. It was available in every drugstore/pharmacy, yet it was purchased only by parents who were deemed *overprotective* by their peers. "Overprotective" at that time meant installing smoke detectors, making your kids wear seat belts, and serving breakfast cereals that didn't contain marshmallows.

To avoid flaying my groin that day with the camp, I stayed ashore. Fortunately, there was a sandcastle contest to occupy me all day.

Being essentially an only child had allowed me to refine my skills as a beach artisan over the years. My focus and the comfort in solitude made me a lock for the grand prize in this tournament.

Others worked in teams with one member rushing into the waves from time to time for a refreshing dip. I spent hours that day by myself, sculpting a faithful replica of the US Capitol building. It had a dome, and I placed a snail shell atop a beach reed for the Statue of Freedom. I sat by it all day, making small adjustments, rewetting where necessary, protecting it from vandals and toddlers, patiently awaiting my tidal wave of glory.

The judge was named Amy. She was a sun-wrecked, gum-snapping, dishwater-blond teen in a side ponytail and faded, safari-print bikini. She smelled like a Peter Paul Mounds factory thanks to the excess of the coconut-scented Hawaiian Tropic tanning oil with which she had marinaded her gaunt frame. For ten minutes she flounced around examining and commenting on the submissions, but she didn't say anything about mine. What could she say that wouldn't come off fawning or give away the ending?

After a short conference with her equally tawdry girlfriend, a frizzy brunette with bad skin, also named Amy, she awarded a sweet frilly blue ribbon to . . .

Kapler. Who else? The four-eyed turd.

His entry? An amorphous series of slopes, ramps, and chutes, which he had shaped and smoothed *using a tennis ball.* At nine months old I could have made that pile of shit.

In her paean to Kapler's monument to mediocrity, Judge Amy said, "It reminded me of what I used to make with my dad when *I* was a kid."

There you go. Because Crapler was able to rouse nostalgia for this floozy's dad, he took home a sweet blue ribbon.

My word, it's like this camp was established to make Kapler feel good about himself. I made an actual *castle*, with a *dome* and a shell for the Statue of *Freedom*! But because I didn't sculpt a catalyst for your mawkish reverie, I go home with nothing but the sand in my crotch. What the hell did this kid have on you people?

Camp eventually ended. Because of my weak showing in the sports arena, I abandoned all my athletic dreams before fourth grade even started. The way I saw it, if I were any kind of athlete, I would have cartoonishly dominated those Yids. Abandoning all hope was a hobby of mine. I was easily discouraged but, in a way, persistent because every time, after a period of licking my wounds, I would revive my original passion and return with undying zeal . . . until the next minor setback.

The school year covering 1980–1981 was also the last year Rick lived at home with my mother and me. He worked sixty hours a week as a CPA and often spent weekends visiting his girlfriend, so I treasured the fleeting time we shared. I spent a lot of time that year following him around, attending his accounting league softball games and then afterward going to dive bars with his coworkers/teammates. I was like the mascot/batboy. We laughed a lot together.

He had always been funny, but over his four years in college his humor had become sharper, also saltier, and insult-based. This transformation was no doubt the consequence of the Beta Kappa Phi fraternity he had cured in for three years.

He was expert in a category of humor he referred to as "bustin' balls." The jokes favored in this genre would be, say, if you wore clothes in colors more flamboyant than gray, beige, or navy blue he'd say, "Nice shirt, Mary!" Or Sally. Or Betty. Really any girl's name that was no longer contemporary would work. In general, showing weakness or femininity was risking his scorn. He did not care for softness, calling anyone behaving unmanly the insult that was topping the charts at the end of the decade, *wimp*. "Wimp" bridged the evolution of that category of slurs from "sissy" to "p—y." While the portmanteau "wuss" had a promising two-year run following a cameo in 1982's *Fast Times at Ridgemont High,* "p—y" reclaimed the throne in 1985 and never looked back.

There was also a sadistic pastime that my brother had imported from college. It was called "flicking." Not boogers but using the same fingers and action you might use to flick a booger or other projectile for distance. You would take your middle finger and build tension by curling it toward your palm and then using your thumb as an energy-stacking lever, you'd let loose a stinging strike on a peer that was painful and occasionally left welts. Rick was good; he could've broken glass with his flick and enjoyed practicing on me. I liked showing how tough I was in withstanding the battery, or rather, I liked that he liked seeing me be tough. This hazing *infuriated* my mom. She would tell him he was going to give me an "aneurysm" or "brain damage."

His response? "Why don't you put him in a plastic bubble?" This was a reference to the ABC made-for-television tearjerker *The Boy in the Plastic Bubble* that starred the guy who played Barbarino, John Travolta.

Sometimes if I expressed distress myself he'd say, "Why don't you go read a book?" This may have been just a generic "toughen up" rebuke but felt pointed when absorbed by me, a confirmed bibliophile.

He was unassailable, sometimes even ragging on my dad. Like, one time my dad rolled a bowling ball awkwardly and Rick said, "Nice throw, Phyllis," which would have been biting even if my dad wasn't named Phil. My father would occasionally warn him about bringing these frat house *put-down* customs home with him, but by that time Rick was gradually dethroning my dad as the leader of the family. I felt the insurrection was inevitable as soon as Rick started calling him Phil during his freshman year of college. I could still go to Dad for protection, but neither of my brothers were at an age where he could punish them.

Another effective formula Rick utilized was what I called the "What are you?" technique. This is where the object of his put-down would do something associated with a pop culture or historical figure and he would then ask if you *were* that pop culture/historical figure. It wasn't especially sophisticated, but it got laughs around the house and neighborhood. An example was one hot summer day while playing outside I kept coming inside to refill cups of water for my friend Finn and me and Rick said, "What are you, Gunga Din?" Finn laughed, so I laughed. I didn't know about the 1890 Kipling poem or the 1939 film it inspired, but it was delivered like a punch line, which was enough to pass for one in 1980. Another "What are you?" was when I opened a candy store in our garage and he said, "What are you, Willy Wonka?"

He made a lot of friends in that frat house. I'd met at least six of these fraternity brothers while he was in college. From his popularity and the delight he radiated when recounting his college antics, I gathered that "bustin' balls" or "put-downs," as my dad euphemized, was the way to get laughs and win friends. When school started, I eagerly integrated these techniques into my act.

My teacher that year was Mr. Arthur Mercier. It was the first time I ever had a male teacher. He was in his early thirties, or at least seemed to be older than twenty-three-year-old Rick but younger than my fifty-six-year-old dad and forty-seven-year-old mom. Mr. M. was a little over six feet tall with a build and bearing that suggested he had played sports that required a helmet. He had thick black hair of professional length parted on the left side and a dashing black mustache. A boring wiseass would have pointed out a faint resemblance to Chef Boyardee.

Over the years, I had become wary of men who looked like him. I had always hated these "man's man" types, and my four weeks at Simchah had reinforced my disdain.

Initially I thought: *Lovely, another mouth-breathing cretin to further erode my confidence.* But Mr. Mercier surprised me. He had a generous, honest smile and warm dark eyes. Within a couple of days, he knew everyone's first names and even apologized for mispronouncing Marcia K's name *Mar see ya* instead of *Marsha*.

My affection for him was cinched shortly thereafter. Whenever a teacher asked for a volunteer to run an errand to the office, all hands went up immediately. There was something about that two to four minutes of independence while walking to and from the office. It provided a solitary contemplative stroll with no one around to question one's passion for stepping only on the red tiles even if it meant some hopping. One morning he picked me to bring the lunch money and attendance sheet to the office, and when I returned, he said, "Thanks, Gah!" like we were pals. If life had been a cartoon there would have been illustrated hearts flying around my reddened face while a heart-shaped heart leaped from my chest and pulsated to a tympani beat.

That year I concentrated on being funny. While the woman teachers I had in the past were mostly averse to flippancy, I figured a male teacher would welcome a sharp-tongued scamp looking to liven things up. I had several gags. Whenever someone gave the wrong answer I'd make the buzzing sound associated with the big red *X* on Richard Dawson's *Family Feud*. I'd frequently *ntz* or roll my eyes at kids who asked stupid questions and sometimes say the retort "Uh-doy" which had recently sur-passed "duh" in usage frequency. I appropriated Rick's "What/who are you?" gimmick every chance I got. To make fun of a boy who brought Wheat Thins to the Christmas party, I said to him, "What are you, *Sandy Duncan*?" after the Wheat Thins spokeswoman of the moment. After a field trip to the skating rink that stopped at Burger King for lunch, Brian L. ordered a Sanka; for the next several weeks I called him Marcus Welby after the iconic TV role of Sanka's spokesman, a fossil named Robert Young.

One time I scolded a boy named Jeff. He was an odd kid who was taken out of class once a week to meet with a calm man with a soothing voice and a beard who must have been the school counselor. During a social studies test about Alaska, Jeff just started walking around the room while we were filling out the test and I said, "What are you, special?" I was bustin' balls like it was the Dean Martin roast of Orson Welles, and I felt I was dropping gems.

The kids didn't see it that way. They didn't know who Sandy Duncan or Marcus Welby were; they just thought I was a weirdo and a jerk. I no longer felt comfortable around my mom's friends, but I didn't feel much better around kids my own age.

Thankfully, on an unseasonably warm afternoon in November (nearly fifty degrees), I received a blessing that would rejuvenate my mood and provide me with purpose for years.

Often when my mother worked at night, she would hire Finn Burns to sit for me. He spoke differently than every other kid. He had a large vocabulary and would use inflated language to describe the mundane, like when he wanted to ride bikes down to 7-Eleven he'd say, "Lewy, fetch ya vehicle and set a course for Sev."

He had a collection of slang terms that either he coined or sourced outside our community because I knew of no one else who talked like Finn.

If a family was rich, he would say, "Oh, Lewy, they're *stuffed,* Lewy. *Stuffed.*"

"Stuffed?"

"Lewy, with dough, Lewy, coin, loot, bread, scratch. Keep up, kid."

He even used swear words in a clever way. Plenty of boys, including Rick, would call certain people "dildos." But Finn put a twist on the term, like when describing the obnoxiousness of a neighbor with this pearl: "Oh, Lewy, the dildoity is breathtaking, isn't it, Lewy?"

Cigarettes were "nails" (shortened from coffin nails); hair was "spinach" or "lettuce"; work was "the rock pile"; a mom was a "moo." Any boss or authority figure was "Mr. Slate" (Fred Flintstone's boss). Legs were "get-away sticks," "wheels," or "pegs."

Sometimes he'd use quaint or formal language, like when pretty girls walked by he would say, "Evening ladies," like he was an old-timey gentleman.

They would sing, "Hiiii, Fiiiiinn!" and you could tell they liked him.

Everyone liked him—mothers, fathers, teachers, jocks, stoners, drug dealers, shy people, loud people, sexy girls, plain girls, brains, ignorami, criminals, priests, nuns, rabbis, drunks, dogs, cats, squirrels. He made you feel good without feeling he was trying to put one over on you. He was versatile, clever, and polite but not above an insult or a swear. I guess Ferris Bueller would be a fair comparison, but Ferris was a prick. Finn was what we call in Yiddish a mensch.

Finn had a resonant, lingering laugh, and he was lavish with it. My family had to be in the exact right mood to partake in

a laugh and their taste tended toward middle-of-the-road, es-
chewing absurdity and silliness. Finn liked all my jokes.

Many days we'd ride our bikes the 1.7 miles to "Sev," where
we'd buy Slurpees and baseball cards. We'd sit on our bikes
or on the stoop in front, fighting off ice-chip migraines and
scanning our change for the wheat-backed pennies Finn called
"Wheaties."

Finn was athletic and a big sports fan; when he babysat, we'd
usually play some sports. So once again I was swearing off my
swearing off of sports. On that gray balmy day in November,
with the comforting smell of burning leaves in the air, he took
me to a playground where we played basketball with a bunch of
his friends. I had no basketball experience before that afternoon,
but in just a couple of hours I was hooked.

Basketball fit every aspect of my disposition. The ball wasn't
fired at great velocity near your face like baseball, and the sport
didn't permit assault and battery like football and hockey. This
was a civilized, elegant, violence-free sport. You didn't need a
helmet or pads. You didn't even need pants.

The sport was aesthetically pleasing as well. I loved the sound
the nets made when we made shots. We called it a *swish*, but
with the park's metallic chain nets it sounded like someone
had dropped a fistful of cheap forks. Activating that rusty wind
chime was exhilarating. Dribbling home that day from the park
I loved how the basketball's bounce echoed so forcefully that it
caused the neighbors' front doors to throb.

Soon I could do some cool dribbling moves like between the
legs and behind my back. Rick taught me how to spin the ball
on my index finger, and within a few hours I could do it and
keep it going by lightly tapping the ball on its equator with my
left hand, my tongue over my lips just like Rick. Within days I
could bounce it off my fist and later my elbow or head and get
it spinning again. Rick and I bonded over my basketball pas-

sion in a way we hadn't when we threw the baseball or football around. I think because of his strong arm, mine felt inadequate. With basketball, he would teach me things, and while he was at work, I could perfect them and show him his tutelage was bearing fruit. I think he may have sensed that this sport was more in line with my physical and mental makeup, so he was especially encouraging.

Another advantage basketball offered, particularly over baseball, was that it didn't require many people. It could even be played alone, which was appealing as I was still struggling to find a reliable everyday friend. Practicing basketball was more engaging than spending time with my meager options for companionship. I was constantly practicing the shooting motions while lying on my bed. My mother let me practice my dribbling drills on the tile floor in her room and skip a leather jump rope in the kitchen. I think her indulgence was the result of my telling her that Larry Bird made $650,000 a year, a figure I determined on the adding machine was over forty-three times what Rick made as a CPA. I wanted to make it to the NBA, a feat Rick informed me was less likely than winning the lottery, twice.

The most valuable benefit from basketball, though, was a rebound of my self-esteem. There was something about how I felt about myself around boys and men after developing some basketball skills that helped quiet the voice in my brain that called me *wimp*, *femme*, or *fegelah*. I hadn't felt bliss like this since *The Monster at the End of This Book*.

Basketball also gave me more common ground with Mr. Mercier when I found out that he coached the school's basketball team. I started playing basketball outdoors every day at recess using one of the class's poorly inflated, warped, goitered basketballs. I had wanted to bring my ball, an orange Wilson Indestructo model that Rick had given me for Chanukah, but my dad warned me that someone "will *hike* it on ya," which I inferred was one of his countless synonyms for "steal." Phil Gulman had a bottomless supply of words for "theft": "hike," "clip," "swipe," "boost," "lift," "pinch," "jack," "nip," "nick," "pocket," "sleeve," "palm," "snipe." It was like being raised by Mickey Spillane. Maybe there was rampant fourth-grade crime back in the bootlegging "Extray, Extray, Read All About It" days, but in 1980 suburbia, nine-year-olds weren't so larcenous.

Every day now, after recess, I'd come back to the classroom sweaty and make sure to recount the highlights of the games loudly enough for Mr. Mercier to overhear. Whenever I tossed papers into the gray metal wastebasket beside his desk I would say, "Bird for three." If I hooked it in: "Kareem!" If I dunked: "Julius Errrrrrving." Mr. Mercier would always smile.

One Sunday in early December my dad brought me to the Basketball Hall of Fame in Springfield, Massachusetts, which cemented my love for the game. We stayed until closing. From the barren gift shop my dad bought me a pair of Milwaukee Bucks wristbands that had an adorable smiling deer that was spinning a basketball on its hoof! I also got two Hall of Fame commemorative pennants, one for me and one to give to Mr. Mercier. It was the first time I could remember looking forward to going to school on Monday.

When Rick heard about this patronage, he chastised me curtly.

"Are you bein' a brownnosah? Nobody likes a brownnosah."

I had never heard that expression, so at first I figured it involved bringing thoughtful, inexpensive gifts to teachers. Why would nobody like that? But from the revulsion in his tone and the fact that it involved the color brown, I deduced that it was doody-related. I wasn't brownnosing. I wasn't trying to get better grades. I had the highest math and social studies scores in the fourth grade. I just really liked Mr. Mercier, and I wanted him to know he was appreciated. Of course it made me second-guess my largesse and arrested the happiness I felt. I think Rick applied a lot of his college experiences to my world. I'm sure brownnosing at UMass was repellent to the people you'd want to be friends with, but this was innocent adulation mixed with panning for a male role model. This was the most amount of time I had ever spent with an adult male—five and a half hours a day, five days a week, versus noon to six every Sunday with my dad, sometimes several hours of that time watching the tedious New England Patriots punt all afternoon. I hadn't liked a teacher since Mrs. Burns two full teachers ago and this man was like an extra father. And I brought him a pennant from the Basketball Hall of Fame. That was the least I could do. For what he was adding to my life and my understanding of manhood, he deserved a spot in the Teachers Hall of Fame alongside Anne Sullivan and Gabe (Welcome Back) Kotter.

For Christmas every year the kids would give the teacher a gift that their mothers had picked out for them. Every other year I just delivered it, but that year I asked to pick it out myself from a drawer of things that my mother had stolen from Murray's during her crime spree there. I didn't know that the items were stolen, but there is no other way to account for the number of graduation gifts that bureau has provided. I gave him a silver Cross ballpoint pen. I made sure to test the pen so that he wouldn't think we were cheap jerks. I hoped he would think of me every time he signed significant documents, like report cards, hall passes, and warning notices.

In 1979 Massachusetts residents joined myopic citizens across the nation in voting to reduce local property taxes. To address shortfalls, municipalities strangled budgets for art, gym, and music teachers, youth sports, after-school programs, and other offerings that made life bearable for people too young to vote. In order to mitigate the results, Mr. Mercier gave us an extra gym class once a month.

On a Tuesday he informed us that the next day at extra gym we would be playing basketball. In preparation, that night at the mall I got my first pair of legitimate basketball sneakers. They were cream-colored Converse Chuck Taylors canvas high-tops, size five and a half. Nine dollars. I don't want you to think that I am so old that any serious basketball player still wore canvas sneakers. Even in 1980 Chuck Taylors were kitschy. The issue was that the classier basketball sneakers, particularly the ones made of leather, were way out of our price range at about thirty-three dollars. Despite their lack of style, I spent the night we bought them adoring them, running my fingers over the soles, and pressing on the firm but springy insole. The off-white laces with the transparent aglets would never be cleaner and sturdier. The outer soles would never be so free of gum, pebbles, and dog crap. And the *smell* . . . oh my. I stuck my snout right in there and savored that rubbery, muscular smell. Sneakers possess that seashell-to-your-ear-type magic. If you closed your eyes and held those Chuck Taylors up to your nose, you'd think you were in the sporting goods section of Sears.

This was a time when only serious basketball players owned basketball sneakers. They were neither fashion statement, status symbol, identity, collectible, or investment. You bought basketball sneakers because you required the support and flexibility for the unique movements vital to competitive basketball. And you *wore* them. Almost exclusively while playing basketball. The idea of hoarding and stashing them was absurd, in 1980 more people collected bottle caps than basketball sneakers. The only Jordan in the NBA was Eddie, a six-foot reserve for the New Jersey Nets. Michael Jordan was a senior in high school. There were players who wore the nascent Nike brand of footwear, but its name recognition was so paltry that most of us pronounced it to rhyme with "like" or "psych." The stars of the NBA, Dr. J, Larry Bird, and Magic Johnson all wore Converse, so I did, too.

Also, basketball sneakers were only worn with shorts or jeans. A person wearing basketball sneakers with a suit was a look I called "Poor kid at a bar mitzvah." The idea of an adult who had never dribbled between their legs nor spun a ball on their finger wearing the same footwear as Kareem Abdul-Jabbar with a tailored suit was inconceivable. We didn't change; sneakers changed. The sneakers available today are objets d'art; what was available to us in 1980 were stick-figure cave drawings in comparison.

I brought my secret weapons to school the next day even though when I told my dad my plan on the phone, he warned me that someone would "filch 'em." I assured him that I would not take my eyes off them. I brought them, still in their box, with the off-white tissue paper inside. I had worn them around the house the night before and driven my mother cuckoo by making the squeaks of stop and start on her bedroom tile until she said "Gah, *genug!*"

We went to the gym, and we played a short game and I missed every shot, all layups. I was crushed but didn't let on, hoping Mr. Mercier didn't see. But he did. After the last miss rimmed out, he said, "Gah, you can't *buy* a hoop!" I had dreamed this would go differently, though I wasn't all that surprised as I tended to choke under the eyes of authority.

Later that night I recapped my game for Rick but I lied about what Mr. Mercier said. The way I told it was, "And Mr. Mercier said, 'You're taking great shots but they're *just* missing.'"

It was very important to me that the world corroborated the promise Rick saw in me.

I spent that especially cold winter practicing dribbling in my mother's room and the garage and going to the local library to take out books about basketball players. Occasionally, I'd shovel out some space at the park after I read that Jerry West and Magic Johnson had done that. The basketball books all shared the same arc. Humble beginnings followed by suffering, then maniacal dedication resulting in basketball stardom and a bland biography.

That winter of 1981, with this goal to chase, I was feeling okay about myself. The rejuvenation lasted until April, right before the spring vacation week, when I received a painful censure of my character. Mr. Mercier gave me a warning notice in conduct. Over the years, I had gotten a couple of these notices for excessive talking, but this one was different. It read "Gary has been making insensitive remarks to other students in class. . . . He needs to show more compassion for kids who aren't as fortunate as him."

My mouth went dry. My stomach shriveled. I knew about compassion; my dad had recently given me a lecture stressing its importance. It wasn't as long a lecture as the one he frequently gave on the importance of throwing the first punch, but he was serious about the topic.

I felt overcome by anxiety in my stomach about this criticism, so I sheepishly went to Mr. Mercier's desk for clarification of my offense. I didn't need clarification; I wanted to check his temperature, see if he still liked me.

He said the warning was because of "For instance, the way you give nicknames and when you make the buzzing sound associated with the big red *X* on Richard Dawson's *Family Feud* when someone gives a wrong answer." He also cited the rolling of my eyes and *ntz*ing and of course "uh-doy." Yes, but do you still like me?

I understood, and I didn't like what it said about me. I hated being teased, and here I was teasing these kids "less fortunate than me." I was ashamed. Also, I had thought Mr. Mercier really liked me, that I was his favorite, that I had impressed him in school and athletically. I had hoped he thought I was "one of the guys." To me this warning notice meant Mr. Mercier thought I was insensitive, cruel, a little shit.

Up until that moment I thought guys *liked* guys who were deft with insults. Johnny Carson loved having Don Rickles on his show. Rick and my mom loved watching Rickles put down the womanizing Johnny and his drunken oafish shill of a sidekick, Ed McMahon.

I spent the rest of the day and the walk home going over my transgressions.

I wished Mr. Mercier had pulled me aside instead of sending the notice. It seemed impersonal, and also I was going to have to get it signed by a parent. If my dad found out he'd be so disappointed in me and might yell. My mother would be irritated, but she's a hypocrite because whenever there's a "man on the street" being interviewed on the news who is unattractive she pretends to be startled like she saw a ghost.

Why'd Mercier wait until I had been working the act for seven months?

And another thing, Mercier, "less fortunate" than me? My clothes all come from my brothers. Every Sunday there's a good chance my parents are going to have an argument about the $110 check my dad writes out right before he leaves, during which he'll say "G-d forbid I die . . ." at least once. Also, I'm pretty sure I'm ugly.

How in the heck did these *less* fortunate get out of bed every morning? I dreaded morning, and according to Mr. Mercier I was the leading brand. I still didn't have a true friend. I saw Finn regularly, but he was more of a guardian angel than a friend.

But by the end of fourth grade I had a plan. If just *watching* basketball players made me feel good, then they must feel good about themselves. They seemed to have a lot of friends, at least ten. I'll become one. How? Well, the lazy biographies I read and reread indicated that *suffering* was a crucial component to success. I've got suffering down. Hard work and sacrifice? I'm in.

I discovered a few important things that year. I couldn't hang out with my mom's friends anymore and feel good about it. I wasn't going to win any friends my age by "bustin' balls." And I wasn't confident enough to be a Finn. I realized that year that I had a capacity for hard work that I could apply to basketball. This would give me purpose as well as the prospect of new friendships. So fourth grade was a turning point. But that's the thing about fourth grade: "You learn so much about yourself."

October 2017

This week I start going over to Will Marmion's house to watch Boston Celtics basketball games. Like Finn, Will took over his mother's home but with his teenaged daughter, McKenzie, instead of his wife. We sit in the same room in which we played Atari Pac-Man in 1982. I don't have the energy to talk much. It feels Herculean to be out of the house after dark. I bring snacks whenever I feel energetic enough to go inside the grocery store.

While I'm there, his company and the surprising play of the hungry young Celtics distract me from the hours of rumination I engage in when I'm by myself. Sometimes after the Celtics we watch a movie we know all the words to. When I leave, I feel marginally better. Tomorrow morning I'll feel like shit, but for a few hours at Will's I have a little life.

Fifth

For the first time since first first, I was happy to be back at school. There was just one reason: I couldn't wait to tell Mr. Mercier about basketball camp. My week at Shoot Straight Basketball Camp was the coolest thing I had ever done. I was away from home for six days and five nights, the longest I'd ever gone without seeing my mom.

I'd tell Mr. Mercier how Georgetown University star Patrick Ewing's high school coach put his arm around me for a Polaroid and that I met Houston Rockets all-star Calvin Murphy and got a picture with him, too. I'd show Mr. Mercier both of those pictures. I'd also tell him that Murphy drove a brand-new copper-colored 1981 Cadillac Seville with a gold plate on the dashboard that said, "Custom Made for Calvin Murphy."

Maybe I would stay after school that day and catch him up all at once. Or better still, maybe I'd present the stories in installments over the next several weeks thereby necessitating multiple visits to my fourth-grade classroom, which was on the same hallway as my new fifth-grade one.

As we filed down the hallway on the first morning, I looked inside the old room so I could wave to Mr. Mercier and watch his face light up.

"Gah!" he'd say. "Stop by later so we can catch up! I wanna hear all about the basketball camp, even if it should necessitate multiple visits."

When I passed by the old room, I saw a woman teaching in there. Mr. Mercier must have switched classrooms or been made principal. I'd have to get a bathroom pass and investigate before lunch.

My fifth-grade teacher was Mrs. Phyllis Schaub. She was a middle-aged Jewish woman with the short reddish-brown hair that drenched that group throughout the 1980s. It was immediately obvious that she wasn't especially strict and wouldn't yell very much, but it was also clear that there wasn't going to be any way to make her laugh because she practiced the detachment that less authoritative teachers had to adopt to maintain order. Artie Mercier was like a fresh young dad. Phyllis Schaub was a tired mom. And not just because she had the same first name as half the world's middle-aged Jewish women. She just didn't have that "I was a kid once, too" energy that the great ones had.

After the books were passed out, I asked for the bathroom pass and I roamed the halls looking for Mercier. Maybe he had to take the first day off for jury duty or gall bladder surgery. I continued to make my list of things to tell Mr. Mercier but now with fear that they'd never reach him. My stomach felt like it did when my mother forgot to leave the key in the mailbox for me.

I could've asked Mrs. Schaub about him, but asking your new teacher about your last teacher felt rude. Also, if there was bad news, I didn't want to get it from this Clairol-soaked chalkie.

After school I went to Finn Burns's house so I could ask his mother, Judy, if she knew when Mr. Mercier was coming back. She told me he took a job teaching in Salem, Massachusetts, nearer to where he lives. He wouldn't be coming back to West Memorial.

He should have told me. I wouldn't have spent the last six

weeks assembling a summary of my summer. I still held out hope that one day he'd visit. Then I'd tell him about camp. I'd abridge it so he'd have time to visit with the other teachers. I'd only tell him about the Houston Rockets' Calvin Murphy and his awesome Caddy. I kept the Polaroid with Patrick Ewing's high school coach in my locker for when he returned for a visit.

I couldn't tell anyone how disappointed I was. Kids aren't supposed to like their teachers. Plus, I held out vain hope: someday he'd visit and make amends.

Without the energizing force of Mr. Mercier, I lumbered through the first few weeks of school, anxious from Sunday at dusk through Friday at two thirty. The only marginally positive change was that my bedtime was made an hour later, to 9:30 P.M., which allowed me to stay up to watch *Bosom Buddies,* starring the fledgling actor Tom Hanks but not late enough to watch my favorite, *Taxi,* on a school night.

I was resigned to dragging ass through another uninspiring year. Then one day during lunch I overheard a round-faced blond boy in a faded New England Patriots sweatshirt talking about baseball cards.

For my eleventh birthday the previous summer my parents had taken me out for tacos and to a baseball card show at the Holiday Inn near our house. Until the moment we entered the "Pioneer Room" I was dubious as to the *existence* of such an enchanted forum.

We walked in and there were about thirty folding tables covered in albums and display cases and boxes filled with baseball cards old and new. I couldn't have been more hopped-up if I had opened a crate containing a litter of pygmy hippos. I was shaking with joy. The small convention was run by men, but men who behaved like children. Some of them even wore replica jerseys of the baseball teams they liked, which I found rather sad but somehow, these oddballs seemed happy.

Ever since that Sunday afternoon I was spellbound by baseball cards. I still played basketball every day—but once it got dark, I retired to my room, where I spent hours organizing and admiring my baseball cards and plotting how to acquire more. I loved the feel of an unopened pack in my hand. The smell of the packaging and peeling open the slick waxy wrapper, then inhaling the ambrosial bouquet of the sugar-dusted rosé-colored rectangle of brittle bubble gum that I never once chewed.

So that day in September, when I heard this boy named Billy Marmion (535-0346) talking baseball cards, I asked him if he wanted to trade some with me. He invited me to go to his house, but it would have to wait until the following day because of course I had Hebrew school on the day we first connected.

The next day, just after 10:00 A.M., we were in math learning the operations involved in adding and subtracting mixed fractions and all that pencil-blunting tedium. Because Mrs. Schaub had to teach math to everyone in the class no matter the skill level, we had to wait on some of the unfortunate kids who had struggled since third grade when six times nine had dashed so many college dreams.

While Schaub helped with some of the less motivated students, I noticed Billy studying the clock from his desk, which was one up and one row over to my right. He started scribbling on a memo pad. He folded the sheet in half and handed it to me. On the top of the page in navy-blue script was embossed: "A Note from Billy." In the lines below, Billy had written, in pencil, large enough to cover the page, "Dear Gary, 4 hours 28 minutes until we go to my house." His penmanship was horrendous, but the message was unforgettable.

Initially the countdown notes came every twenty minutes. By 2:10, when the class atmosphere got a little looser, he started sending them every couple of minutes and then, when there were only five minutes left, he kept writing and tearing off pages in a frenzy. I was laughing because he was really exerting himself trying to keep up with the time, like the Bugs Bunny episode when Bugs played all the baseball positions in a victory against the heavily favored Gas House Gorillas. He passed me nineteen notes over the course of the day, all of them beginning with "Dear Gary." Rick would call him a brownnosah, but I loved it.

We walked to his house, which was about a mile from the school and a mile from my house. His house was about the same size as mine, but he had a basement instead of a garage. We went inside, and he called his mother at work. This seemed like a routine, which I envied. In the mornings on days my mother wasn't going to be home after school she'd just yell, "The key's in the mailbox" as I walked down the driveway.

Billy's home smelled of Merit cigarettes, fresh dairy, and pasta sauce. There was a slight trace of dog and cat paraphernalia within the bouquet. Overall, a comforting aroma.

We traded baseball cards for a while. He had an awesome collection, though he didn't take great care in protecting them or organizing them. They were just thrown into a big box that had once carried snow boots. The cards weren't separated into years and teams like all of my cards, and they hadn't been placed in a Topps Super Sports Card Locker made of premium vinyl that you could only get by sending a wrapper, four dollars and seventy-five cents plus seventy-five cents for shipping and handling and waiting four to six weeks (it took all six weeks) for delivery. Not only did Billy not separate his baseball cards by team, they weren't even separated by sport! He had hockey and football mixed in with *Empire Strikes Back* and *M*A*S*H* cards like some sort of g-ddamned freak show. Also, he was indifferent to the trade value of his cards, too generous. A kid who hadn't learned during now three years of Hebrew school that G-d would smite him for offering less than fair value for a Rickey Henderson rookie would have robbed Billy blind.

After the trading finished, Billy took me to his basement, which he called "down cellah." It had a damp-dirt, garagey, hamster-cage smell (it was actually a rabbit named Harvey). Delightful. Under dim fluorescent lighting we played two different games called "hockey," neither of which had even the vaguest connection to actual hockey. First, we played a game where you controlled the players with metal rods connected to two-dimensional players who could never get control of the puck. This was a two-player game I'd always wanted as a gift but had never requested because a friend was not included. After the rod hockey we played another faux hockey called air hockey, which was sublime. Before the ubiquity of video game systems, I coveted air hockey the way I would Atari about six months later. Arcades had air hockey tables that were similar in size to foosball, but Billy's air hockey was about three feet long. You plugged it in, and a supernatural cushion of air poured out of tiny vent holes embedded in the "rink." The hum was soothing; a plastic disk the size of a kid's hand would float on the air stream and you would attack it with a round paddle with a knob in the center that looked like a derby-style hat. You'd try to slap the disk into a slot in the wall of your friend's side. I will never understand why this electrifying game doesn't dominate the tabletop-sports genre. Maybe because it required virtually no skill, strategy, or technique. Which to me was a good thing. Who wanted to dedicate their life to becoming decent at Ping-Pong or pool or darts? In my estimation those were dead-end sports for con artists and drunkards.

Offering rod hockey, air hockey, and an Invasion of Anzio military playset (plastic army men), Billy's basement was like a toy store. The Marmions were not much wealthier than us, yet his toy and game collection was downright decadent. His dad was a salesman and his mom worked full-time, but he was an only child, meaning the toy budget was not depleted by older brothers. I would have gladly given up one brother if only for the air hockey. Max was in his junior year at UMass studying hotel and restaurant management. Rick had recently married a college classmate who my mother frequently roasted to her girlfriends by saying the wife had received her M-R-S degree after majoring in "pre-wed." This would get big laughs but *had to be* old jokes; they sounded like Joan Rivers.

I called my mom to pick me up just before five. I had determined over the years that this was the exact right time to leave a friend's house. I didn't want to make mothers think I was fishing for a dinner invite, but this was generally the time when moms would start dinner prep and you wanted to secure an invite at a juncture when she could still stir some more stock into the cauldron.

I liked eating at other people's houses. Other than Passover my mother served food that came only from cans or the freezer. Also, even when my brothers were home, nobody ever ate at the same time as anyone else in my house unless it was a birthday or the commemoration of the Exodus. It was like living in a house of middle-aged bachelors.

I could have walked home, but I was always frightened to walk through unfamiliar neighborhoods because of the common suburban hazards: German shepherds and teenagers. As I waited for my mom to pick me up, I thought about my good fortune: not since first first grade, when I danced frantically to the "Alley Cat" song with Luke, had I had such a fun time. I wouldn't tell my mom yet because I didn't want to jinx it, but I believed I had a new best friend.

I couldn't believe my luck. Beyond the baseball cards and the FAO Schwarz–ian basement the thing about Billy that made him irresistible was that he was so funny.

He would sing *"Harvey* Nagila" to his rabbit, even though he wasn't Jewish. I'm not sure if it was just for my benefit, but that type of clever song parody killed me. Billy also had a real gift for nicknaming, a skill highly valued among boys my age. He called Mrs. Schaub "Mrs. Snob." The other fifth-grade teacher, Mrs. Cronin, who was always clearing her throat to get kids to quiet down, he called "Ahem-Head." He called the oafish principal with a fondness for wearing blazers over turtleneck sweaters "Herman Munster." He called Wally Mitler "Hitler." A boy named Doug Cares he called "Who" Cares. Some of his nicknames went too far, like his nickname for the alcohol-ravaged custodian Mr. Dropo whom he called Reverend Jim (from ABC's *Taxi*), the kid who had the last name of Penezous, whom he called "Penis," and his name for a chunky neighbor kid named Matt Grimm, whom he called "Fat" Grimm. He got away with it, though, partly because he was overweight himself but also because he had a charming air about him when he was launching his insults, not unlike Louie from *Taxi*.

One Friday afternoon my mom picked us both up from school and made a stop at the Warren Five Cents Savings Bank. My mother liked Billy immediately, owing to his quick wit, easy laugh, and that she was probably as desperate for me to find a friend as I was. We sat in my mom's car while she went in.

Outside the bank, Billy made up a joke about how nobody who went in there was allowed to deposit any more than a nickel and that my mom was in there so long because a guy had a quarter and they had to call Warren, the bank owner, to calm everybody down.

Then Billy started making fun of people who walked out of the bank. A lot of the jokes were formulaic—such as "Look at this guy's face!"—but he also had a real gem that afternoon. When a woman wearing a shabby turquoise ski hat exited, he said, "Nice hat lady, did your dog knit it?" She couldn't hear him, we were inside the car with the windows rolled up, but I pictured a dog knitting while wearing a bonnet and reading glasses way down low on its snout, and I couldn't catch my breath.

By the time Halloween season arrived Billy and I were best friends, talking every chance we got during the school day and hanging out at his house every afternoon. Then he asked me to trick-or-treat with him!

When I asked my mother about it she said to me, "You don't wanna trick-or-treat this year, do ya?"

Despite its sentence structure, it was not a question.

Over the years, my mother had frequently used this trick to thwart my interest in things. "You don't wanna . . ." plus the activity she wanted to smother. A few years prior she had put an end to celebrating my birthday with kids' parties invoking "you don't wanna." I hated putting my mother out and was sharp enough to infer that she was done planning and paying for birthday parties for me, so I said no I didn't want a birthday party with kids at it. But I *did* want a birthday party with kids at it that year, if only because it always increased my toy inventory.

But on her trick-or-treat referendum, I held firm. You bet your ass I want to trick-or-treat. I've never looked forward to it more. My best friend asked me to go with him and his *husky-*sized corduroys portend a productive harvest of the neighborhood's candy fields. This should keep my candy coffers full through Veterans Day. This would be the first time I tricked and/or treated with a friend rather than one of my impatient, bored brothers. Also, that year, Halloween fell on a Saturday, a serendipity that would not repeat for the rest of my candy-begging career.

Foolishly I entrusted my mother with the costume selection. She brought home something called a Kooky Spook's inflatable witch costume from CVS. It was a costume I had seen advertised on UHF and scoffed at its inanity. It was a disco ball–sized inflatable yellow head with a long pointy orange nose and a black witch's hat, all made of vile-smelling vinyl. You blew it up and fastened it on top of your head. They gave you a tub of oily crud to make your face "disappear" but the sludge was impossible to apply evenly, and so I just looked like a coal miner with a pool floatie on his head.

Her ability to disregard my interests was uncanny. I loved the Boston Celtics, the Incredible Hulk, and the Muppets, and she thought, *Witch!*

Billy dressed as a vampire. His mom painted his face white and slicked his hair back with Brylcreem, and he had fangs and a white tuxedo shirt with a cape. He looked like Dracula. I looked dirty.

Our pillowcases filled up quickly with an array of '80s candy staples—the usual fun-sized bars and common candy fare. My favorite candy at the time was ZotZ. ZotZ had a hard candy shell, but the center was made of whatever active ingredient makes Alka-Seltzer fizz. Also, it contained sherbet. It was my favorite non-bar candy, and while it may seem gimmicky, it was the apex of '70s candy innovation and delectability. ZotZ was a superstar of the '70s and early '80s but then nearly impossible to find, the Peter Frampton of candy. The fact that it contained sherbet is apt as much like ZotZ themselves; sherbet's market penetration peaked in 1980.

The most common candy I received was Smarties. They must have been very inexpensive. When you're all out of candy but still need a fix to ward off withdrawal, these were the methadone to my candy-bar habit. When trying to come down off Three Musketeers I'd turn to Smarties. It can't be an accident that they were shaped just like pills.

The only candy you could throw in my bag and I wouldn't eat was Bit-O-Honey. Bit-O-Honey was a sadistically arduous candy, not so much chewed as *gnawed*. A typical reaction to a Bit-O-Honey novice was to say, "Oh, it's stale" but *no*, even a fresh Bit-O was as rigid as bathroom tile.

Late in our journey we had heard a rumor from an Indiana

Jones that the Strausses were passing out *Slim Jims. Full-sized.* This was soon confirmed by a Papa Smurf who had earlier tipped us off to the Surrettes' dealing of *full-sized Three Musketeers.* He had been reliable in that case.

In total it would add a mile to our trek and sounded too good to be true, but this type of unorthodox Halloween distribution was worthy of investigation. I'd never even considered cured meat sticks as legal Halloween tender.

We got there and a Strauss flipped a single Tootsie Pop into our pillowcases. This felt more like the ending to a fable: don't believe everything you hear, even if it comes from the two most trusted men in pop culture. The confectionery anticlimax having sapped our strength, we called it a Halloween.

In addition to being degrading, the vinyl headpiece on my witch inflatable made me sweat profusely, so I was grateful that Billy was ready to end our quest. When we got back inside his house, the lights were low. There were candles out but not of the skull or Jack of the lantern variety.

His parents were celebrating their sixth wedding anniversary over a fondue pot. Instead of telling us to beat it, they invited us to join them. Despite a pillowcase full of candy, the best treat that night was sirloin bits dipped in hot Swiss cheese. Perhaps the universe had denied us the Slim Jims because it had a worthier meat in store. I'd never heard of fondue before that night. It was awesome, although something my mother would deem too complicated to replicate. It took a woman who would paint your face like Dracula to make fondue.

I hadn't considered the arithmetic regarding Billy's parents' sixth anniversary until later that fall when we were walking back to class from a trip to the main office. I can't remember why he had his birth certificate on him, but he showed it to me and pointed out that it had a different last name than what he went by in school. In a furtive tone he explained that he'd had a different father before. The fondue sharer was his stepfather. I was touched that he trusted me with that information.

He didn't seem ashamed the way I was about my parents' divorce. I always told kids who came over that my dad was at work. Along with the fondue and the "note(s) from Billy," I knew he was a better friend than I was used to. We were everyday friends, and I was so grateful.

As 1970s sitcoms had taught me, good times are fleeting. Things are looking up for Laverne? Wait twenty-two minutes. Billy and I continued to be friends, but in January an antagonist arose to undo my peace of mind.

Bobby Swan, a short wiry boy with dark brown hair approached me one day and said, "You're dead after school."

He was using one of the two established methods for proposing fights at West Memorial. He had chosen the more direct version. The other one was "Meet me on the hill after school"— said in an angry tone.

Bobby and I had actually been friendly since third grade. We had been infielders together on the same Little League team, just two years before. I had gone to his last birthday party. It was at McDonald's, and we had both condemned a guest named Tom Sanders for ordering a *large fry*. Though it was never explicitly stipulated, every decent child understood that you should limit your birthday party order to the small sizes. We had bonded while ridiculing the oblivious greed of that twerp.

But less than two years later, shortly after Christmas break, he dead-after-school–ed me. I don't know why. It's not that I don't remember; it's that he never gave a reason. He may have had one, but he didn't share it with anyone. I really couldn't think of anything specific I had done to warrant it, but I didn't want to push for a motive. I had an inkling it would be something along the lines of "I just don't like ya." Nobody needs to hear that. Though

I could have understood it. There were plenty of reasons to not like me. When a teacher asked the class a question, I *loved* having the answer. I was obnoxious while playing basketball, always dribbling through my legs, and just like my friend Finn, chirping *two* in falsetto whenever I made a shot. I also frequently referred to myself as the Incredible Gulk.

I was certainly irritating, but none of my quirks needed to be violently corrected. I should have just had limited appeal, *which was the case*. I was friends with Billy and friend*ly* with a couple of other weirdos in my class who were crazy for Dungeons & Dragons and home computers. Mind you, I didn't ever play their beloved game. D & D intrigued me, and I owned a set Joanie got me at a yard sale, but once again it required several friends, and the classmates who were aficionados only once invited me to join them. Plus, it flirted with the occult, which since my Wally days had scared the hell out of me.

Initially I was sure I could get out of getting killed after school. Over the years, kids would make threats like this, but they would let it pass after I made a good joke or did something nice, like maybe pick them for kickball or give them a pencil or a Hostess fruit pie.

Soon, though, after several more days of taunts, I realized he wasn't going to change his mind. I had even tried to reminisce about l'affaire de grand frites hoping to appeal to some nostalgia.

The only thing I could do once I realized that my fate was sealed was try to delay it, holding out hope that a relaxing weekend or an act of G-d could dissuade him from beating me up.

I was tempted to fake sick to stay home from school, but my memories of doing that in second first were too strong. I was too ashamed of the weakness of that version of me to try it again. This isn't to say I responded to the threats with any strength or resolve; instead of resorting to truancy, I applied several stalling tactics and excuses, and, G-d bless him, Swan agreed to every one of my petitions for postponement, even my most flimsy and embarrassing excuse, "I can't fight today; I have Hebrew school."

His hostility never receded, but I was grateful for his forbearance regarding scheduling, especially his respect for my religious deferment. He could have just followed me out of the school, pushed me down, and beat the snot out of me. He seemed to be following some obscure honor code requiring he receive my consent before pummeling me. It's possible this was inspired by the samurai in the miniseries *Shogun*, which had been a sweepsweek bonanza for NBC one year before.

I had never been in a fight. I had never hit anyone in the face. How do you punch someone in the face? That seemed so *intimate*. I would never have thought about pinching another kid's cheek or mussing their hair or *hugging them*, G-d forbid, but I'm going to drive my fist into their face skin as hard as I can? Also, what if I hit him in the face and he didn't fall down crying? For all the time my father spent encouraging fighting and bragging about his mid-1930s boxing skill, he spent maybe eight minutes showing me how to throw a punch. Even if I can summon the rage to throw a punch, what if it has no effect?

I rode a string of excuses and snow days into February. By February vacation, a weeklong recess Massachusetts public schools granted every winter, I knew I had to get it over with if only to eliminate the stress. I was losing my mind, sometimes wishing I were dead. I had wished I were dead periodically over the years, most ardently in second first when my teacher had been my tormenter. That time my father had interceded. Now the torment seemed more dire, but I knew my father would not come to my rescue. He would just tell me to fight. I knew I'd rather die than invite the humiliation of losing a fight in front of what I imagined would be the entire school and maybe even some of the less compassionate staff.

On the Saturday night before the end of February vacation,

Rocky was on television. I had seen it in the theater years before but this time I watched with serious focus. It inspired me. If Rocky—an unlucky club fighter, a self-proclaimed "ham 'n' egger," a lonely man, in a dreary studio apartment who confided in his pet turtles—can go fifteen rounds with the heavyweight champion of the world, then I can go to the hill and fight a boy at least ten inches shorter than me. I felt recharged by this plan . . . on that Saturday night . . . at the beginning of vacation . . . with the *Rocky* theme still fresh in my mind.

I was inspired to do some training, which involved ten push-ups and ten sit-ups and jogging around the house twice. I did this routine on four occasions during vacation. I was ready.

When I saw Bobby on Monday, I said, *Okay, today we'll meet on the hill after school.* The hour hand spun wildly 'round the classroom's industrial clock like an airplane propeller. All day I wasn't thinking about Rocky or my tremendous height and reach advantage. What I was thinking about was something Bobby had told me two years ago during a Little League practice. His brother, a kid who was such a ruffian that they put him in a school for bad kids, had told him you could kill someone by uppercut punching them in their nose. The nose bone would spear their brain. I hadn't thought much about it at the time, but now I couldn't think of anything else. *I'm dead after school.*

It was a gray day and chilly. I left school that day and made my way to the arena, the flat section six yards wide atop the steep hill overlooking the west side of the school. There was a crowd of about a dozen kids in attendance, a decent showing and a function of a couple of factors. First, kids don't have access to live entertainment, so to have this free spectacle in the afternoon and on their walk home was a boon to sadistic voyeurs. Second, my stalling efforts had created a nice buzz.

The two of us faced off within a circle created by the audience. I decided not to throw the first punch, reasoning that I shouldn't make this kid angry. What I did instead was grab him by the wrists. There would be no way for him to punch my nose bone through my frontal lobe if I secured his hands. What next? No idea. The wrist grab was not a grappling strategy but another procrastination technique. My muddled thinking was this: *As long as he's not hitting me, I'm okay. He can't* hurt *me if he can't* hit *me with his* fists. Boy was I wrong.

I didn't see stars literally, but there was some kind of electrical explosion in my brain, like tiny lightning bolts across the inside of my eyes. Before I even realized what happened I was on the ground, disoriented and horrified.

What happened? Well, forty years later it's still a little hazy, but it seems that, as soon as I seized his wrists, he leaned back and then smashed me right below my left eye, with his *forehead*.

Without a single punch I was on the dirt/grass of the hill. Crying. I wasn't crying from the physical pain; that hadn't kicked in yet. I was crying from shame mixed with the objective unfairness of it all. Why did there have to be so many witnesses? This would have been plenty mortifying without the ringside fight fans. I was also feeling deeply disturbed by the arcane maneuver he had employed.

The next thing I heard was a boy's voice from the crowd say, "Let him up, he's crying."

Is that a rule? Cry, game over? If it isn't a rule, it should be. Like "tie goes to the runner" and "employees must wash hands before returning to work." Either due to the authority in that boy's voice or perhaps the rule's validity, Bobby didn't hit me after *crying* was called.

As bad as this horror montage was, it had not yet reached its nadir. At about the same time that the fight was called for crying, an adult arrived to break things up.

I don't remember what my mother said to all the kids to get

them to disperse, but it was the same tone she used to get neighborhood cats off our backyard furniture and had the same result.

We walked to her car. I didn't know she was picking me up that day or else I would have postponed again. I don't remember any comforting inquiries into my condition. She was angry. I'm not sure what she was angry about, maybe making her wait, muddying my jeans, and putting myself in a position to get into a fight.

She drove her maroon Chevrolet Chevette, Detroit's uninspired answer to the VW Bug, and parked it in a lot right in front of the school, then went in and told the principal. Even though I told her it was over, that nothing could be done and that her tattling to the ineffectual Principal Munster wasn't going to help. In fact, I said while drying my eyes and withering down in the front seat, it might inspire retribution and further disgrace. Having your mother break up a fight then squeal to the principal is tough to recover from. J-sus Chr-st.

I went to school the next day. I didn't want anyone to think I was destroyed. I *was* destroyed, completely, but not going to school would make them think I was aware of how embarrassed I should be. I never looked forward to going to school, even on half days, but to show up the day after a public defeat so one-sided—I hadn't even thrown a punch—I must say that took some fortitude. I didn't feel that on that day, all I felt was bruised and weak. I considered suicide again but then decided that instead of feeling bad the kids would all think I was crazy and maybe make fun of me for being so weak. I didn't need that type of abuse on top of the black eye. I'll spite them by *not* killing myself.

Where had Billy been during all of this? He wasn't even in school on the day of the fight. His family had taken some extra days on their February vacation. Had he been there, I was sure Billy would have given me a pep talk. He would have reminded me how much bigger I was than Bobby and maybe outlined some strategy.

That Saturday I went over to my dad's condo for dinner. In the kitchen he noticed the bruise under my eye. He asked me what happened, and, understanding G-d's stipulation as to honoring thy father, I told him I got in a fight. I didn't want to tell him, but I never lied to my father except about how late I stayed up the nights before his Sunday visits. I braced myself for the story of how he had run home crying to his father after he got beaten up by some kids in the Bronx in 1933. Instead of comforting him, his father asked him, "Who got into the fight, me or you?" Then my grandfather had told my dad to figure it out for himself.

I was also prepared for him to explain that I would have to avenge this or else be tormented by the shame of this defeat until I graduated. That this kid would antagonize me until I won a rematch.

But he didn't bring up any of that. He said, "I'm sorry that happened to you, son." It was a relief. It felt like he knew me. It was my favorite thing he ever said to me.

Billy was surprised by my loss. "You're so much bigger than him! Why would he even pick a fight with you?" Billy couldn't understand why Bobby wanted to fight me.

I understood. Some boys are targets for other boys' aggression. Bullies can smell fear, weakness, devotion to Mommy, an abnormally lengthy possession of a blanky. Over the years I had seen kids who I recognized immediately as future victims. I considered myself lucky that I had up until that week avoided a headbutt to the face. I understood it though I wouldn't have said it; no one would have accepted that type of insight from an eleven-year-old boy.

Billy knew my favorite song, "Who Can It Be Now?" by Men at Work. My favorite baseball player, Rod Carew. Favorite Celtic, Larry Bird. Favorite football player, didn't care. Pro wrestler, Captain Lou Albano. My favorite condiment, mustard. Monster, Yeti. Dressing, Thousand Island. But he didn't know that I was afraid of fighting, being hit by a baseball, and the dark. Why would I tell him? He could tell everyone in school.

That wouldn't be the last fight I got into in fifth grade. Word must have gotten out about my fragility because in March a kid my age started picking on me. Danny Booth was a short pale kid with braces who had moved into a house at the other end of our street a couple of years before. He had a Southern accent, but I can't remember from which of the rebel colonies he hailed. He wore jeans and a jean jacket and work boots, which was the outfit for kids who wanted to be hooligans but couldn't afford leather jackets. He also always wore a cheap plastic replica of the Boston Red Sox batting helmet. This helmet was part of a trend in baseball souvenirs that had thankfully fizzled out by that time, but this backwoods hillbilly still wore it. Once again it was not clear why this kid wanted to kill me, though he provided a hint when he included "Jew-beggar" among his taunts while instigating the fight. I must say, I was not bothered by his explicit anti-Semitism. If it weren't so hateful, I would have laughed because of the insanity of the suffix, "beggar." I was no more a Jew-beggar than I was a Jew-*gardener*.

I resisted his incitement for a couple of days and then got fed up one day as he followed me home with his best friend Luke Arcuri, owner of the stomped Speed Buggy lunch box from the first day of kindergarten.

Luke stayed out of the fight but walked alongside Booth the whole way home, like his manager. As we approached the pathway through the playground, I had an idea on how to delay this fight for one more day. Just before the steep paved ramp going down into the pathway, the sidewalk ran along a small ravine to the left. With everything I had I shoved him down the slope. One moment he's barking out what he's going to do to me, and the next, he's somersaulting backward into a gully! The perfect time of year for it with the rotting dead leaves and underbrush covering the ground. Then I sprinted down the path and to my house two-tenths of a mile away. I was thrilled by the lunacy of it. If I wasn't so scared, I would have been cackling all the way home. I couldn't enjoy it. If I finished second in the race to my house he was going to beat me up that day. Fortunately, I was a speed demon and easily made it home before he caught me.

Less fortunately, the key was not in the mailbox and nobody was home. Booth arrived and was furious and covered in muck. *Here we go again.*

We squared off by the basketball hoop on the street in front of my house. He must have had the same misgivings I had about throwing a punch because he didn't throw any. I have no idea how I built up the nerve, but with my right arm I got him in a headlock. His stupid helmet plocked on the street, making a sound like a dropped Frisbee. *Immediately* he started squawking and moaning, ready to surrender. Over a headlock? *Why did you pick a fight with me if you're vulnerable to such a primitive hold?*

"You gonna leave me alone?"

"Yes!" he groaned.

I was shocked but shaken. I had overcome the fear enough to apply the cinch but not enough to keep my knees from knocking. As cartoonish as it sounds, "knees knocking" is a real phenomenon.

"I let go and you *never bother me again.* Got it?"

"Yeah!"

I let go. He kept his word. I won, I guess, but it didn't feel like victory. It felt like I had pulled off a prank. It made no sense. He was so convinced I was beat-up-able, almost as convinced as I was. Then on an impulse, I reflexively subdued the pisher with a move I'd seen champion Bob Backlund use on Channel 56's *Championship Wrestling,* and he gave up. Fearing vengeance, I didn't gloat. I never told a single soul, until now. What was there to tell? I was relieved that I wouldn't have to deal with his taunting anymore, but I felt no satisfaction. I felt bad for the schmuck. It had to have been humiliating. First you get covered in twigs, moss, and decaying foliage, then get throttled in the middle of the street by a "Jew-beggar." *What is the draw of fighting?* I wondered. Having someone at my mercy was sickening. The shaking took time to subside, the chemicals secreted during the tussle took time to dissipate. I'd need to adjust my behavior, keep myself to myself and Billy. I continued to enjoy Billy's insulting nickname-based humor and absurd jokes, but he could get away with it whereas I had to be careful, and also I felt guilty about ragging on people ever since Mr. Mercier let me have it in that warning notice the spring before. Billy was carefree, light, calm. Nothing worried him, no one intimidated him. I felt scrutinized and on guard all the time.

As I added friends from outside our neighborhood through basketball and another season of Little League, I became concerned that Billy would insult another friend. It was tricky to manage the feelings within groups. I'd never get fully comfortable with it.

Fifth grade ended in late June. I stayed home from school on the last day. It was only a half day, and there were no tests or anything important. The only person I wanted to see was Billy, and I was going to hang around with him all summer anyway, so with my mother's approval, I skipped.

At around 1:00 P.M. the doorbell rang. I was in my room reading *The Westing Game*, a book about an eccentric millionaire who left a fortune for anyone who could solve the mystery presented in his will. My mother answered and was friendly to whoever was at the door and then she yelled, "Gah!"

It was Schaub! She wanted to deliver my exceptional report card in person. I was shocked. I had never even had a real conversation with this woman with whom I spent every day for an entire school year. I said thank you, but I was brusque and can't imagine I looked her in the eye. She gave me a hug. I wished I was the type of kid who could have said something nice, but the truth was I didn't understand why she hadn't just mailed it. Mercier, my idol, disappeared like the proverbial fart in the wind without even a goodbye, but Mrs. Schaub, who I was mostly indifferent to, hand-delivered the report card to my doorstep. But instead of appreciating Phyllis Schaub's warmth and generosity, I wondered what was wrong with me that Mercier never visited.

This was the last year that I was not concerned at all with girls. I was concerned with only three things. How can I get more baseball cards? Am I getting better at basketball?

But most important, *don't get in any fights.* Years before it was released, I came to the movie *WarGames'* sage conclusion, "The only winning move is not to play."

October 2017

There is no cell service at my mom's, and my mom has no internet, so in order to send and receive texts and emails I drive to a location with some coverage. On a good day I can get four bars at Symphony Park. Most mornings, after I walk and feed Sandy and Igor, I drive about a mile from my mom's house and park the car next to the basketball court. I'll drink iced coffee from my twenty-four-ounce cup and tend to texts and emails and return some calls. I can get cell service elsewhere, but those places hold no magic.

There's long been a delusion involved in my depression that makes me fantasize about time travel. I daydream that I can go back in time and consciously enjoy the times when I felt better and avoid all the pitfalls and missteps that I believe have doomed me to the state of mind I am trapped in.

I know that a time/space portal is beyond my means, but I imagine that I will see someone or have a realization or recapture a feeling that may rekindle the light I once felt there. The time and place I imagine returning to is October 22, 1983, here at Symphony Park.

Sixth and Seventh

I had a fun summer. I went back to the basketball camp and roomed again with King Bucknall and also played on a Little League team. I loved baseball, just like my dad and brothers. Mostly I loved throwing a baseball around once a week for as long as my dad's fifty-five-year-old bursitis-compromised arm held out or with Rick for as long my arm held out.

The backyard throws and catches had been the extent of my baseball experience when my mom dropped me off for Little League tryouts on the first Saturday morning of April vacation that year. It was a beautiful day, but thanks to an early-spring blizzard the week prior, the field was covered in around ten inches of snow. The infield had been shoveled or snow-blower-ed to allow us to field grounders.

There were three skill levels within the Peabody Little League organization. Majors was for the best players. Minor A was for the next best players. And then there was Minor B for the rest of the kids, the worst players, the "move *ins!*" the "easy outs," the "lookahs," the "whiffahs." Little League developers didn't bother to adopt the school reading group policy of issuing humane names to the divisions. If the Little League elders named the school reading groups, the lowest reading group would be called "The Shitty Readers."

The decline in dignity from Majors and Minor A to Minor B was steep. If you made Majors or Minor A you received a complete uniform consisting of a shirt with the team name on it, matching pants, matching hat, and finally, and this was obnoxious, color-coordinated *stirrups* to go over your socks.

Minor B kids got a T-shirt that had "Little League" on it. No pants. No matching hat. *No stirrups.* Stirrups had to have been a deliberate slap in the face to the Minor B–ers. You couldn't have sacrificed an electron of glitz and gotten Minor B kids hats that matched their T-shirts? You had to spend another $1.05 on decorative sock garters?

The biggest difference was in the team names. Majors and Minor A used the names of Major League Baseball teams: Cardinals, Angels, Athletics, Mets, Twins, Astros, and so on. The Minor B teams were named the Bears, the Lions, the Cougars, and the Mustangs—two zoo animals, a Mercury, and a Ford. They just couldn't bear to show the lousy players a splinter of compassion. It would have cost them nothing. It's not like Major League Baseball had given their "expressed written consent" to use their names but stipulated, "You may use our names for everyone except those wedgie-picking zeroes in Minor B."

The fortunate thing that year was because it was my last year of Little League they had to put me on a "majors" team. Thanks to that team, I had more friends than ever: *three.* A boon! Most of the kids I met in Little League went to the McCarthy School, which was the school I had gone to for kindergarten. The previous June, McCarthy closed and transferred their students as well as their principal to West Memorial School. This gave me more friends and acquaintances in my school than I ever had before.

The downside of this migration was that their seventh graders were more advanced in terms of boy/girl interaction. Seventh-grade girls and boys from McCarthy were already calling each other on the phone and meeting each other at malls. Quickly our native seventh graders caught up. Girls were calling boys! What if their mother answered?

The kids in my grade made their own leap by playing a game at recess called "boys chase the girls" and its popular offshoot "girls chase the boys." I immediately recognized this primitive adolescent sexual pageant as a portent of personal stress. I watched in fear, alone on the ramshackle basketball court.

I had noticed girls before that year, but I was clinging to the comforting notion that the reckoning was still in the offing, hopefully high school. I knew a few things about the mating convention. The previous year I learned that "goin' out" was the terminology for what the sock hop era called "going steady."

Nobody dated. You were either "goin' out" with someone, which meant an exclusive relationship, or you were single. There must have been some clandestine "hookin' up," which at that time was called "scoopin'," but it was rare. You asked someone to "go out" with you and instantly you were in a monogamous, committed love affair. I never saw much of what the arrangement entailed. It seemed to mostly be writing "XY Loves XX" all over your brown paper-bag book covers.

My approach to dating, like most of life, was to look to my older brothers for guidance, not by consulting them but by rigidly following their path. Although one time, I did consult my brother Max on dating. Max was nine years older than me; I figured he'd have some insight. His response made me realize he was no more adept than I was.

I asked him: "How do you ask a girl out?"

He told me to say, "Would you like to grab a bite some time?"

You're shitting me. Grab a bite? Out of respect for his age, I didn't laugh in his face. His advice may have been effective were I planning to take a girl for a malted at Schwab's lunch counter in 1936, but these gals were dancing to a faster beat. Fortunately, I was smart enough to dismiss this nonsense. My word, if I said what he suggested it would have become my nickname. I'd be Gary "Grab-a-Bite" until I fled the region in disgrace.

My mother was not with it, either. She had always derided neighborhood kids and teens she worked with at the mall for being "girl crazy" or "boy crazy." She would often *boast*, "My boys never dated in high school," like it was an achievement, the result of good parenting. It was no plan or preference. My brothers weren't desired until they got to college. I accepted the same fate. Rick had married a woman he met during his senior year at University of Massachusetts. Max was a senior and had a girlfriend he met during orientation, also at UMass.

It wasn't that I didn't want girls' attention or affection. It looked like a lot of fun. But I knew how I felt around girls: anxious, self-conscious, and certain that they could sense every shaky, sweaty, eye-averting atom of it. I had worked diligently the past couple of years to develop a personality that would be of interest to *boys*. And just when I had some momentum, adolescence ambushed me with this bedeviling new audience.

Now I'd like to briefly address an element of male adolescence that a less self-conscious writer would feel more comfortable sharing. If you sense what's coming and feel as uneasy as I do, or you're my mother, I *beg you* to skip ahead.

Had the late Philip Roth not so thoroughly and masterfully documented the onanistic tendencies of the working-class Jew boy (see *Portnoy's Complaint*), it would be right here that I'd air my affair with a palm that, blessedly, has a gift for discretion. The culture had not yet widely illuminated the activity, so I believed I had invented this sport I was simultaneously delighted and tortured by. I was unaware that my secret passion had a *name*. I would eventually find out it had a thousand names.

It started one day in fifth grade, when I was home alone with the flu. I felt a novel and insistent urge while watching teen pan-elists in provocative burgundy turtlenecks on PBS Channel 2. I attended to the urge, quickly becoming an enthusiast. I don't want to disclose the frequency, but, friends, let me just say this:

If I had attacked the guitar with such vigor, I'd be Muddy Waters.

There was guilt and shame, and I was convinced I was a de-viant, not because of anything I had heard or read but because of my familiarity with the Old Testament. Something that felt this good but involved lust and fantasy had to enrage G-d. I was frequently bracing for a swift punishment from Hashem until my father explained that it was normal "as long as you don't do it a hundred times a day." A hundred? No, not a hundred.

This frenzy of desire intensified my anxiety any time I was around girls. I had no idea how to play to this new crowd. Girls didn't care that I knew where every NBA player went to college. They weren't going to be impressed that every Sunday I helped the manager of the Sears carpet department sell baseball cards at flea markets. Most important, they didn't find funny what I found funny, which that year was *SCTV, Newhart*, and me.

I had seen how the boys they responded to behaved, and I was appalled. A lot of burping, swearing, and body-function jokes. Easy stuff. The more vulgar and vociferous the boy was the more popular they were with girls. Their athleticism, wit, and earning potential were nonfactors.

Being loud, raunchy, and/or overconfident were specifically the traits my father and brothers had railed against. Be humble! Be unassuming! Nobody likes a braggart! Stop showing off! Al-ways be polite and respectful around girls and their moms. The dissonance was infuriating.

I feared that my new friends, who I had only had since the previous summer, were going to either abandon me to spend more time with girls or abandon me for not helping to attract girls. I could sense that more than wit, basketball skills, and loyalty, going forward, acceptance by girls would be the chief qualification for acceptance by the boys in my life. I felt like I needed to win over girls to maintain the friendships I had worked so long to cultivate.

My distress over dating first came up while I was playing basketball on the street in front of our house. Max, the gorgeous Mr. Fixit, had sunk and cemented a pole and installed the hoop a couple of summers before. After a vandal (I'd bet money it was a teenager standing on top of a car, none of those assholes could dunk) broke off the rim and stole it, Max designed and built a steel apparatus he affixed to the backboard that allowed me to remove and rehang the rim every night using a garden rake.

While I was shooting baskets, a seventh grader I knew through some of my Little League friends, Jimmy Velez—who everyone called Otto (another Billy nickname masterpiece)—drove his bike by on his *Salem Evening News* delivery route. We talked as I shot free throws. He was a short, chunky boy but had immense confidence and was very popular with both boys and girls. He had a girlfriend named Diane LeBlanc who was the prettiest girl in the school. She had long blond hair, blue-green eye shadow all over the lids above her green eyes, and elaborately ribboned barrettes in her hair. Also, a collection of Jordache blue jeans so tight that if worn by an '80s sitcom tween would prompt a "Where do you think you're going?" from her ornery daddy.

As we were talking, a black Ford Maverick drove by playing a song called "It's Raining Men." That summer I had thought of a joke about that song that involved another pretty girl in Jimmy's class. Her name was Tracy Breen, and she, too, owned several pairs of snug jeans plus a pair of commendable boobs.

As the Doppler effect distorted "Hallelujah! It's raining men, AMEN!" I said to Jimmy, "I wish it would rain Tracy Breens."

I thought this was funny and, more important, would let him know I was hip to his scene. He laughed and so I dropped the kicker: "I'd go outside with a bucket."

Otto chuckled, then added, "Y'know Froggy got second off'er?"

Froggy was a dope of an eighth grader whose wrecked voice engendered that pitch-perfect sobriquet.

Second base I understood thanks to my roommate at basketball camp the prior two summers, King Bucknall. King was an African American kid from Brockton, Massachusetts. The basketball camp was mostly African American boys and girls from Boston and Cambridge, Massachusetts. King was the first Black person my age I became close friends with. I had several Black neighbors, but there were only six Black students in my entire school that year. It was just a few years into the violent racism accompanying desegregation in the Greater Boston area, but I didn't feel any antipathy at camp. The only thing I picked up on was that Black kids hated Larry Bird and the Boston Celtics.

King shared with me two unforgettable pieces of information that summer. One was that Black people had to apply cream to their skin regularly or else they got "ashy." Being "ashy" in his school seemed to be the equivalent of wearing "floods" in mine.

The second thing that he put me on to was that kids in his school were dating and they measured levels of intimacy through a baseball analogy.

He called this system "the bases." According to King, first base was a kiss. Second base was being in a girl's room. Third base was being on a girl's bed. A home run was "the works."

I understood that "the works" was sex, but my parents had only superficially addressed the birds slash bees with me. My entire understanding of sex came from an *ABC Afterschool Special* I had watched in second first called "My Mom's Having a Baby." It delicately explained some of the terminology—"sperm," "penis," "vagina"—but thankfully the children's program couldn't cover the intersection of these improper nouns. Overall, the lesson from King was tame. Other than home and first, the bases seemed quaint. I was relieved, right up until this newsie on a Huffy started dishing about Froggy.

I said, "Whoa! Froggy got into Tracy's room? What a *stud*."

"No, it was at a party at Alyssa Grey's house."

I was confused. How could he get credit for second if he wasn't in Erin's room? Otto must have sensed my confusion because he then clarified the bases while I stifled my horror.

He told me the bases were:

First: a French kiss.

I had no idea what a French kiss was but couldn't let on. I found out later that it involved the tongue, which made it no clearer. What could you possibly do with your tongue during a kiss? *Ichhhh.*

I sank a fifteen-foot shot taken from atop a rusty manhole cover.

He continued.

Second base: up the shirt.

I gritted my teeth to keep my jaw off the pavement. *Please tell me it's the back of the shirt. There is no way twelve- and thirteen-year-old girls are letting these brutes put their hangnail-ridden fingers on their boobs. Personally, I wouldn't feel comfortable even if it was the back of the shirt. My hand on that much skin? Oy gevalt.*

I shuddered but managed to swish another shot from the crack on the street that I considered the three-point line.

One aspect I had trouble digesting was this: Froggy had croaked about the double he hit with Tracy to so many people that it reached a nobody like me. I wouldn't have told a soul. For the one millionth time in seven years of consciousness I learned: there's no justice.

Otto continued. Third base: down the pants.

With this base Otto made a gesture toward the front of his own gray corduroys.

I dropped the basketball. It rolled over into the sewer grate and stopped.

At least with second, his gesture had been ambiguous as to where on the body the hand went. With third, even if it was the other side of the pants . . . it was still a private area intended *solely* for husbands and obstetricians. Also, now that I knew third was this invasive, I knew second just had to be up *the front* of the shirt.

My mouth was dry. My hands were shaking. I would have been less horrified had he told me Bubble Yum was made from people. I still had to nod along like the information was reasonable, but my word. Maybe all this groping is done over underwear? Still.

Home of course was sex, which I took pride in letting Otto know I knew already. But second and third base ruined my day as well as the game of baseball.

The anguish of the boy/girl thing climaxed in April at a school dance for sixth and seventh graders. I wore canary-yellow chinos, and a lemon-yellow Polo by Ralph Lauren polo shirt, both left behind by Max. I put a dab of his English Leather aftershave on both sides of my scrawny neck. Fortunately, I did not have to shave or apply deodorant yet, as while I was close to six feet tall, my endocrine system seemed to be devoting itself to making my pants and shirts too short rather than making me hairy or smelly. I was deluded enough to think I'd get compliments on my style if not my aroma.

There was only one comment: a girl named Kelly Feeney asked, "Does the word 'clash' mean anything to you?"

It didn't. I gathered from context that two different yellows were not stylish.

I sat in the wooden bleachers with some of my friends and ogled the couples. I made jokes to some of the boys who were left out like me, but it was sour grapes and graveyard whistling. I was painfully envious.

It got worse, the onset of hell heralded by the opening beat to Quiet Riot's pop-metal atrocity "Cum On Feel the Noize." The philistines *rejoiced*. In 1980s suburbia, crude double entendres and lewd misspellings was what passed for edgy.

Conditions continued to deteriorate. When the shrill singer got to the line "Girls *rock* your boys!" a clutch of grade-seven Jezebels drowned out the amps by wailing the following parody: "Girls *wanna f*— the boys!"

Had I a string of pearls to clutch, they'd be powder. I recoiled in indignation at this *smut*. Where were the authorities?

Over the next few minutes, the girls repeated the bawdy stanza *five more times*. I was shaken, and grateful that my mother was not community oriented enough to chaperone this bacchanalia. Or my *father*. Phil Gulman would have overturned the DJ stand and throttled him for provoking such wickedness.

Not soon enough the soiree wound down. The DJ put on a slow song, and the couples danced sternum to sternum, pelvis to pelvis with their lovers.

I watched as they swayed to Journey's megahit "Faithfully." I felt guilty looking at them while they basked in their prime. It felt Peeping Tom–y.

A boy named Jeff Scarpacci caught my eye and then reached down and pretended he was squeezing his girlfriend's rear. The animal. If I had a girlfriend, I would never grab her rear. Certainly not *in front* of people, not even in *mime*. But the catch-22 was, that type of weaselry was what girls liked, provided the boy was disruptive in class and didn't even know what a catch-22 was.

The couples gazed into each other's eyes. If you didn't know better, you'd think the lyrics—about the strain that rock-and-roll arena tours puts on a new marriage—was resonating with them. I blame Steve Perry. His clarion alto could make the alphabet into a tearjerker.

> *I'm forever yours . . .*
> *Faithfully.*
> *S-T-U-V-W . . .*
> *X-Y-Z.*

I knew in my brain these relationships would be lucky to last through the current marking period, *but my heart,* raised on *The Love Boat* and candy heart *Be Mine*s, felt that "forever yours" *deeply.* My eyes leaked. It hurt to swallow. Mercifully, the lights remained low as the DJ deftly transitioned to Styx's synth-pop claptrap "Mr. Roboto."

I went home, sad, ruminating on how these horny Rickey Hendersons were going off to steal more bases while I would be sorting baseball cards and reading the Chronicles of Narnia alone in my room.

Sixth grade ended, seventh grade began, and a familiar malaise returned when the days got short. My collection of friends had ebbed significantly when two-thirds of them went off to junior high. Billy was my only friend left.

I was prepared for a drab year, but then on October 22, 1983, my mom and I went to the bar mitzvah of my friend/neighbor Andy Freedman (535-1402). He lived less than a tenth of a mile away, but thanks to some finagling by Phyllis Freedman, he went to a different and better school. I was dreading the event, convinced I would be spending the day being ignored and/or ridiculed by kids from another district.

This was the first time I had been back to Temple Ner Tamid since my bar mitzvah on June 4. Perhaps my return as a man pleased our Creator because it is clear He smiled on me that day. Almost immediately on entry, a boy named Chris Damone (535-4212) rescued me from being my mom's date for three hours. Chris was at least seven inches shorter than me but had a muscular build and a deep, kind of raspy voice. His puberty was playing out differently than mine. I was built like a strand of angel hair pasta. Chris was more of a rigatoni. He was olive-skinned, with black hair, blow-dried and parted down the middle. He had dark brown eyes and long eyelashes. We had played on a Jewish Community Center basketball team together the previous winter, and he was a classmate of Andy Freedman. He was thrilled to see me. I was surprised because I'd done little to distinguish myself on the court that season. Why would he like me?

Chris and I sat together during the service and at the reception. We talked about basketball and school. He told me that everyone hated him at his school. He had somehow angered the in group. This puzzled me because he was a terrific athlete, friendly, had clear skin, and had told me at the JCC banquet that he had a girlfriend who he "got tit off of." More confusing was that I had never heard any young person outside of TV and movies be candid about their social circumstances. I felt safe telling him I had only one real friend, Billy.

He laughed at the things I said, like when I said this was not a lunch but a lunch*eon*. He asked what the difference was, and I said, "Silverware."

He convinced me to go to the kid's party that night but most providentially to meet him at a basketball court near his house to play basketball in between the luncheon and the evening's pool party for the kids. Normally, following that type and length of social exposure I would need a trough of Kellogg's Frosted Mini-Wheats and a six-hour nap, but Chris's warmth recharged me. I was giddy.

My mother gave me directions, and I rode the 1.2 miles on the red Huffy twelve-speed I'd bought at Toys"Я"Us with my bar mitzvah windfall.

The basketball court sat in a treeless two acres called Symphony Park. There was a baseball field, a steel jungle gym and swing set, and two steel basketball hoops with the customary corroded chain nets.

There was also a drinking fountain that seemed to have been modified to put out factory fires. You couldn't use it alone. One kid would turn the spring-loaded valve while the other muzzled the violent geyser by interlacing their hands over the spout. Then the torrent flooded your gullet through a gap in your hands. This was better than school drinking fountains where you had to perform fellatio on the spout to get a hint of a quench.

There were also four light posts surrounding the court, which Chris said would allow us to play until midnight that coming summer. We were making plans!

We played two-on-two for over three hours, having been joined by some other kids who went to his school. In between games he reconstructed the mechanics of my jump shot. He was very patient and kindhearted while directing the adjustments, which involved adjusting my release point and putting more backspin on the ball. He was genuinely excited for me when it clicked. Thanks to his encouragement and tutelage I played the best basketball of my life that day.

I had never met anyone my age who was so confident and generous with instruction and *praise*. I concluded that Chris was either very lonely or the devil.

I hadn't looked forward to a party since I became afraid of kids in second first, but thanks to my new acquaintance, I was excited to go to this post–bar mitzvah pool party. I showered, even though hygiene was something I suspended every weekend and many weekdays. It wasn't that I thought that any girls would like me or my scent, I was worried that Chris's enthusiasm would dim if I became a social liability. I had an opportunity to audition for a new crowd that was unfamiliar with my act. I put on my crimson, white-lettered Phi Slama Jama T-shirt from my expansive collection of T-shirts associated with basketball and a pair of navy-blue sweatpants with three red stripes down the legs over a "bathing suit" that was a pair of gray gym shorts over my underwear.

At the party, Chris introduced me to some kids, including some of the girls. He had a lot of friends for someone everyone hated. That afternoon, he introduced me to Lori Kremer (535-0720). Lori was a thin, reddish-auburnish-haired girl with skin a color reminiscent of a bottle of Bermuda sand Joanie once brought back from vacation for me. Lori had a smile that if the lights had failed us in the 'gogue that day, Andy Freedman could have read his Torah section by it. She wore a white sweater and jeans. The jeans weren't aggressively tight, so I wasn't frightened.

Chris introduced me as "my friend Gary." Odd to be introduced that way, as his "friend." I didn't really have a protocol for determining whether someone was a friend, but seeing a kid once in nine months wouldn't have met the criteria. He must have been very lonely. Or the devil. Then Chris told her that I was awesome at basketball, and I blushed, denying it in a real *Aw, shucks* manner. It was easy to pretend I wasn't that great at basketball because I wasn't that great at basketball.

Lori asked how I knew Andy, the bar mitzvah boy, and I said I lived near him but went to West Memorial School, *but* I was in the final year of my sentence. She laughed. Lori said her family went to Temple Beth Shalom, which was the reformed offering 1.3 miles from our Temple Ner Tamid.

Chris asked what the difference was between the two temples and I said, "At Beth Shalom, they don't teach any Hebrew, and they only go to school there once a week. At Ner Tamid I'm a C student, at Beth Shalom, I'm the rabbi."

We got on a school bus that took us to an indoor swimming pool. No dancing! I'd rather have girls see my rib cage and outie than watch kids my age dance. Someone was playing KISS 108 FM on a boom box radio and Prince's "1999" came on, which was inevitable in 1983. Most of the boys groaned, and a cassette of the insufferable Led Zeppelin cover band Def Leppard replaced it.

I then took a huge leap of faith. I confided in Lori that I *loved* "1999" and just about everything Prince Rogers Nelson sang, going all the way back to "I Wanna Be Your Lover," four years prior. This was a risk because almost all the kids my age were proud devotees of "hahd rock." Anything that didn't have distorted electric guitars or hostile lyrics was condemned as "disco." Those suspected of being disco fans were called one of countless homophobic slurs. Lori loved Prince, *and* Earth, Wind & Fire, *and* Donna Summer *and Soul Train.* There wasn't a funk, R & B, or dance band I confessed to that she didn't love. I pointed out to Lori that most kids our age hated R & B music, and she said very seriously in just over a whisper, "I call those kids *morons.*"

We laughed. At one point that night I said to Lori, "These all-day affairs wear me out."

Her eyes scrunched, her face turned red, and she laughed hard into her dainty alabaster hand. Heaven. Later she asked me if I had a theme for my bar mitzvah and I said that the theme was "Let's get this done for under eight hundred bucks." More laughs. What a discovery. My taste in music, my impoverished background, my jokes, my *me,* all were appreciated by a young woman.

After that party I would talk to Lori on the phone whenever I went over to Andy's house. I couldn't call a girl from my house. My mom was prone to picking up the phone without warning. She couldn't conceive of anyone else using the phone. Worse, she had a habit of lingering when she picked up. I didn't want any girl to know I had a family, and I didn't want my mom to know I was talking to girls. I had guilt about growing up and leaving her alone.

I never asked Lori "out." She was too easy to talk with to risk losing her as a friend. I knew she liked me, but who could tell if she *liked* me liked me? I'm sure she was the type of person who could gently rebuff a suitor, but was I a suitor who could accept being gently rebuffed? And would she still like me if she knew what a limited social portfolio I came with?

That day would be the genesis for every positive experience of my teens. My development socially, athletically, and every close friend I made sprang from that day.

It was the best day of my life and led to even better days both at that basketball court and as a direct result of it. Thanks to that park I met my all-time closest friend, Jason Hurwitz (535-5424), and a dozen other people I either stay in touch with now or wish I could. Up until that day I had been *resigned* to play basketball in front of my house by myself until I left for college.

I spent every day over forty-five degrees there until I was seventeen. That basketball court was an antidepressant long before antidepressants had entered my vocabulary and brain. What I didn't realize was that the park didn't make me feel better because I made jump shots or stayed on the court winning games, it made me feel better because I was *outside, with people,* and sweating. Once again I had not learned the right lesson.

During the winter in seventh grade, my grandfather Morris Gulman died. We weren't close. He and my grandmother Jeannette had moved to Florida long before I was conscious. That tells you everything. If grandparents truly enjoy you *or* your parents, they don't move to that godless swamp. To your grandparents, seeing you more than once a year is not worth the 5 percent in-state income tax they save. They'll say it's the weather. It's *you*. You aren't compelling enough. The good news: your share of the inheritance will be a shade fatter. For every thousand dollars the grammy who loved you would have left, the snowbird will leave you a thousand and *fifty*.

I only bring Granddad up to share this: following his death, I made a change in my life requiring considerable effort and sacrifice. I gave up one of my favorite hobbies. I was worried about repercussions from beyond if my grandfather were to survey his progenitors and witness me practicing this activity. I abstained for all of seventh grade through April of eighth grade. Until then I had thought going without leavened bread for eight days a year was tough. To resist that urge for that length of time, during that stage of puberty, is like quitting cigarettes the night before your hanging.

Chris, it turns out, was, as I feared, the devil. He had a vicious mean streak. As charismatic as he could be, he was difficult to be around. I believed my access to him was predicated on my wit, but eventually my drollery wasn't doing it for him, and he fired his jester with a blithe "You're not funny! Stop tryin' to be funny!" That ended that "friendship." *I'm not funny? Son, you're not in reality.*

I'd have preferred an ice pick to my jugular. He lost interest in me when his popularity resumed. He must have realized how niche my female audience was. It was only Lori.

October 2017

For years I drank coffee every morning and it made me especially charming and creative. From March 2015 until this morning, it had no effect other than to ward off a painful withdrawal headache. Today the coffee works again for the first time in over two years. I feel awake, optimistic, like *me*, but after a cup of coffee, the ideal Gary. If I feel like this every day, I'll have a life. Riding this caffeine high, I remove the stack of bills from my most recent hospital stay, and call the number, which I know by heart.

I have more than thirty pages of bills and invoices, all at least ninety days overdue. They total over $40,000 and are for just a portion of the electroconvulsive therapy (ECT) treatments and the associated anesthesia I had undergone before moving back to Massachusetts. I have avoided them, leaving many billing envelopes unopened for months. I've considered just paying them all, so I won't have to face the ordeal of contesting the charges with my insurance company. I'll be bankrupt, but it will relieve the anxiety these calls generate. But then being broke again will bring about new stresses, anxieties, and regrets.

I have called several times since I moved back to my mom's, and they have me call elsewhere, and when elsewhere suggests I call the first number I called, I would give up, afraid I was in an absurd loop and would wake up as a cockroach. I catch a break that day when a customer service rep named Carla says my bills should have been covered by insurance. She is the seventh person I have talked to.

She patiently has me read the date of service and claim numbers, eighteen digits long, literally eighteen, on the bills and after each one she says, "Yup, that one is covered," with pep in her voice.

Not since Rhea Perlman on NBC's *Cheers* has a Carla brought me so much joy. I am welling up with gratitude and relief. I stay on the line to commend her to her manager. My brain had built this frustrating paperwork into a terrifying catastrophe. It is a torture my brain has been inflicting on me for a long time.

Eighth and Ninth

I spent every single day of the summer after seventh grade at Symphony Park either playing basketball by myself or with anyone there from 10:00 A.M. until dark, rain or shine. Sometimes I went home for dinner and came back to play under the lights. Before bed each night I jumped a leather rope for an hour in the kitchen, then practiced a series of speed-dribbling drills on the tile floor in my mother's room.

I didn't go to one movie all summer because I didn't want to waste any time. I skipped *classics*: *Ghostbusters, Karate Kid, Indiana Jones and the Temple of Doom, Gremlins, The NeverEnding Story, The Natural, Purple Rain*, and *Revenge of the Nerds* all had to wait until they came to my friends' and neighbors' premium cable channels. I was on a mission.

In September I started at Higgins Junior High School, which housed eighth and ninth graders from all over our city. It was about a thirty-five-minute school bus ride from my house.

When I started there, I had two ambitions:

1) Make the basketball team.
2) Don't get murdered.

It was the first time I was going to a new school since first first. It was also the first time I took a bus to school since kindergarten. This change was far more stressful than the previous ones. My new school had a horrific reputation. Over the years I'd heard stories of drug dealing, weapons, and assaults on students by students. There were also credible reports of assaults on *teachers* by students. Billy called it "Rikers." My friend Lori Kremer from Andy Freedman's bar mitzvah put it best when she said that the first bus ride to Higgins felt like we had been sent to "juvie."

I also had an odd compulsion going on at the time. I was convinced that G-d controlled my fortune moment to moment. I started praying in the morning and at the end of every day and intermittently throughout the day. I'd apologize to G-d for my lustful or cruel thoughts about my classmates. I'd thank G-d for a good grade or for playing well or finding a key in the mailbox when I had forgotten mine. When I woke up I would say, "Thank you for letting me live again today, Lord." It wasn't that I was grateful for being alive. I was frequently miserable, but I was scared to death of dying. Yet when I faced a crisis in ninth grade, I told no one, not even G-d.

Higgins Junior High was the biggest junior high school in New England according to a kid who told me that. It seemed possible. There were more than a thousand eighth and ninth graders. There was also a large group of students enrolled in the adjoining vocational school. These kids, known as "voc-ies" (rhymes with "smokeys"), were aged fourteen to nineteen, mostly boys, and while I'm sure there were young people who wanted to become auto mechanics, carpenters, and plumbers within their ranks, most of them looked to be awaiting sentencing.

The voc-ies were segregated from gen pop, but there was a hallway that led to their wing of the sprawling two-story building. We were told during an orientation tour that under no circumstances should we walk down that hall. The implication was that if we intersected with these brutes the administrators would not be responsible for our death. The orientation had a ten-minutes-into-a-horror-movie feel, where the adult warns the teens about doing the thing that leads to their demise one scene later.

I called the voc-ies the Sweathogs. If you were between five and forty in 1975 you know what a solid reference that was. If you were over forty, you were dead. If you were under five or not born, try to imagine a time when there were only *three* TV channels. Whatever was on the previous evening's prime-time sitcom lineup, even something as uninspired and corny as *Welcome Back, Kotter* would be discussed, analyzed, and reenacted by parents, students, and teachers. Do not go back and watch *Welcome Back, Kotter*. It doesn't hold up. One of the catchphrases was: "Up ya nose with a rubbah hose." Oof. Yet every Thursday night, thirty million people laughed at that tripe. About three times more people than watched *The Sopranos* finale.

I did have the occasional run-in with some of the voc-ies. They would sometimes take a class with us. They were always unprepared and frequently disruptive. They had little use for books other than slamming them out of my hands in the hallway. It was their version of popping Bubble Wrap. I was a hoarder of quizzes, tests, worksheets, and handouts, which I stuffed in the pages of textbooks, so every few days I'd have to gather a *Don Quixote*'s worth of loose-leaf while the entire school left grimy Fila prints on my quizzes.

The Sweathogs were probably not any more likely to harm me than the kids on the college track. It was a case of snobbishness. Most of us were taught that without a college education we'd be destitute, so that's how we saw these kids who knew at fourteen that they wanted to work with their hands rather than prepare for the SATs.

The first day at Higgins I saw a fight in the hallway. The winner *pile-drived* his opponent's head into the tiled corridor floor. This was a maneuver I'd seen only on Saturday morning TV wrestling and it was common knowledge that pro wrestlers used a trick to protect the skull and spine of the pile-driven. No trick here. The assaulted had a racquetball-sized lump reddening on his forehead. But what happened when the school bell rang was more unsettling: the victim, the perpetrator, the audience, *everyone*—they just went to class.

Though they weren't formally introduced during the orientation assembly by lunch, I knew the names of the three guys you needed to avoid to survive. This also meant avoiding anyone affiliated with them. Fortunately, much like Joker and Penguin, the bullies' underlings chose wardrobes similar to their employers. They favored leather jackets and nylon pants with dozens of zippers, none of which had any utility. They wore gold "rope" chains no thicker than a number two pencil. The predominant 'do was short hair spiked up with Dep or Dippity Do gel.

To stay safe you needed to avoid the crews of the bullies but also their relatives, girlfriends, and neighbors. One kid, Leo Kalinowski, got knocked unconscious by a hellion named Nunzio (not his real name) because he said something lascivious to Señorita Pedro, a young Spanish teacher Nunzio was fond of. This makes it sound like Nunzio was a gallant character, but this was an anomaly. Nunzio's victims were usually chosen at random.

Billy put Nunzio's record into perspective when he said, "Remember the kid who pile-drived that kid this morning? *That* kid is afraid of Nunzio."

Nunzio's most infamous offense was shooting a kid at an amusement park. With a gun. If he had just *brought* a gun to an amusement park, it would have been terrifying. He used it. At an *amusement park*. The wounded was a teen from Lynn, a border city of ours nicknamed "the City of Sin," and not just because it rhymed but partly because it rhymed. The old threat "You're dead after school" wasn't hyperbole with Nunzio.

Nunzio had a soft spot for bloodshed, but he practiced your traditional burger, fries, and a Coke hooliganism as well. He once took my friend Mitchell Page's clarinet case, unlatched it, then scattered the contents down a stairwell. All poor Mitchell could do in response was mutter a sarcastic "Thanks, Nunz," gather his parts, then take detention for being late for biology.

Nunzio was not his real name. I would never take a chance that he would read this and want to revisit our brief relationship. In fact, the incident with the gun was not his real crime. It's a felonious equivalent I've substituted to make it harder for him to figure out he's Nunzio.

He was five foot seven, skinny, with close-cropped gelled hair. He was a stylish dresser. A day-to-day look that favored red suede Pumas with fat white laces, the tongue arranged to stick out over the cuffs of relaxed fit Guess jeans. He rotated an extensive collection of I.O.U. sweatshirts. I.O.U. was a brand sold throughout the '80s to gangsters and their fans. The sweatshirts were covered in graphics announcing *I.O.U.* and buzzwords such as "ORIGINAL" or "FASHION"; they were often multicolored and used colors for boys that only boys not afraid to be kneed in the balls for wearing (purple, orange, yellow) could risk wearing. They were expensive, more than thirty dollars. The ensemble was finished off with a dousing of Drakkar Noir (pronounced Drakah Noyah in these parts), a compelling cologne sprayed from an oblong black bottle.

Nunzio was a year ahead of me when I got to Higgins, but bad grades and absences due to suspensions and arraignments had slowed his progress. That was one of the dangerous things about junior high. High school incorrigibles eventually turned eighteen and either dropped out or were locked up. Junior high kids were still too young to be culled from the pack.

I wasn't as dapper as Nunzio (not his real name, seriously). I wore sweatpants and a T-shirt every day. The T-shirt always had a basketball camp or a Georgetown Hoyas logo on it. I wanted there to be no delay in getting to a court every day after school. I also wanted every teacher and student to know what I was about. In the absence of any other distinguishing traits, I chose to be known as a basketball player. I wasn't cute or tough or super smart. While I still made some friends laugh in the cafeteria, I was so overwhelmed by the danger I felt that I was careful not to draw any attention. There was another dimension to my lack-of-fashion choice: I believed I needed to earn my right to wear nice clothes. I was already big enough to wear the orphaned elements of Max's tasteful preppy wardrobe, but I didn't feel I deserved to dress nicely until I achieved something. It was only much later, long after I made the team, that I started wearing pants without elastic waistbands and shirts with collars.

My gym teacher that year was also the coach of the basketball team, which made every gym class a kind of tryout. No matter what sport we were playing I made every effort to stand out so that the coach would think I was a good athlete.

In late October he dumped out a bag of ragged orange basketballs and we played a game of five-on-five. Official basketball tryouts weren't until the Monday after Thanksgiving, but I was prepared to show the coach what I was capable of. That late-October morning in gym class my obsessive preparation, along with being six foot three, gave me a silly advantage over every boy in that gym class.

My play must have looked like magic. I swished twenty-foot jumpers and baffled the stoners with ostentatious ballhandling, behind-the-back passes, and reverse layups. The kids and the gym teacher gave me feedback that exceeded praise: they were *laughing*.

This teacher who had been polite but not friendly up to that day told me that my mother should invest in a larger mailbox to accommodate the letters I'd be getting from college basketball coaches. I had basically made the team six weeks before the try-outs. The coach told me I was a lock. I told no one so as not to jinx it or provoke a g-d who violently punished hubris.

Over the next several days after that gym class, every male teacher told me that they heard I was the next Larry Bird. I assured them I wasn't. It's no feat to look good when playing against kids who have played basketball only on Atari.

On the second Friday after Thanksgiving, I officially made the freshman team. Making the team was more relief than anything resembling happiness. It didn't make me feel good about myself. I just knew I would have been crushed by not making the team. Once practices and games started, I beat myself up for not dominating and for being shoved around by some of the more physically mature and aggressive players. This was the beginning of a pattern with me. I'd put all my energy toward an objective. During the development phase I was determined, eager, joyous. As expectations rose, I became self-conscious and E-string *tight*. Under scrutiny my confidence vanished and with it my power to perform the most fundamental aspects of the sport.

In a game in which we completed an undefeated season, I got in with a few minutes left. I had a breakaway, no one near me. When I got to the free throw line I took one stride forward, one dribble, planted my left foot, raised my right knee toward my chest, shot with my right hand toward the upper right corner of the square . . . *thud, clank, thud* . . . rebound Somerville. A shot I started every workout by making over and over for thirty-six makes. I'd made that shot thousands of times the previous summer. That afternoon, with no one *near me*, I bungled it. I had enough time to explain algebra's order of operations to a voc-ie, and I still missed. I was a choker. Take me to the park, and I'll dazzle you all day long. Put me on a court with a timer, an opponent, and a ref and I'll let you down. I went home and cried.

For the first time in my basketball life I was not lauded for being dedicated and talented but criticized, castigated, and condemned for being passive, timid, "soft." I knew that! Why do you think I dedicated my life to this noncontact sport?

I played on five different basketball teams that fall and winter: a Peabody Jewish Community Center League team, a USY (United Synagogue Youth) team, the St. Adelaide's Church team, and Higgins Junior High's eighth-grade team and its freshman team. The quality of my teammates was in indirect proportion to the number of days of Rosh Hashanah its players observed. Although, my Catholic Youth Organization (CYO) team started two other Hebrews, earning the team the nickname Saint Beth Shalom's.

Because of the need for rides to and from the various practices and games we played I got to know a lot of parents, especially my mother. My mother had moved from the mall Hallmark store to the employee cafeteria in Sears. She worked the cash register, poured hot and cold drinks, and toasted then smeared various spreads on various breads. She was beloved. Everyone from the store's top-selling appliance man, Warren Worth, to the HR manager, Pam Sharkey, greeted her with an enthusiastic *Barb!* Her boss was a blind friend of hers named Mike McDonald, who short-order cooked and was as funny a man as I ever met. He paid her five dollars an hour "under the table." She stole at least that in juice, Lorna Doones, Peggy Lawton brownies, Hostess Fruit Pies, Donettes, napkins, plasticware, Oreos, Thomas' English muffins, Snickers, Twix, Milky Ways, Nestle's Crunch bars, ROLOs, Ring Dings, and Drake's Swiss Rolls. Our kitchen was stocked like a 7-Eleven. Yes, she stole from a blind man.

She would pick up Mitchell Page (the victim of Nunzio's clarinet attack) and me after freshman team practices and games every weekday around six, after she finished at Sears. She would always bring Mitch and me a cold glass bottle of Veryfine cranberry apple juice, courtesy of (Mike) McDonald's. Veryfine was a regional juice company that was the first juice purveyor in my community to offer such exotic beverages. It was buried in the '90s by Snapple's manic blitz through the juice rack.

I was used to having drinks in the car, but to Mitch—one of eight kids whose mother couldn't pick us up because his dad used the family's only car for work—this drink was ambrosial. He was so grateful, always telling me how nice and funny my mother was. It reinforced my inkling that my mother was unusual. No other carpool drivers provided refreshments. She always called him Mitchy, which I found sweet. It felt like she was in my life like she was back when Billy or Wally would be around our house. With basketball taking up all my after-school time, those days were over.

Poor Mitch. He was dental-tape thin at a time when being skinny as a boy was buh-rutal. We had a similar build: PEZ dispenser–y. That school year, 1984–1985, we saw a lot of heartbreaking images of Ethiopians suffering from famine. Pop stars banded together to record "We Are the World," sending millions of dollars in aid to the victims of drought and civil war. Teenaged boys in my city did their own part to raise awareness about the tragedy by derisively calling every ectomorph "Ethiopian."

Ever since my fourth-grade warning notice for being mean, I had significantly reduced my ragging and ranking, as well as my busting of people's chops and/or balls. I didn't like how the boys made fun of Mitch. Of course, I never said anything. I was just grateful they weren't attacking me. It could very easily have been me they were calling "Oxfam America." I was just five or ten pounds heavier, marginally better at basketball, and only less nerdy in that I didn't play a woodwind. Mitch's presence distracted them, like a rodeo clown's.

Ninth grade felt like just a change in teachers and classrooms. Same anxious feel as eighth. While I didn't look directly into its eyes, there was a specter of a future where I wasn't good enough at basketball to play in college, so I made up my mind at the beginning of ninth to expand my opportunities by being a good student. Thus a goal of making the honor roll was added to "don't get murdered." Both goals took commitment and creativity to realize.

English was the only class that was challenging. The teacher, Mr. Ray Crean, was demanding. Every Friday we were tested on ten vocabulary words we received the day before. The test involved using all ten words, properly, in a coherent essay or story. I overcame the onerousness of the assignment with the aid of *Webster's Pocket Dictionary*, which gave concise definitions and synonyms for every word we saw. It started my lifelong devotion to finding a better word.

My favorite class was German I. I chose it because during eighth grade we had a quarter-long sampling of German, French, Spanish, and Latin, and Herr Victor Passacantilli was so charming and talented that I decided to study a language as cacophonic, impractical, and imbued with anti-Semitism as German. There was a fortuitous bonus to choosing German, which was that Lori Kremer also chose to sprechen Deutsch.

Lori's versatility and amiability transferred seamlessly to junior high school, where I don't think there was even a monthlong period that she didn't have a boyfriend. She was like the Finn Burns of girls my age. Everyone loved Lori. Thanks to German class, I got to see Lori every day, so we could talk comedy and *Soul Train*.

One other stroke of luck for ninth grade was that we were given free time, during which we could go to a study hall or the library and do homework. I devised a scheme that allowed me to play basketball during school hours. This privilege would ultimately cause tremendous stress.

Next to the main gym there was a separate smaller basketball court in a space called the auxiliary gym. It was rarely occupied. I asked the coach to let me spend my study period playing basketball. He agreed with two conditions. I was not to tell the other players, and I would never let anyone else in the gym while I was playing.

I started playing in there twice a week. It had no windows, but it was cozy: the scent of floor wax and sweat, the iambic beat of leather on maple, and the *fwit* of my jump shot spinning through the off-white dreamcatcher.

It was heaven. And the stipulations seemed easy to abide. Don't tell my teammates, and *"Anybody* comes in, you tell me."

No sweat. Who would ever want to use that gym?

Nunzio (not his real name, and I can't stress that enough). He walked into the gym on a Friday in February accompanied by Leslie L. and Kimberly S. I knew the two girls well because I'd lusted after them for two years. They were also ninth graders. They did their hair, painted their faces, and dressed identically. They both had long bleach-streaked brown hair that was gelled, moussed, teased, lacquered, and Aqua Net–ed into a font reminiscent of bound carrot greens. Makeup-wise, they applied their senior prom face every morning. They may have worn perfume, but it was overpowered by the 'Net, which came with a smell but also a physical component. A whiff of Aqua Net, particularly when it was misting from the can, felt like a koala cub had grabbed onto your larynx for safety.

Every day these ladies slid and shuffled down the hallway floor tiles in fluorescent-pink pumps, the snap of cinnamon Dentyne adding a percussive track to their movement. For pants they wore black stretch pants with stirrups. On top Leslie had a fluorescent-pink sweater over a ribbed tank top, also fluorescent but yellow, and Kim had a red sweater over a white ribbed tank top. Both exposed their black bra straps. At fourteen even partially exposed bra straps were as stimulating to me as the Playboy Channel. More stimulating, as for me, the Playboy Channel meant flipping to channel sixty-one and watching scrambled video of soft-core sex.

I am not sure what they wanted when they entered my gym. I figured they were there to drink Schlitz malt liquor, smoke cigarettes, and take a bunch of drugs. I didn't have enough imagination to conceive of sex involving an odd number of participants.

This was exactly what the coach swore me to alert him to. It was also a test of my loyalty to basketball. I had heard stories of great basketball players having the keys to the gym when they were growing up. Keys to the gym and a lanky frame seemed to be the main ingredients to NBA stardom. Would Larry Bird or Kareem tell?

Immediately after they entered the gym, I snuck out silently. Then I told. I said to the coach, "There's someone in the gym."

Then I race-walked to the library and signed in. I hoped I was so insignificant that Nunzio wouldn't be able to identify me. We'd never had a class together. We had just two classmates in common, Mitchell Page and his clarinet.

It was fifth period when I left the gym. I wasn't relaxed but I couldn't imagine I had anything to fear, at least not in the short term. I went to sixth-period computer class with Mr. Yohansky (whom Billy had rechristened "Mr. No-hand-sky" the year before, after Mr. Y lost an index finger while teaching woodshop). Then I went to seventh-period English class. As I was entering the doorway, a basketball teammate named Diego "Bombo" Rivera said the three words every student, teacher, and staff member organized their lives to avoid hearing.

"Nunzio's aftah you."

Dear G-d.

This was serious. This wasn't childish tattletaling. I was a snitch, a rat, a fink, a canary, a stoolie, a squealer, a narc. I had denied the most violent kid in our city a cigarette or drugs break. Or worse, I had cockblocked a three-way. I was on the run.

I went to school the next day enlisting a plan that used everything I learned when I wanted to be a bodyguard after John Lennon's murder when I was in fourth grade. I would never take the same route twice. I would avoid being in the hallways with large crowds. I would always be aware of my surroundings. This meant lingering after each class, relying on the quality of the post-class questions I asked. When I did have to use crowded hallways, I would sidle up to any teacher or administrator and use them as a human shield. I also stopped drinking milk and water to avoid ambush at a urinal.

I skipped school when I could and in early March I volunteered for a program where I helped elementary school kids go through one of those ropes courses with a zip line like the one where Kapler learned so much about himself. That got me out of school five straight days. Life on the run was exhausting, though it did add this solid extracurricular to my transcript. But I knew, based on my fifth-grade bullying experience, the stress involved in flight over fight would undo me.

The irony is that by telling on Nunzio (not his real name), I was forced to abandon the basketball gym during study hours for the rest of ninth grade. I couldn't chance it. Our schedules had lined up once. I happened to have study hall at the same time Nunzio had scheduled a bacchanalia, an orgy, a ménage à trois. He could want access again. I had to be elsewhere.

I went to school for two more weeks without incident but felt like a gazelle at the watering hole—shaky, anxious, apprehensive, overwrought. On Thursday, March 13, I got a reprieve. That morning I sat in biology class with excruciating intestinal pain. I'm sure my immune system had been compromised by stress, sleep deprivation, and dehydration. This wasn't like the stomach pains I had from anxiety in second first or when I incited a bully in fifth.

A word on farting in school: farting was as ostracizing as picking your nose, greasy hair, frizzy hair, unibrows, bad breath, body odor, short pants, tight pants, baggy pants, pants worn too low, pants worn too high, pleated pants, plaid pants, polyester pants, bell-bottom pants, thrift store pants, eyeglasses, crossed eyes, braces, yellow teeth, gapped teeth, crooked teeth, small teeth, big teeth, big noses, acne, acne scars, or an erection in the shower after practice. I don't know *why* nobody ever farted in class, far worse sins were carried out, I just knew not to. But now the pain was so severe I couldn't hold it in. Maybe no one would notice.

"Oh my G-d. What's that smell?" a girl screamed.

When I came to, the teacher was kneeling beside me and talking in a gentle tone. Elisha Hopkins's purse was under my head. I had farted, then fainted. *Thank G-d.*

My mom picked me up, and within an hour I was watching the first round of the 1986 NCAA basketball tournament on ESPN while eating canned raviolis à la Chef Boyardee. I had the flu and had fainted from fever, distracting everyone from the stink bomb I'd detonated but, even more fortuitously, giving me a break from Nunzio for one day at least.

I felt better by Thursday night but got out of going on Friday, invoking: "You don't recover from a faint in twenty-four hours, Ma!"

I went back on Monday.

For a couple of weeks I remained slippery, cunning, vulpine even. My concern had been reduced to the level of the bar mitzvah thank-you notes I had put off the summer after sixth. But then I would find myself enjoying something and think, *Oh shit. I almost forgot, adolescent Sonny Corleone is after me,* and I would grind my teeth.

And then one afternoon in April, there he was, wearing a flamboyant I.O.U. top. This one was heavily accented with lemon-yellow hues. Despite his foppish, natty, dandified ensemble, I was shaking. There may have been some people nearby, but the tunnel vision accompanying my hysteria blurred them. Or maybe it was just me and Nunzio. I thought of running, but I was too tired. The sun was shining through one of the few unbroken windows in the building. He smelled good.

I said nothing. He said nothing. My eyes fluttered in preparation for a punch in the face, and I clenched my abdominals just in case he liked to work the body first. Somehow, I didn't cry. I thought for a moment that maybe he forgot all about the betrayal or didn't recognize me.

Then he furrowed his eyebrows, smirked, looked past me, and from the left side of his thin-lipped mouth said two words, "Whydja *tell*?"

He didn't seem angry. I would describe his attitude as "repulsed," "repelled," "revolted." I felt *relieved*. I felt ashamed and weak, too, but I had felt that since I was seven. The impact of the incremental disgrace was negligible. After the six weeks in my self-imposed witness protection program, I had no residual dignity to lose. I suppressed a desire to drop to my knees and wrap my arms round his ankles in thanksgiving.

Then I answered his question truthfully. Averting my eyes from his, I said, "I didn't wanna get in trouble."

He seemed befuddled mixed with amused, the way I imagine a shark would react to a dolphin's explanation for why it occasionally surfaces for breath. I wanted to thank him but felt that would make me seem weaker, so rather than forfeit my last atom of dignity I turned and walked to Civics. He stayed behind to consult with his henchmen Mario Palmacci (not his real name), Sal Passanissi (not his real name), and Adam Peckerman (his real name). They must have had some business to discuss.

The return of the aroma of lawn mowing in the air and the extra daylight joined with Nunzio's clemency to revive my mood. Maybe a year or two before I would have beaten myself up for running from a fight. I had accepted some of my limitations, yes, out of self-preservation, but it was progress.

I found some qualities that I liked about myself. I wasn't popular, but nice people like Billy, Mitch, Lori, my five coaches, und mein Herr Passacantilli liked me. My mother enjoyed the extra time we spent together. I had made the honor roll four quarters in a row and wrote some strong stuff in a daunting English class. Other than a couple of skirmishes in my war against self-gratification, I had mostly honored Adonai.

My mother had wanted to take me to a real restaurant for making the basketball team in eighth grade, but I didn't have time until the spring ended my weekday basketball commitments. By that time the initial eighth-grade glee had been overtaken by the realization that *making* the team wasn't enough to make me feel worthy of a restaurant meal. But after getting straight A's in the fourth quarter of ninth grade I felt I'd earned a sit-down meal. I put on Max's deserted aquamarine rugby shirt and his best tan corduroys, and we went to a Saugus, Massachusetts, Mexican food restaurant I had been craving for years called El Torito's (the Little Bull). I got a beef burrito and dipped a thousand tortilla chips in chunky salsa. My mom got a hamburger; she didn't eat spicy. It was a celebration reminiscent of the time my parents took me for my eleventh birthday to the baseball card show and then to Paco's Tacos in the mall food court. I'd been Barbara Gulman's sidekick for fifteen years. This was the last dinner that was just me and her.

I finished ninth grade with my face and dreams intact. It didn't feel like a promotion from junior high to high school as much as being released for good behavior.

November 2017

Around Thanksgiving I am feeling well enough to work as a comedian again. After I told Joanie and Will and Finn, my close friends knew why I had moved back to Peabody, but I hadn't felt comfortable talking about my illness onstage until that fall. Working meant traveling away from my mom's house but then after flying back, I'd be back in the bedroom. One night, after returning from some shows in the Midwest, I am looking at the 1986–1987 varsity basketball team photo from sophomore year of high school. I was standing in the back row, the tallest player at six feet five inches. The picture was taken right after a game I played in.

Right after the game ended, a photographer herded us in front of a white-painted cinder block wall. As everyone was being arranged for the picture the boy standing to my left ridiculed me for having just missed a wide-open dunk. He called me a "big dork," which burned. My default response was to laugh it off, but I didn't find it funny. I was *seething.* Nobody would know. In that team picture I stand out because of my height but also because every other player is mean-mugging the camera while I am grinning, broadly. Tenth grade was mostly a nightmare that I grinned my way through, but when that misleading photo was taken, I had already met my very first girlfriend. I just hadn't talked to her yet.

Tenth

Tenth grade was the last year I spent most of my free time with my parents. Every Saturday night my dad came over and we'd split a large pepperoni pizza and watch a movie on the VCR we got that year. This doubled the amount of time my dad and I saw each other, and I was grateful for the visit. It was the closest we'd ever been. My father would tell me every couple of weeks that if I would rather "hang out with the guys" he would understand. But the guys weren't doing anything I'd rather do. My oldest brother Rick and his wife were expecting their first child, so I rarely saw him. Max was engaged and planning a wedding, so he was a similar case. I was still very close to my mom but was at that age where I was embarrassed by it and resented her input regarding everything she still tried to maintain influence over, which was mostly my clothes and my hairstyle. I preferred my hair short—a crew cut—which reduced the frequency of my visits to Aldo, an affordable but sadistic barber who would scorch my scalp with the blow-dryer while bludgeoning me with his hairbrush.

My mother didn't like my hair short: "You look like a buzzid (buzzard)."

On the night before tenth grade I was excited. I was hopeful that this would be the year I got a girlfriend. I wanted a girlfriend but told no one and said it only to myself, silently, in my head. I'd grown another two inches since the end of ninth grade to six foot five. No corresponding weight gain, however, which made a girlfriend a long shot. I weighed 170 pounds.

I dipped a scruffy toothbrush into a Dixie cup of warm water, then rubbed the bristles over a dwindling bar of Ivory. I removed hundreds of hours of blacktop abuse from my basketball sneakers this way. White Nikes, royal blue swoosh, size 14. You'd never know how old these shoes were if it weren't for their threadbare laces. They weren't *Jordans*. *Jordans*, known back then *only* as *Air Jordans*, had existed for almost a year but at sixty-five dollars were way beyond our budget. They'd also violate the principles of my sneaker philosophy, which was: you should earn the sneakers you wear. I was outraged whenever I saw a boy who *dabbled* in basketball wearing Air Jordans. In a just world, you would have to try out for your sneakers. Want a pair of Air Jordans? Take off from the free throw line and dunk a basketball. You don't get to wear the same shoes as Michael Jordan just because your father is a dentist.

The sneakers scrubbed clean, I turned to the next day's outfit. I was growing fast, so it was important to check the fit of clothes bought even a few weeks ago. I used the bathroom by the family room. It was also the laundry room and home to the most reliable toilet in the house. I yanked out the price tags from a Ralph Lauren polo shirt and a pair of jeans.

The shirt was from the Ralph Lauren factory store in Lawrence, Massachusetts. Crimson-red and royal-blue horizontal stripes, canary yellow logo. The most alluring feature of the shirt was that it was vertically ribbed but ribbed subtly, ribbed responsibly. There was a sensible gap between each rib. Just a gorgeous g-ddamned shirt. It was marked down from seventy-five dollars to fifteen because it was an "irregular." The label on the neck was sliced to indicate its discount status.

The jeans were Levi's 501 blues. My mother called them *dungarees*, which infuriated me. I hated that word. It was dated plus three times as many syllables as "jeans." And it starts with *dung*.

The pants had a button fly, a charming regression. Over the years I'd grown indifferent to the zipper, remembering it only when I forgot it. This retro detail made me look forward to putting on pants for the first time since a fifth-grade dalliance with overalls.

There were two mirrors in the narrow bathroom. One square and frameless above the sink, one ornately framed on the wall behind me. The angle they hung at forced on me an endless arch filled with clones of me. The outfit fit. Looked good. Maybe my romantic pessimism was premature. Then, I turned my body to examine how far the shirt fell down my rear and was *horrified*. A feeling I hadn't had since I first heard my voice on a tape recorder at Wally's house. But *so much* worse. It was the first time I'd seen my profile. That's *me*? There was a plantain in the middle of my face, and it was repeated to infinity. Dear G-d.

Let me get a second opinion. I created a makeshift mold of my nose by laying my index finger over its slope. I removed the finger and examined its curve. My fear was confirmed. It was hooked. Like a capital *D*. I could have handled the slight bend of a parenthesis. But it's a GD *D*. I had inherited the "Wasserman hook," a nose shape bequeathed to everyone on my mother's side and both my brothers. I had been a fool to think I would elude the curse.

The next morning, adrenaline and anxiety had me out of bed on time. The previous night's encounter with the echo mirror had chastened me, reinforcing my commitment to secrecy regarding my romantic desires.

I poured cinnamon Life cereal into a ceramic mixing bowl, then added whole milk from a red-capped gallon jug until the crisscrossed wheat squares floated. I returned to my room to dress and give my Life time to tenderize. In fifteen minutes, I was dressed, cereal bowl sinked, teeth Colgated. I headed outside to walk the quarter mile to the bus stop.

My mother followed me outside with a cheap camera. The first-day-of-school picture was not a tradition for us. Picture taking was rare in my family. There were no photos from any basketball games, Cub Scouts, Little League, bar mitzvah, or any birthday after age ten. Coverage of my birthdays one through ten was sporadic. It wasn't *as* easy to "develop" pictures back then, but it was easy. You just had to drop them off at one of a dozen retailers who offered affordable film processing. Some were run out of parking lots in toll booth–sized huts called Fotomat.

We were on the lawn, documenting the peak of my ugliness. She was annoyingly insistent. I gave token resistance: "I'll do it after school. The light'll be better," I said.

She replied with two of her greatest hits.

"I don't ask for much. Is this so much to ask?"

Then she said, "You're a one-way street."

I folded and stood for the pictures.

I wanted to evaporate. It was painful inside my head. There was the previous night's discovery inside the never-ending vanity along with a more familiar sound. Since the onset of adolescence, I'd had a steady soundtrack playing in these circumstances. It was the voice of a nation of teenagers united in ruthless appraisal of my every movement.

"He thinks he looks *good*! He *likes* those clothes! Thinks he's *sexy*—look at this dork, virgin, toucan, posing for his mommy!"

I felt off, aware of my body. No idea where to put my arms or hands, a clear sign that a young man does not believe in himself. I put my hands in my pockets. It felt phony, the horde blitzed: "Look at 'im trying to look *cool*!"

Hands on my hips.

"What a tool! What are you, Superman now?"

There it was again, the "What are you _____?" formula. It was still the go-to put-down in my house, neighborhood, and school.

You put on a necklace: "What are you, *Liberace*?"

Do something generous: "What are you, *Gandhi*?"

Identify an unusual woodland creature in the forest: "What are you, Marlin *Perkins*? . . . Joan *Embery*? . . . *Dr. Dolittle*?"

It always got a laugh because of the strength of the formula, but it wasn't clever.

Can we just get this done? What if kids walk by and see this? What if they mock me in front of my house? In front of my mother.

"Can I go now? Please."

My mother went into her dismount, the classic: "You're so *odd*."

The shoot complete, both of us fully aggrieved, I grabbed my Converse duffel bag and arrived at the bus stop early.

I got to school and received my homeroom assignment, and Lori Kremer was in it! I would get to see her first thing every morning, some motivation to make it to the bus on time. The homeroom teacher handed out our locker combinations.

"Don't give it out to *anyone*," the homeroom teacher warned us.

I wish. How I envied the couples who shared lockers. Sharing a locker was moving in together. Reuniting between classes, meeting for a quick smooch or, in wilder cases, a closed-eyes make-out. Your lover could keep books and supplies in there that were for classes closer to your locker than to hers. I could say things like:

"I think I left my scientific calculator in my girlfriend's locker. Can I have a pass to get the scientific calculator . . . the one in my girlfriend's locker? It's right down the hallway, my girlfriend's locker is."

I headed to first period at 7:35 A.M. The teacher, Ms. Carmody, said *r*'s as *w*'s and *w*'s as *r*'s in the most unfortunate class to have that particular impediment: geometry. Kids were barely stifling laughter as she informed us of the ruler, protractor, and calculator requirements. Kids suck. The issue is that the higher functioning, kinder students had qualified for trigonometry in tenth, so Carmody and I were stuck with these morons.

Second period was Mrs. Elizabeth Congdon for world history. She was probably nearing the end of her tenure, as she was the oldest teacher in the school by a decade. She had very long brown-and-white hair that she wore in a ponytail. She passed out a few pages stapled together, and I encountered the word "syllabus" for the first time, which made me feel like a college student.

Third period was English with Mrs. Eunice Yost. She was a small blond woman who had a sweet way that I liked instantly. She was closing in on sixty, or just past it, round face and cheeks. She'd have made a great three down in a set of Russian nesting dolls. I would describe her vibe as Miss Marple–esque. I would not be surprised to learn that she solved murders in her off-hours.

Fourth period was German II with Frau Patricia Power.

Frau Power had short frosted hair and wore large sturdy glasses. She generally sported well-worn white canvas sneakers, and gray slacks. She was rigid, cold, or maybe she was just fully committed to immersing us in Teutonic culture. Nevertheless, I'd always look forward to that class because Lori Kremer was in it. I was still crazy about Lori, like most of the boys in our grade, but *never* let on. Lori was a treasure of the class of '89. She was as funny as ever, with her boisterous laugh, and was the only other person in my life who knew all the words to Run-DMC's *You Be Illin'*. While Lori and I were friends, I never saw her outside of homeroom and German. But I didn't see most of my friends outside of school. Nobody had a license, so unless parents drove my friends and me to a movie or the mall, we rarely hung out outside of school.

Seated behind Lori was a girl named Kristel Holland (535-3459). She had sandy hair down past her shoulders, large bright aquamarine eyes, a lightly freckled fair complexion, and a charming dimple in her chin like Marion Ravenwood in *Raiders of the Lost Ark*. She went to the same school as Lori since kindergarten and went to our junior high, but I had never seen her before. She was exquisite. In about 190 days we'd become inseparable. That day we said nothing.

Lunch started after fourth period, at about 10:40. To accommodate the sixteen hundred plus students, there were three separate lunches. You went to lunch depending on where your fifth-period classroom was located. Seconds after exiting the lunch lines with a peanut butter and grape jelly on Wonder, I extrapolated the social order of Peabody High School. It was clear from the seating of the cafeteria.

At each sitting the seniors occupied the tables farthest from the lunch line with one table belonging to class royalty, the stars of the football team. They were mostly seniors and were accompanied by their girlfriends, who were mostly gorgeous. These teen clichés go by different names at different high schools. At Marilyn Manson High they were known as "The Beautiful People." At S. E. Hinton's Pony Boy High they were the "Socs" (pronounced Sōsh). At Peabody High School they were called "the cliquers," pronounced *clique-ahs* because of the Boston accent. There were some exceptions made for a star hockey player or a teen gangster, but unless you were a member of the illustrious football program or approved by its members, you didn't sit at that table.

I knew most of the boys' names in the clique through youth sports or elementary and junior high school. If you didn't know their names, it was easy to learn them because their talentless courtiers eagerly hollered their teammates' names every few minutes. They did this to get their attention but primarily to siphon prestige from the familiarity: Pat! Jeff! Lee! There was an implicit "I'm friends with _____" beginning these pathetic howls.

Once I had the name, I figured out who was dating whom by matching the name with the script sewn on the left shoulder of the jackets the girls flaunted. As staggeringly corny as it sounds, girls wore their boyfriends' letterman jackets. Navy-blue wool coats with a white vinyl accent wrap below the shoulders. Over the heart, a powder-blue chenille capital *P*. Quickly I realized that I went to school in an Archie comic.

No matter the weather, the cliquettes wore their boyfriends' coats out of pride but also probably a desire to discourage unwanted suitors. "You can talk to me, but I must warn you, the owner of this coat will slam you into a locker. It will be loud, and it will be uncomfortable."

The football players without girlfriends wore the coat all year long, hoping to entice a girl into adopting it. It was especially sad in June as they schvitzed their way toward vacation.

Seating from the clique-ah table outward was based on status in that everyone not sitting there had none. Geeks, dorks, dweebs, Eugenes, Waldos, and other nerds did eat lunch, of course, but they didn't have a section. They just sat wherever the clique-ahs didn't.

The only other demarcated section in the cafeteria was for the *druggies* and *burnouts*. They sat in a classroom-sized area to the left as you approached the food service lanes at round tables fanning out from a jukebox. They wore denim or leather jackets. They looked sullen, even while joyfully air drumming along to '80s glam rock hits that averaged out to Whitesnake's "Here I Go Again." I never saw any of these kids eat. Maybe they were hungry but didn't have the money for music *and* lunch but were too cool to brown-bag it. I get it. You can't flout societal norms and prepare a nourishing lunch.

The burnout quarter had a pungent aroma made up of stale cigarette smoke combined with Aqua Net hair spray. The smoke came from the jackets and hair exposed to the climes of Door 9, the student/faculty smokers' lounge. On this outdoor patio just outside the clique-ah section, teachers and hoodlums intersected, Road Runners and Wile E. Coyotes bonding over a common vice. There may have been some amiable interactions but, at least in my mind, they avoided eye contact, knowing that any warmth would be exploited in remedial English.

That first day, I entered the seating area and scanned the young adult collage for a safe place to sit. Thank G-d, I caught sight of some other basketball players, including Mike Womack (531-5114), a handsome albeit underweight eleventh grader sitting at a table in a clique-ah suburb right on the edge of the clique-ah line. Mike was the biggest wiseass I knew. During summer league basketball in July, while arguing a toupeed referee's call, he was thrown out for saying to the official, "Yaw blind! And last summah, you were *bald*."

Mike dressed immaculately thanks to his skills at swiping designer apparel from his job in the men's department at Jordan Marsh. He sat next to his best friend Rob "Sully" Sullivan (531-5969). Sully was a football player but not a starter and, like Mike, a junior. So he sat in the suburbs, too. He was nearly as tall as me but had a sturdier, muscled build, and a crew cut, but his sharp proportional features (gentile) could accommodate short hair better than mine. He had deep-set blue eyes, a superhero jaw, and Irish complexion. Handsome. His only physical flaw was a scar on his forehead you could shelve an EraserMate on. I had seen him a couple of times at the mall with Mike but knew him only enough to raise my eyebrows and nod when I saw him. He was confident and talked like he was trying to be heard over a police siren.

This seating position appeared fortuitous. *Look at me! I'm just one table removed from the clique-ahs and I'm only a sophomore. This could elevate my status, it could be like a letterman jacket. And why shouldn't I sit here? I'm coming off an ascendant summer on the basketball court. My game is* nice. *And furthermore, if my father hadn't been so intractable about me repeating first, I'd be a junior. I belong here.*

Sully felt otherwise. His territoriality kicked in, so he decided to haze the underclassman. "You gotta shave that mustache. It is just awful." He guffawed abrasively. "You gotta know how awful that mustache is. We may have to hold you down and shave it for your own good."

Bullies. They can smell prey. Even through air drenched in fish sticks, they can smell it. A timid kid need not say a word to beckon their torment. Just sit there. Your bearing alone will draw mockery like suburban fathers to car trouble. I can't imagine this is still a phenomenon, but growing up in my neighborhood you could always summon automotive consultants by lifting the hood of your car. Like deer hearing leaves rustling, the rusty spring creaking of a hood rising alerted every potbellied, farmer-tanned, dipstick checker within earshot.

Until Sully's derision I hadn't even considered shaving. I was preoccupied with several other flaws that required shame. It was maddening. I could have given this kid a dozen other flaws to slam. Even if I shaved the downy wisps, I was still six foot five, 170 pounds, and had styleless hair, no muscle, a large crooked nose, and a mouthful of braces. I was a friggin' disaster from every angle.

Sully's campaign lasted another three days. I was hoping that he would relent so that I could sit at a coolish table with my teammates, but I underestimated his commitment to eradicating my feathery 'stache.

Maintaining my policy against negotiating with terrorists, I relocated the following Monday and sat with some kids I knew from Jewish Community Center basketball. At this table I had approval bordering on reverence. The popularity came from my three years of running roughshod over any basketball league with a menorah on the uniform.

These kids were not popular around school, and yet they had a confidence, an ease. This was common at my school: upper-middle-class Jewish boys having healthy self-esteem. I attributed this self-possession to that lesser-known Hebrew miracle, Jewish sleepaway camp. I loved those guys. They weren't as popular as Womack and Sully, but they were funnier and shared some incredible stand-up comedy tapes with me: Emo Philips, George Carlin, Richard Pryor.

My fifth-period class was called Chem Study. I loved chemistry. I got great satisfaction from applying the formulas and pleasing the teacher, Mr. Paul DeCourcey. He was an early-forties man with wiry, wavy salt-and-pepper hair and a mustache. Americans outside of Sully were pretty much neutral to mustaches by 1987, so DeCourcey was considered neither dashing nor creepy. DeCourcey had a good sense of humor, which that year meant doing a decent Dana Carvey's "Church Lady" from *Saturday Night Live*.

Nowhere near soon enough it was Thanksgiving. It felt like I should have graduated by then. Loneliness breaks time.

For all but a few Massachusetts schools the football season culminated on Thanksgiving, the perfect holiday for staging those bloodthirsty pageants. Compounding the fiendishness was that so many Massachusetts communities, like the state itself, took their name and school mascots from Native American culture. Fittingly, this Thanksgiving, Peabody vanquished the Saugus *Sachems*. With that victory Peabody High clinched a berth in the Division I Massachusetts state championship, the Supah Bowl. Their opponent would be Winchester High School. The Winchester High School . . . *Sachems*.

The high school basketball season started on the Monday after Thanksgiving, elevating my morale a pinch. The first week of practice, we couldn't play until after 8:00 P.M. because after 5:00 P.M. it got too dark for the football team to practice outdoors, so they commandeered our court. I didn't get home from practice until 11:00 P.M. every night that week, further deepening my resentment toward these philistines. It's not enough that you get all the girls, you also have to make me miss *Newhart*?

Our basketball "coach" was a five-foot, two-inch tyrant named Ron Bitter. He fancied himself a Bob Knight type. But Knight was not just a monster, he was also a master strategist and gifted teacher. Bitter was neither. He was slight of build with a paunch, beady dark eyes, waxy pink skin, and a hairstyle identical to the plastic one fastened to the head of the dad in the Fisher-Price Little People play sets. If only he wasn't so cruel, he could have been dismissed as a buffoon.

I made the varsity team and during preseason I was holding my own and earned a mention in the local newspaper's season preview, where I was called "a diamond in the rough." A six-foot-three junior named Sean Dunne was set to start at small forward. Nice kid, although he practiced in the so gauche '80s Hawaiian shorts known as *Jams*. J-sus, put on a pair of gym shorts, you preening dandy. A week before the season started, Sean landed wrong in his Air Jordans and broke his right ankle. So Mike Womack would start at small forward and I would be the first player off the bench. I was terrified.

First game of the season was against Brockton High School. They were ranked number one in the state. Before our game I watched from the bleachers as their junior varsity routed ours. Off the opening tip one of the Brockton JV players, a freshman named Curtis Bostic, drove the length of the court for the first of several thunderous dunks. With that one dunk the young man surpassed the number of Peabody dunks that season. This was the *junior* varsity game! I wanted to throw up.

I entered the varsity game six minutes in, replacing Womack. First time down court I caught the ball on the left wing. I felt like my head was submerged in gelatin. My ears hummed from the blood rush. I took one dribble, then spun toward the baseline getting a step on my defender, number 23, who happened to be Troy Bostic, the big brother of the JV Dr. Dunkenstein. I jump-stopped into a crouch, leaped straight up, and fired at the glass from eighteen feet. The ball banked off the square and *tchtchsh* through the nylon. *Holy shit.* I'm a star. It got better. There was a whistle. I'd been fouled!

"Foul on number 24."

Wait. I'm 24. Shit. Offensive foul.

A horn blew. Womack raced in, pointing toward me contemptuously, signaling my banishment. At halftime, Bitter, his face morphing into France's *The Red Balloon*, blamed me "a sophomore moron who decides to go one-on-one," for our double-digit deficit. He threw his clipboard across the room for emphasis. I spent the rest of that night and the next nineteen games watching from the flaking cobalt-blue wooden bench.

I dragged myself through the next three months, trudging through practice every day. To my dismay, the team did well enough to make the state tournament, extending my purgatory by at least one game.

The final game of the regular season was on a Friday night, in the late winter. I was dressing in the dismal flickering fluorescent-lit visitors' locker room. I pulled my sweatshirt on. As I finger-combed my hair back, I felt a thick, scab-like sore. Odd, I would remember suffering a deep gash to my scalp.

On the bus ride home, I found another sore on the back of my neck and several more in my scalp. I was achy, exhausted, yet I hadn't played a single second. Aggravating my discomfort, the team and cheerleaders were celebrating the victory by reprising their sickeningly hokey cheers. Without the field house to cushion the cacophony, the blare was torture. I hated them *and* the imbecilic Beastie Boys cassette they blasted. Today, I *revere* the Beastie Boys, and they have said their debut album was parody misinterpreted as frat-boy anthem, but I wasn't sophisticated enough to pick up on the satire. To me at sixteen, they sounded like culture-appropriating, misogynistic assholes who "went into the locker room during classes . . . went into your locker and . . . smashed your glasses." I was an early rap and hip-hop devotee, but I believe the context in which I first heard the Beasties kept me from immediately embracing them. I resisted them, until the moment I found out they were New York Jews. I quickly abandoned my mistrust and saw them as a band that would outgrow their teen debauchery and become innovative, influential artists who went further in making Jews seem cool than anyone since Moses split the Red Sea.

The next day my condition worsened. My mom took me to a walk-in health clinic to get the rapidly spreading blisters checked out. The nurse guessed that it was scabies.

"It's not scabies," I told her.

"How do you know?"

"'Cause we're not in Alcatraz."

We laughed at how funny I was, but it hurt. I had a violently sore throat and ached everywhere else. As a bonus, these sores were aggressively itchy. A doctor diagnosed chicken pox. She promised it would be hellish because I wasn't a child. It was. I cried from the pain for days. Still, I considered it an equitable exchange for freeing me from what turned out to be two more basketball games.

I got a week off from school, during which my mother was as attentive as she had been when I was home sick as a child. She got me several topical salves and antihistamines to combat the itch. Once the fever and the itches and aches became tolerable, I must say I enjoyed the TLC. My dad visited a couple of times and brought me eight packages of baseball cards, something he hadn't done in years. Only delusion kept me from realizing this was the end of my childhood.

I went back to school, my body and face covered in thick scabs. I probably could have gotten excused until my skin cleared up, but I was getting good grades and didn't want to screw it up. I didn't care how repugnant I looked. What could happen, I'd get *less* attention from girls? I'd never kissed a girl and I couldn't conceive a scenario where I ever would.

After recovering from the pox, I returned to my routine of playing basketball every day. I'd decided to work harder. That's all that was missing, more practice. It had always been part of my response to setbacks. I would first feel discouraged, hopeless, suicidal, then lick my wounds, and rededicate myself with more discipline and effort. I hit the courts with more fire than ever before.

A couple of weeks into my new commitment, at our team's end-of-season awards banquet in mid-April, "Coach" Bitter sat down next to me. He was smiling. I smiled back! I figured he'd probably ask how I was feeling and encourage me, tell me he expected big things from me next year. With three starters graduating, he was going to need me. While smiling, he put his arm over my shoulder and told me, "Don't bothah comin' back next ye-ah if ya still a f—in' pussy."

My mouth was burlap. My smile gone. Basketball, my love, had rejected me via this gargoyle in khakis.

It was April. I wouldn't touch a basketball again until July 5. First time I'd gone even two days without basketball since fifth. I needed a new love.

I had come to rely on basketball to feel better. Have a bad day at school? Go out and shoot. Feeling down about my future? Shoot jumpers until it got dark. Every afternoon, head up to Symphony Park to play against whoever was available or run myself ragged when it was just me. Come home and shoot some more in front of the house. Wintertime, shovel out the street, build snowmen to shoot over. I was depositing effort into an account I would cash in one day.

For most of my life I could feel better by thinking about a time when I would feel better. For years it was contingent on basketball stardom. Realizing that basketball would not redeem me, that it would contribute to my pain, I was devastated. I was sad, lonely. Watching basketball, reading about basketball, talking about basketball had occupied my mind since I was ten years old. Now thoughts about it filled me with despair. Basketball was supposed to solve my problems, bring me confidence, recognition, a route to college, a girlfriend. It all felt delusional. A girlfriend? A girl who would fall in love with a benchwarmer? I withdrew, submerged in self-pity.

Once again, sitting on that beer-bottle-green shag rug in my bedroom, I started to rebuild. Where I once endlessly pored over sports cards, read book after book, organized stuffed animals, drew with crayons and markers and sculpted with clay. I sat with my back against the bed and listened to the Steven Wright tape Andy Freedman had given me, over and over on the General Electric boom box my neighbor Margie Graff got me for my bar mitzvah four years prior. I had forgotten how much humor had soothed me. Those tapes were painkiller and vaccine. I laughed, which lightened me, but hearing the laughter from the audience and knowing something about how that felt, inspired me.

I became obsessed with jokes, their components and the components of the components, the words. "Obsession" is not the right word. My interest in jokes and comedians wasn't a neurosis. It wasn't interfering with my schoolwork or alienating me from friends. I just couldn't get enough of this joy. It was restorative, redemptive. This comfort, this bliss I got from laughter and its creation wasn't obsession, it was love.

One Friday afternoon that spring I pressed play and record at the same time on the Margie boom box. The first bit I recorded was a parody of a show called *Lifestyles of the Rich and Famous*. My mother never missed the show. It was an extension of her deification of the rich. One of her favorite things to do growing up was take us for rides through affluent neighborhoods. "To our right, another house we'd never be allowed in."

I abhorred the lifestyles of the rich and famous even before it became a show.

My spoof was called *Lifestyles of the Broke and Hopeless*. Like most amateur comedians of the day, I did a decent impression of the prophet of voyeuristic materialism, Robin Leach. It was basically nasally shouting with a stock British accent. His rhythm was easily replicated by stretching out the final word of every senteeeeeence. I went around the house holding the boom box and commenting on all the evidence that poor people lived there.

"Let's visit the bathroom, where this bar of soap is actually a sliver of Dial *fused* to a bar of Ivoryyyyyy. This bottle of Prell's life has also been extended through an infusion of shower water. It's now certain to last these losers another eight to ten shampooooooos.

"Now, we move to the kitchen, where in this overflowing drawer the thrifty homeowners store America's largest stash of fast-food napkiiiiins. Wendy's, Burger King, Pizzeria Unoooo. The selection is nothing short of decadeeeeent."

Continuing the remote piece, I took the boom box outside to my mother's claret-colored Chevette, opened the door, and declared, "Beneath this slice of living room shag lies a hole in the floorboard you could shove a size fourteen sneaker throooooough. Only Fred Flintstone had a larger hole in his automobiiiiiile."

I put a few more impressions and routines on the tape. One was a fake ad for a product called "stick in the door." It was inspired by my mother's fanatical insistence on wedging a broomstick handle in the sliding glass door to thwart intruders. She recognized no incongruity in her concurrent policy of leaving a house key in the mailbox.

I played the tape for best friends Billy, Jay Hurwitz, Andy Freedman, and Lori—and it was a hit. They had favorite lines and repeated them. They asked to borrow the tape. They looked at me while they were listening the way I looked at magicians. I was proud and fought to hold back a smile.

On a Friday in May, our German II teacher, Frau Power, had divided us into groups to practice conversation. Frau, as I called her, wore a floral-print blouse, and her usual white canvas sneakers with gray woolen slacks. She was recently back from a long medical leave. She felt we were behind so tolerated no nonsense.

I sat with Lori and her friend Kristel Holland near the back of the room, our desks facing one another. I had known Lori since fall of '83. I'd never talked with Kristel before except for an occasional hi in class and two smiling waves in the hallway. What a smile! Straight, shiny white teeth and a twinkle in her eyes. She had her sandy hair in a bun and looked adorable. She was quiet but not shy. The steadily rising sun was making it warm. She took off her denim jacket and draped it over the desk. She was wearing a thin white blouse buttoned to just beneath her clavicle. We completed the assignment early.

As we waited for some of the stragglers to catch up Lori asked, "Ya see *Cheers* last night, Gah?"

"Yes! Oh my head, so funny."

I then made this observation: "Why is the *Cheers* song such a downah? Hilarious show, stahts with a song—makes me wanna kill myself."

The girls laughed.

I sang mournfully and quietly so as not to antagonize our

dour Frau Power. "'Making your way in the world today takes everything you've *goooooooot*.'"

I drenched the "got" in gloom. Lori's face tightened. She hunched forward into her laugh posture. Her laugh was high-pitched, her face reddening. She covered her mouth with the back of her delicate pink fist. While I loved making Lori laugh, this show was for Kristel. She was new to my work. Her eyes squinted and their merry glint further energized me. Her laugh was contralto, deeper, from her chest. I'd bet there was a smoker in her house. I liked her.

I was hyperaware that Frau Power loomed fifteen feet behind me, seated at her desk. If she interrupted, she'd wreck my timing, dignity, and, crucially, the climax this routine deserved. My back was to her, so she couldn't silence me with a glare. I'd be getting the hook any moment, either from Frau or the wickedly shrill beep that signaled the end of fourth period. That beep had been maliciously tuned so as to inflict the entire school with tinnitus every forty-five minutes. I had to entertain the girls while reading their bearing to see if the Power was afoot. Safe for now. I did the next part sotto voce, pretending my right palm was the sheet music. My left hand cupped imaginary headphones. I peeked at the clock to see how much time was left in class. It was going to be close.

"That poor singer they hired . . . 'everything you've *gooooootot*.'"

Kristel smiled, turned to Lori for affirmation. Lori laughed. Kristel added her bass to the harmony. I shook my head, closed my eyes, still pretending to be on the verge of tears. I blew up my cheeks, then vigorously exhaled an anguished sigh.

"After he finished singing, the whole studio was in tears, *sobbing*. He's like, 'Thank you. Now, if you'll excuse me, I'm gonna go eat a buncha poison.'"

I concluded by dabbing my eyes with the sleeve of Kristel's jean jacket. How *audacious*. It smelled like teenaged girl, nonaerosol hair spray, bubble gum–flavored Trident, and maybe a hint of cigarette? The girls were giggling loudly. Everyone was turning around to see what was so funny.

The Frau barked, "Herr Gulman! You're outta control. Settle down. This isn't playtime."

I was dizzy. My face was burning. My belly dancing. The long, mechanized beep ended class. G'night, everybody!

Through a grin I said, "Entschuldigung, Frau."

I made teenaged girls laugh. I got in trouble. And it was Friday. Ich bin im Himmel. (I am in heaven.) Soon, it got better. Much better.

Textbooks were being turned in. In the cafeteria, junior clique-ahs were seizing the throne from the graduating monarchy. I walked taller and faster now with the finish line in sight. My braces, recently pried off, were no longer foiling my winsome smile. Andy Freedman just got his driver's license. Lori and I were congratulating him, and he promised to take us to the movies next Tuesday.

As we disembarked for the summer, I threw away this sentence toward Lori: "Ask that girl Kristel to go."

"That girl." That'll throw 'em off my track. "Ask that girl Kristel to go" was an abridgement of the truth, which was: "Ask that girl who I think is so lovely and nice. *You know,* the girl who laughed so hard at my *Cheers* joke, a moment so precious I'm not sure I'll ever forget it. Kristel, the girl for whom I take a calculated route to seventh period every day because, twice, we crossed paths and she said hi and smiled and my face was warm for the rest of the afternoon? *That* girl. I believe her name is Kristel."

The following Tuesday afternoon I sat outside on the back patio for an hour and got a great tan on my face. I looked much better with a tan. I put on a white-and-peach thin-horizontal-striped polo shirt that my brother Max had left at home. It made me look less skinny because it was tight around my meager biceps. I shaved and, after I shaved, I splashed on Brut by Fabergé aftershave.

Early evening, it started to rain. But for the first time since I can remember, the rain didn't make me feel lonely. I was too optimistic about the night to feel lonely. We picked up Lori at her house and then headed over to Kristel's.

We drove to Kristel's just after dark. It was a modest, one-level suburban home. Similar setup to mine but, unlike in my house, the front picture window curtains of their house were open so you could see inside. The interior was bright, again a contrast to my house, which, when I left that night, was lit only by the family room television set. Every light in their house was on, even in rooms they weren't in.

Their front door opened into what the Hollands called the parlor. My family would call it the living room. I liked *parlor*. It conjured the gentleman caller from *The Glass Menagerie*, though I'm sure Tennessee Williams didn't pronounce it "pahlah" the way the Hollands did.

I entered and instantly sniffed a fragrant mingling of cigarettes and dogs. Kristel's mother enthusiastically greeted Lori, Andy, and me. She and Lori embraced warmly. They must go back some. Kristel wasn't ready. The mother introduced herself as Vicki. She was so nice that I forgot that this was the first time I'd ever been in the home of a girl I liked. Vicki had a young voice, warm smile, and a laugh that may all have been designed by the universe to quell the distress of teenaged boys. She had short blond hair, a little spiky, and just the right amount of makeup for a mom. For some reason I always believed that mothers of pretty girls must be mean, but Vicki dispelled that instantly. If a tornado warning had required us to take shelter the rest of the night in the parlor, I would have rejoiced.

A short while later the source of the cigarette scent entered. Paul Holland had graying curly hair in a Julius Caesar cut, a sunburnt, pinkish face. He was barefoot, wearing jeans and a polo shirt. He greeted us, gruffly bellowing: *"Where are you taking my daughter?"*

Here we go. What the Chr-st. I needed Alda and this guy was givin' me Eastwood. Oh well.

Then he burst out a booming Winstons-soaked cackle. His smile revealed deep smoker's creases surrounding crinkly twinkling eyes identical to his fetching daughter's. I loved this guy. I'm pretty sure he was lit.

Once again, I was aware of how these people were *so* not Jewish. Jews don't greet dates after a couple of St. Pauli Girls. This was too great. What if this becomes a thing? How have I gone this long without this experience? I now knew what it felt like to be one of those guys who hangs around with girls after school, at night. I wish it were a date, but I think dates require more overt asking out, and I'll bet usually you have the date's phone number.

The dad said, "I'm Paul."

I said, "Good to meetcha. I'm Gary."

I chose "Good to meetcha" over "Nice to meet you" so I wouldn't come off soft. After some chit and chat and a short discussion about how tall I was, Kristel entered from the bedrooms area. She was wearing faded blue jeans and a white sweater and had clearly spent time preparing. Her hair was blonder and more styled. If she looked like this in German class, there was no way I would have had the chutzpah to "ask that girl Kristel." As adorable as she was in class, her beauty had been amplified. She glowed. Kind of like fall leaves when you drive west an hour before the late-September sun sets. I'd had this feeling in my stomach before—when my brother Max drove too fast over a dip in the road and one time when I sank a buzzer-beating elbow jumper to beat St. Francis Xavier of Winthrop in the CYO state semifinals in eighth.

My mind was sprinting. *This girl is too good for you, so don't get your hopes up. But maybe she doesn't know that? This is some boys' lives. They do this. Why can't you? Stop. Just put on a good show tonight. Enjoy the evening. That won't be enough. This exists. How do I go back to watching videos and getting pizza with my dad every Saturday night? This happy family, this well-lit house with this redolent montage of tobacco smoke, teen perfume, and incontinent pups.*

We went to the multiplex in Revere, Massachusetts. Entering the theater lobby, I deployed some movie jokes I'd honed over the years:

"Do you smell popcorn?"

And "Let's hurry. I don't want to miss the newsreel."

I deftly maestroed the seating in the theater. It was partly luck, but I would have tackled Andy if he sat between Kristel and me. I made a fun show of wiping off Kristel's movie seat before she sat. I sat to her right and on the aisle. I intentionally bumped my elbow against hers as we set up on the shared armrest.

"You want to share, or do you wanna arm wrestle for it?"

She laughed.

When they showed a preview of the ridiculous *Masters of the Universe* starring Dolph Lundgren I quipped, "I smell Oscaaar."

"I think that's popcorn," she snapped back.

I laughed. *This is so great! Look at us, sharing the holiest genre of humor,* the inside joke. *Calm down.*

I thought of telling her what a start her father gave me with his "Where are you taking my daughter?" but I worried that she'd say, "He does that with all the guys who come to pick me up for dates. And let me tell ya, boy-o, there are tons of 'em.

It's outta hand. I don't have another date-free night until after Halloween."

On two occasions during sweet moments in the movie I tenderly rested my head on her right shoulder for half an instant, and blessedly, she didn't recoil in revulsion. I was drunk with delight. I'd never tasted alcohol, but I could understand why you would turn to it when the feeling I had that night was disrupted.

She smelled like heaven. It was Forever Krystle, a fragrance I recognized from the Sears perfume section. Krystle was created for and promoted by Linda Evans, the fifty-something star who played Krystle Carrington on the prime-time lux-fest *Dynasty*. *Kristel* wore *Krystle*. What fifteen-year-old wears a perfume peddled by some aging soap star? It didn't matter. She could've rubbed OFF! Deep Woods behind her ears, and I'd have been bewitched.

The movie was *Roxanne,* and along with Andy's driver's license it tied for the MVP that night. This reimagining of *Cyrano de Bergerac* starring Steve Martin and Daryl Hannah was the perfect film for my scheme. A big-nosed guy who loves a blond girl takes her to watch a movie about a big-nosed guy who loves a blond girl. Despite Steve Martin's grotesque proboscis, Daryl Hannah fell in love with him. And why? He was *funny*.

I don't think "miracle" is overstating it.

On the ride home it was drizzling and cold enough that Andy turned on the heat. It was almost July! I was floating in a state of elated contentment following the so very strong argument for falling in love with me I gave that night. We all had a great time, and I was like the master of ceremonies.

"Is it too hot in here?" Lori asked.

I said, "Yeah, it's too hot, Andy. Oh wait, I see the problem," I slid the heat lever left, "You had it set to *cremate*."

More laughs.

"Kristel, you gotta hear Gary's tape!" Andy said.

"I want to hear it!"

"Okay, sure," I replied.

This is good. Don't blow it, kid.

We pulled up to Kristel's house. At no point did I say we have to do this again sometime or even acknowledge what a special night it was. My plan was more subtle than that. Nobody could know my intentions in case these feelings were not reciprocated.

We dropped Kristel off.

Lori yelled to her, "Kristel, I'll call you!"

To myself: "Me too."

I called on Sunday, July 5. I waited until dusk, around eight o'clock, because I wouldn't be interrupting dinner and what if the parents go to work early on Monday? I didn't want to wake up my future in-laws with a call after 8:30 P.M. on a Sunday. Another reason was that I figured she wouldn't be home at that time on a summer Sunday. Her not being home when I called was a good outcome in my mind, although the fact that she wasn't home on a Sunday night suggested an active social life, which might mean she was too popular for me.

My thinking was: if she wasn't home, she would get a message that I called. She'd then have to decide whether she liked me enough to call me back. If she didn't call me back, then she didn't like me, and after seventy-two hours of moping I would get back to dork status but with a new awareness of how exciting even just being in a girl's parlor can be.

Before I called, I jotted down some notes, a couple of questions/comments I could make in case the conversation lulled.

I would definitely ask: "How was your Fourth of July?"

That would allow me to mention the fireworks display I saw while with "some friends" at Nantasket Beach, which would make me sound like a very worldly person who travels up to seventy-five minutes from home and has friends in different area codes. I'd leave out the fact that I met the friend at a leadership conference associated with the history department.

Then I went around to all five phones in the house and unplugged them from the phone jacks. Except the kitchen phone, which was mounted on the wall. It's hard for young people to understand but growing up we shared a single phone number with our entire family, and they could pick up any phone in the house at any time and join your private phone call. Also, we memorized the phone number of everyone we were friends with or related to and every business we called regularly.

The unplugging of every phone would prevent my mother from picking up and dialing and then shouting, "Sorry" and asking, "Who is it?" and then "Do I know you?"

Of course you don't, Ma. I've never brought a girl home and you don't go to my school, so you definitely don't know her. Also, my mother would regularly have extensive conversations with wrong numbers. I was so terrified of Kristel finding out that I had a mother.

I found "Holland, Paul" in the phone book, then pressed 535-345 on the maroon touch tone in my brother's room. I took a half dozen deep breaths, and, with a swarm of butterflies circling my stomach, I pushed the last number in the number, 9.

As the phone rang, I repeated aloud the mantra, "Please don't be home. Please don't be home."

I had decided to open the call with "Can I speak to Kristel, please?" if the father or her sister answered. I wouldn't use "May I" because I didn't want them to think I was an intellectual or a fairy. I would use "May I" if it was the mother because I felt she would be impressed with the politeness. Also, I decided to use "speak *to* Kristel" rather than "speak *with* Kristel" because I felt *with* made it sound rehearsed and like I was going to lecture her—"May I have a word *with* your daughter?"

I never used the most popular opener with people my age, which was "Is [insert name] there?" I always felt that sounded dumb and left the possibility that some wiseass could say, "Yes, she is," and then hang up. No, I knew what I was doing. I also determined that I would end the call after ten minutes so I wouldn't run out of material.

The only parts I didn't have planned: *How do I figure out whether she likes me?* Her returning my phone call would only be circumstantial evidence. She might just be polite and/or just wants to be friends. *And how do I arrange to see her again, alone?* I decided that "the Tape" would be the thing. I would casually ask if she still wanted to borrow that comedy tape I made.

Two rings. Maybe nobody's home! Three rings. There was no caller ID at that time so I could still bail out. Then there was a click and a recorded voice. An answering machine, very rare at that time and so not a contingency I had prepared for. I had to think quickly.

"Hi, ahm, this message is for Kristel. It's Gary Gulman"—I added the last name, not taking the chance that she calls another Gary back, which in retrospect was silly because there was only one other Gary in our high school, and he was the captain of the football team, so if she had been expecting a call from him then I was out of the running anyway—"Call me back at 535-4169 when you get a chance."

Take your time, there's no pressure. I'll be sitting around waiting for your call no matter how long that takes. There's no way I'm leaving this house until I hear back.

And it was over. All I had to do now was obsess, and second-guess the message I left. I waited by the phone only until ten knowing that, unless she was a psychopath, she wouldn't call after 10:00 P.M. on a Sunday.

The next day I slept till noon, which reduced the amount of

time I had to wait for her to call back. It's a trick I learned over the years from fasting for Yom Kippur. The bonus to this scheme was if she called while I was asleep, then not only did I look like I hadn't been waiting for her to call, maybe she'd think I was up late the night before drinking beers and getting second off girls.

I didn't leave the house all day. No way was I going to let my mother answer, and unfortunately, my mother quickly put the kibosh on my latest attempt to unplug every phone in the house. I would have to be on alert. Every time the phone rang, I would holler "I got it!" and hover over the phone. I had to balance my desire to not appear anxious with not allowing so many rings that my mother picked up. I would pick up after three rings and in the middle of the fourth ring. If you pick up on the third ring you were nowhere near the phone and you certainly weren't trying to psychically elicit a call from a girl you had fallen in love with during a four-hour non-date. Every time the phone call turned out to be for my mom I would badger her to hurry off the phone because although call-waiting may have been available at that time, to this day, you can still call my mother's house and hear the last busy signal in America.

Kristel called me back around 5:00 P.M. and without prompting she asked to borrow the comedy tape I made. We made plans to meet the next day at the basketball court at Symphony Park, which was a half mile from her house. I rode my bar mitzvah twelve-speed, and while I waited, to temper my excitement I shot some baseline jumpers (they require the most focus) with my basketball. She arrived and asked me to come over to go swimming. Things were moving fast!

I walked with her and my bike to her house. In my haste, I left behind my basketball at the park. When I realized it, I thought that sounds like something out of a lazily written story.

November 2017

There is no internet at my mom's. She is eighty-four years old and has never used email or a smartphone. She's never owned a computer.

The other place beside Symphony Park I go to check email and social media is the Lynnfield Public Library, two miles from my mother's house, in the neighboring town of Lynnfield, Massachusetts. It is as well maintained and elegant as it had been when I first went there in preschool to borrow the 33 rpm album Mister Rogers's *Won't You Be My Neighbor?* It's where I had taken out hundreds of books over the years, including the Chronicles of Narnia; *The House with the Clock in Its Walls; The Hobbit; The Outsiders; The Westing Game; The Hotel New Hampshire; Goodbye, Columbus; The Bell Jar; Their Eyes Were Watching G-d; Slaughterhouse-Five; Night; To Kill a Mockingbird; The Catcher in the Rye; The Bluest Eye.* I'd used the encyclopedias and microfilm and -fiche to research and write four or five papers every year.

One of the most disheartening aspects of my illness was that for nearly three years I hadn't been able to quell my anxiety long enough to read a single book. Before this episode I'd read fifty books or more each year. When I started to feel a little better in the fall of 2017, I was overjoyed to find that while I still couldn't read, I could listen to audiobooks. The Lynnfield library offers an app where I can download audiobooks for *free*. The audiobooks, especially first thing in the morning, distract me from my catastrophic rumination, soothing my anxiety. I also find that they make long solitary walks and the light jogs I have started less grueling and lonely.

Eleventh

Eleventh grade was the first year of school I had looked forward to since fifth, the year I was jilted by Mr. Mercier. It was mostly because I started eleventh with a real girlfriend, Kristel. A "call every day" girlfriend. A "drive to and from school in a red 1980 Ford Fairmont that Max had left behind" girlfriend. An "our-song-having ('I Need Love' by LL Cool J), hold hands in the hallway, walk to class and depart with a tasteful kiss *on the lips*" girlfriend.

It had become official during a bike ride home from a large half-pepperoni pizza at Captain Pizza (535-2600) with her and her older sister on July 20. On the night of August 18, at a beach in Salem, with the smell of fried clams and September in the wind, I said, "I love you."

And she said, "I love you, too."

It lasted all the way to New Year's.

Jewish New Year's.

It ended October 4, 1987, a Sunday. It rained all day. I didn't come out of my room.

From my brother Max I received the following consolation: "Girls are fickle at that age. That's why I never dated in high school."

Oh, *that's* why. My father's contribution was even more obtuse. He said in response to my devastation, "She wasn't *that* pretty."

My mom was the only one who said she understood. After my parents divorced, she never dated again. I was sure that would be my fate as well.

I was crestfallen over the end of the day-to-day companionship. And then teen mileposts would arise and intensify my woe. First was the class Halloween party. I had fantasized about attending in a couple costume, like Michael and Stephanie from *Newhart*, or Sam and Diane from *Cheers*, or Mary and Percy Bysshe Shelley from that night Mary wrote *Frankenstein*. We'd take pictures, and in those pictures, I'd know where to put my hands.

The skills I mastered while avoiding Nunzio (not his real name) in ninth were valuable for avoiding Kristel. This time I was eluding only a figurative knife in the gut. I saw her in person just a handful of times the rest of high school.

Lori and I talked on the phone about it for the first couple of days, but I didn't want to be the friend who whines about their ex every time you talk to them. Kristel stayed on my mind into college, but a week after the breakup, realizing nobody wanted to hear about it, I never mentioned her again.

Around Halloween, the classes started playing basketball in gym. I was showing off a new trick I'd perfected over the summer. I stood directly in front of the hoop, holding a basketball, then jumped as high as I could. At the apex of my leap, I cocked the ball behind my head with both hands until it touched the back of my neck. Then I stuffed it through the hoop, grabbing the rim with both hands until the force, plus my weight, forced the rim to fold down on its spring-loaded mount. It snapped back with a satisfying *gugunk,* and the near-empty field house's echo amplified it. Adrenalizing. It felt like an act of vandalism. Everyone in gym class noticed. I did it until the gym teacher told me to "cut the shit, kid."

Moments later two young men of identical height, build, hair length, and cocksure gait approached me with grins. They introduced themselves as the Jetsyns, John and Joe. I found out later that was not their real surname. They had been dubbed the Jetsyns because "they were not of this world."

I'd noticed them around school since the year before. They were assistant football coaches. One of them had subbed for my art teacher the previous fall and spent the class reading a Silver Surfer comic book. I knew by the adulation their players showed them and the carefully scissored sleeves on the sweatshirts over their tank tops that they were very cool.

They both had chins that would look right jutting from Batman's cowl. They had long eyelashes, wavy shoulder-length hair, deep tans, and muscular definition reminiscent of the heroes in the Marvel comic books they read. They were twins and twenty-eight years old, the exact same age as my brother Rick, but where Rick was finishing up a master's degree in taxation, last year the Jetsyns had assisted in coaching our football team to the state championship. They were wearing tank tops that read "Peabody Football 1987, Not Rebuilding, Just Reloading."

"What's your name, brother?" asked John, the more extroverted of the two.

"Gary."

"Gary what?" said Joe, the more restrained and marginally more grounded.

"Gulman."

"Gul Man! All right. You're what, six foot six?" asked John.

"Yeah," I said, and looked away.

"John Jetsyn should guess heights at the Topsfield Fair, brother," John said.

I laughed.

"Why does the Gul Man not play football?" asked Joe.

I said, "I'm a basketball player," and nodded toward the rim I had been abusing.

Then John got serious. "You're a waste, Gul Man."

I smiled and laughed.

"Look at me," he said. "You let the Jetsyns get you on the football field. The Jetsyns will change your life, brother."

I had that fluttering stomach, bashful grin, blushy feeling I got around compliments. It was a strange feeling. I always had an inkling I had something unique to offer but felt uneasy whenever anyone tried to confirm it.

"You're missing out, brother. You're missing out on newspaper articles. You're missing out on recruiting visits, scholarships . . . *girls*."

I saw print as a dying medium, but the last two items on that list would have solved two major anxieties for me. An image of my ex-girlfriend flashed behind my eyes.

Luckily, I instantly recognized this promise as something so far-fetched you'd reject it from a made-for-TV movie. "Nebbishy teen loses girlfriend, becomes football star, wins back girlfriend."

Then I imagined bringing this pipe dream to my mother and brothers and the quick work they'd make of shredding it. My father would have encouraged me if I told him I was going to build a nuclear submarine in the bathtub, but the rest of them would squash my dream with a noxious blend of their cynicism and skepticism.

"I appreciate it, guys, but I'm not a football player. I'm a basketball player. I'll break my neck or blow out a knee. You wouldn't want me on your football team. Ask around."

The Jetsyn named Joe said, "The Jetsyns will bulk you up, teach you how to *deliver* hits, brother. You'll be the one breaking necks and bizzin' people."

"Bizzin'?"

They laughed. John said, "Gul Man, the bizz is the harmonic

sound you hear in your head following a solid helmet-to-helmet collision. *Bzzzzz.*"

They laughed. They were describing brain trauma and giggling. What in the f— kind of people are these?

They reminded me of the college basketball coaches who spoke at my basketball camps, charming and at ease talking to teenaged boys.

"I can't, but thanks, guys. I appreciate it."

"How about this, Gul Man? If Joe Jetsyn beats you in a game of one-on-one, you play football."

I liked this new moniker, Gul *Man*. Better than Gah. Better than Gulman. I liked the attention and the idea of a way out of drawing sad clowns in my notebook all day but knew myself better than these guys did. I was not a Gul Man. I was a Gulman.

"What do I get for winning?"

"The Jetsyns will leave the Gul Man alone."

We laughed.

"Gul Man, the Jetsyns will be as Galactus was to Norrin Radd. The Jetsyns will turn you into a superhero."

They were the oldest people I'd ever heard discussing comic books. They were the first men besides my father to tell me I was something special. And they were the first people I'd encountered who referred to themselves in the third person. They were appealing in the way that all loquacious, upbeat men are to the teenaged Gary Gulmans of the world.

In the expansive field house, on the hoop closest to our locker rooms, Joe Jetsyn and I played one-on-one. Game to eleven by ones. Win by two.

Final score: 11–5, Gul Man.

It wasn't that close. I was a basketball player. Joe was built like Captain America. He was a good athlete, but I had played basketball every day since I was ten.

I won the bet, but for the rest of junior year, every time our paths crossed, they welched on it. And I loved every minute of it.

I'd see them in the stands at my basketball games and around the gym locker rooms, where they'd be consulting with the head football coach or joking around with some of the players. I figured they'd just be benign irritations, leaving me a lifelong alternate reality to ponder while silently lamenting my obscurity at a giant university and later at a business someone else owned. It was nice to be pursued. But it was safer to play "what if" than high school football.

I attended all my classes every day that year but only harmonized with my English class. A ninety-eight average in tenth grade English and my dad's forceful persuasion of my guidance counselor got me promoted to an honor's level English class in eleventh. It was the first time my dad had to fight for me since his upbraiding of Rand in second first. I was warned, "Don't get less than a B or they'll send you back down for twelfth grade." This challenge would have been enough to motivate me, but it was a blessing that the books were inspiring and the teacher even more so.

For eleventh-grade English I had Mr. Story. *Seriously.* It was like having a geometry teacher named Ms. Shape. He seemed around forty years old, though to a seventeen-year-old anyone between thirty and sixty seemed around forty.

He had a full head of gray hair brushed straight back with a suggestion of a middle part and possibly a blow-dryer. He had a prominent, straight nose, with an enviable chin and jawline, and a build I could see finishing a 10K without immediately collapsing. He only wore cotton button-down shirts, a third of which were plaid, tucked into brown-belted tan chinos over versatile thick-soled brown shoes.

His erudition and large-framed glasses kept his manly features from intimidating me. I always felt most comfortable around men who wore eyeglasses. But more than his disarming appearance, Mr. Story radiated an ineffable warmth. He was generous with smiles and praise and possibly owing to the caliber of the students, he didn't waste any time on discipline. He didn't have to deal with kids who I called "Is this gonna be on the test–ers." Those pen-hoarding whiners sucked the life out of me and had to be disheartening to serious teachers. I had Mr. Story first period every morning at 7:35, and despite persistent sleep deprivation, I looked forward to his lectures every day.

I think we started the year covering the transcendentalists, who were sepia on paper, but Mr. Story knew the verses to spotlight and turn into refrains. His dark eyebrows would rise with his voice as he *sang* such pearls as:

> *Whoso would be a man must be a nonconformist.*
> —Ralph Waldo Emerson

> *The mass of men lead lives of quiet desperation . . .*
> —Henry David Thoreau

> *It had been necessary for him to swallow swords that he might have a better throat for grapes.*
> —Stephen Crane

It was the eloquence that made the sentences memorable, but it was Mr. Story's enthusiasm and sonorous elocution that signaled to me that these words were worth remembering, that you could build a virtuous life by heeding the wisdom within 'em. I loved this guy. A man *should* circulate an inventory of quotes like this and, moreover, live his life according to the precepts pervading the work of these immortals.

I read extensively that year: Emerson; Frost; Hawthorne's

Scarlet Letter; Poe; Crane's *Red Badge of Courage;* Steinbeck's *The Red Pony;* Hemingway's *The Sun Also Rises, A Farewell to Arms,* and *For Whom the Bell Tolls;* Fitzgerald's *The Great Gatsby,* almost exclusively straight white males, two women, one queer man (Thornton Wilder), no Jews, Langston Hughes representing all of us minorities.

It was a department-mandated syllabus seemingly devised to force me to interrogate my manhood. My conclusion? These men would hate me. Especially Hemingway, and not just because he was a brutal anti-Semite. I was nothing that meshugenah cared about. Not a hunter, a womanizer, a boxer, a bullfighter, or a drunk. I was a virgin who hated guns, fights, war, booze, smoking, animal cruelty, and arrogant men. Steinbeck was compassionate, he would have liked me.

Of all the books we read, the one I thought about the most was *The Great Gatsby.* It covered two things I was consumed with: rich people and the past.

I saw myself in Nick Carraway. Nick was an observer, someone who needed an invite, pathologically honest, careful, and, like me, "full of interior rules that act as brakes on my desires." My calling was not to be a great man, but maybe I could be a great man's neighbor.

Unlike a lot of teenaged boys, I didn't relate to Jay Gatsby. Although I had a Daisy, and I loved going back in time. I ruminated over the last line, how the past would anchor us all *"ceaselessly."*

My favorite line in Gatsby was "They're a rotten crowd. . . . You're worth the whole damn bunch put together." I contemplated that passage while I brooded at a rehearsal dinner for my brother Max's wedding.

A few weeks before the wedding, on a Friday night, the bride's cousin, an heir to a knockoff-shoe mogul, gave a rehearsal dinner. Within my family my conduct at that fete remains infamous to this day. It was held in a posh Boston condominium in Charles River Park. On the multilane artery approaching the aristocratic subdivision, billboards advertised it with this corny slogan: "If you lived here, you'd be home now."

I remember the entire condo and all its contents being gray. This was due to a combination of the muting my melancholy did to colors and that nearly everything in the uninspired space was gray.

The guests on our side were Max, Rick and his wife, my dad, and my mother. The bride's side was her, her commercial-carpet-selling father, her mother, and a brother, also a rug slinger. In addition, her aunt, uncle, and cousins—all members of the pirate penny-loafer monarchy, the Binders (rhymes with finder)—were there. Knowing what everyone did for work long before you met them was customary in my family. I could *not* give a *f*—.

My mother always gave rich people the honor of including their last name whenever they were mentioned. KennyBinder and RuthBinder, as well as their unimpressive kids, ToddBinder, DanielleBinder, and KyleBinder were given this veneration. My mother never mentioned them without including the full name, like the last name was a *title*. (I've changed all the names to protect myself from my mother's outrage.)

I liked my future sister-in-law, but I had an instinctual and robust resentment of rich people. Unless you earned it through sports or eradicating disease, I loathed you. Much like F. Scott Fitzgerald, "I have never been able to forgive the rich for being rich, and it has colored my entire life and works."

My family, especially my mother, revered the wealthy. And like many poor people, she was convinced that money guaranteed bliss. Her favorite joke to pass off as her own was, "Next time I marry, I'll marry for love. The love of money."

I had heard her tell that joke hundreds of times. It was her "Take my wife . . . please." To my family, wealth equaled happiness, but more aggravating was that they believed money also implied *wisdom*. Everything rich people did was automatically correct.

"They must be doin' somethin' right!" they'd insist.

This attitude exasperated me. In my limited experience the "wisdom" of rich people arose from being propelled from the testicles of a very rich man. In the case of my sister-in-law's cousin's family, the father's uncle, Harvey Binder, had made an obscene jackpot by manufacturing and selling cheap bootlegs of designer shoes. Ooh, what a genius. It infuriated me to see how obsequious and solicitous my mother was of these mediocre cobblers. Who would even want to be rich from *shoes*?

I was bored immediately. There was no one to talk to about anything I talked about: basketball, rap music, stand-up comedy, and the TV show *Newhart*. The nearest in age to me were twenty-something spawn of the copycat-footwear magnate. They talked a lot about skiing. I despised skiers. I found skiing elitist, decadent, a "sport" designed in every facet to prevent the poor from defiling their precious white world, the phonies. Every torn ACL and broken limb was cosmic judgment for their opulent f-you to the working class.

I was stuck in a room with skiers tepidly celebrating the union between a carpet wholesaler and a drapery guy. Nobody talked to me. As a child there was usually someone at gatherings who was happy to see me, and my heart would dance when I saw them. These heroes knew how to remove their thumb, turn their eyelids inside out, or shared my enthusiasm for the episode where Bugs Bunny outwitted the gangsters. There was no one for me.

The entire night, no one said anything funny, though there was plenty of laughter. But it was all that "You meant to be funny, so I'll laugh out of civility" laughter. The only genuine laughter were the guffaws my mother got from using me as a prop for her mildewed quips. Like when offered a drink she said, "I don't drink in front of the kids, and when they're not around, who needs it?" which she stole from Erma Bombeck or Joan Rivers or whichever put-upon Jewess she was plagiarizing.

The rubes roared and flattered her with various versions of "Oh, Barb, you hot ticket."

Hot ticket? Oh my head. She's a Borscht Belt *hack*. She should be followed around all day by a drummer cracking rim shots. You fools. You saps. Have you no compassion for the ventriloquist's dummy who endures these moldy routines night after night?

By the way, if we're just retelling jokes we heard, nobody at this party could top me. I'm the funniest person here, and it's not even close. Raise your hand if you made a cassette tape of jokes that got passed around school! If I were willing to put aside my integrity, I could whip this wake into a frenzy.

The shindig was catered. A young woman, wearing banquet-server gear—black vest, black slacks, black bow tie over white shirt—probably a college student, was walking around with trays of hors d'oeuvres prepared by another woman in the kitchen. I couldn't accept any. I was embarrassed to be part of this group. I wanted to tell her I was proletariat like her and when the time came . . . off with their heads.

I was a hypersensitive, self-righteous, insecure, irritable, insufferable teen. I'm sure I was exhausting to be around then. My only defense is that I didn't like being around me any more than anyone else there.

I'd been up for school that day since 6:00 A.M. It was hard to stay awake even when I *wasn't* a hostage at a dullard convention. I was constantly fatigued from late-night homework, basketball practice, and an undiagnosed nap instigator: major depressive disorder. I was sad, bored, and tired. If I were home, I would've been an hour into a depression nap.

But I couldn't sleep until we were in the car ride, heading home. Two hours, *at least*. I asked my mother if I could put on the Celtics game. She answered with the look she gave me whenever

I told people what Uncle Norman did for a living, a V-ed brow over squinted eyes over a scrunched mouth, which, despite my being a foot and a half taller than her, still made me heel.

There wasn't a magazine rack or a bookshelf to fill the time. Even prisons have libraries. I may go insane. I thought to myself if only I were an old man I could just nod off on the sofa, drooling and snoring blissfully. That's when I noticed space between the sofa and a sliding glass door; the slider opened on to a balcony overlooking other doorman buildings. After dismissing a leap from the railing, I recognized promise within the narrow clearing abutting the glass slider, definitely enough space for repose.

No way. My family would be horrified, probably admonish me in front of the whole haughty throng. Then I'd have to sit there, face stinging in the aftermath of my censure.

But I'd be *behind* the couch. Maybe no one would notice. Why can't they put on the Celtics? You're telling me these windbag ski Jews are gonna do or say anything as compelling as a Larry Bird fadeaway?

Another case where if I had a girlfriend, I'd be okay. I wondered what my Daisy was doing. Probably holding hands with some teenaged Tom Buchanan at a party for gentiles. *I could cry . . . that might stir things up. I've never seen that before. I'm too old to cry to get out of something. I'd like to jump off the balcony, but what if I regretted it on the way down? There's no undoing that, and if I lived, there'd be more regrets.*

I could go for a walk. I'm too tired, and I don't even know how to get around this city, and I'm not a person who goes for walks. Thoreau would go for a walk; Emerson, too. Solvitur ambulando! Not for me. If I got lost and was late coming back, they'd all rip me. "Where were *you?"*

Then they started making hackneyed toasts to the bride and groom.

Someone actually said, "Max, remember the two most important words for a husband are 'Yes, dear.'"

Oh boy.

I'd like to make a toast: "To the rubes who buy your cheap shoes! If they had any fashion sense, right now we'd be splitting up the check at Denny's."

Screw this. I couldn't tolerate another instant of consciousness. I folded my acid-washed jean jacket three times, fashioning a tacky little pillow. Then I placed it on the grayish-beige Berber carpet and laid myself down. I reclined on my back, then folded my hands over my chest. I believed that would be the genteel way to take a nap behind a couch at a cocktail party.

And I slept. At least ninety minutes. My family must have weighed the discomfort of reprimanding me at a party with the impudence of my doze and chose to let me sleep. I woke up to the hot coffee smell signaling the bitter end of this frigid wingding.

I've absorbed much scorn for that floor show.

I've been called rude, an embarrassment, an ignoramus, a big baby, *odd*. By everyone but my dad. Couldn't have been many more labels than that because the collective lexicon of my family is meager. They're not readers. I would have added "petulant," "rancorous," and "sullen."

There were kids in my class smoking and drinking and doing drugs and getting each other pregnant, and I was getting shit for taking a load off at a yawn contest. For the first time in my life, I showed no contrition. I was proud of my stand. It was the only rebellious act of my teens. I saw my nap-in as a protest of classism, materialism, and four-flusher-y. If I had been sixty years older, they'd have brought me a blanket, but because I was a teen I was an outcast.

"Oh, Gary, how *dare* you? How *could* you? *Why* would you? What is *wrong* with you? We could have been accepted by these rich people!"

Oh, *harumph*.

There was not a single person interested in talking with me. I had done cool things. I was the only person there who had dunked a basketball and made out with a non-Jew. I had dreams *in progress*.

You want to ignore a bright, talented, sensitive teen? Fine. I'll sleep through your shitty party for rich people and their cheerleaders.

A few weeks after the nap I was at the wedding. I was depressed mostly because I had wanted to have a date for the wedding. I wanted someone to dance with, not unlike my favorite '80s soul monarch, the enchanting Whitney Houston.

Nobody would know that just six weeks ago I had a girlfriend for two months, two weeks, and four days. They'd just see me hunting for a corner slice of cake and think I was an ugly, immature failure.

The wedding and reception were held at the Pine Brook Country Club in Richie Rich Weston, Massachusetts. It was a country club for Jews but was so Waspy. There were round tables covered in linen with linen napkins that these fancy-pants snobs all put on their laps without their fathers even making them. Who was dropping all this food in their laps? The napkin in the lap is bullshit. If they were serious about protecting their clothes and not just signaling sophistication, they would stuff the napkin into their collar as a bib, but that would make them look like the hillbillies who make their shoddy slip-on shoes.

I had to get there like six hours before the wedding to take pictures, in a tuxedo. The interminable photography session was overseen by the bride's mother, Elaine Besser. I didn't like having an old Jewish woman tell me to smile any more in eleventh grade than I had in tenth. In each photo I struck a pose I called "No, I will not 'cheer up.'" Every picture I was in, I ruined.

I had fantasized about wearing a tuxedo to a prom with a lovely blond girl named Kristel. Instead, I donned the formal wear to walk my mother's mother, Lillian "Nana Lil" Wasserman, down the aisle. Nana Lil was a homely woman, her profile reminiscent of my favorite drawing, the hag who also looks like a fair maiden. But my Lord, there be no angle that turned this hag fair. She had a large fleshy nose grown at an elbow-macaroni arc and a chin hell-bent on shaking hands with that schnoz. She was nearly bald but fought back by collecting the surviving white whisps and pinning them under a bulky gray store-bought bun. This hairstyle and Bozo-thick war paint inspired her most fitting nickname, "Madame," based on her resemblance to the lewd hand puppet of the same name.

Lest you feel sympathy for Lil, I'll share with you two things she said to my mother over the years.

While shopping for my mom's wedding dress, Nana said to the saleswoman, "Get her the biggest dress you have."

My mom was humiliated and cried. Seventeen years later, when the marriage ended, Lil struck another knockout blow: "I should've never made you a wedding."

And there I was, in a tuxedo, not enjoying my ascendant youth at a prom but walking a white runner with Medusa in chiffon. Surrounded by country club Jews, people who *owned* tuxedos.

It all felt like penance for dating outside my caste.

I didn't even have the option to alter my consciousness. Maybe I could have offset my misery by sneaking booze or finding a hippie cousin to smoke a bone with. Almost every teen I knew had been an avid drinker or pot smoker since ninth grade. I had never taken even a sip of beer, and never smoked anything. I don't think I had ever lit a match. I may have been the only member of my generation to abide by the "Just Say No," nonsense of the Reagan/Bush years. The United States government spent a trillion dollars to keep *me* off smack.

I had a few reasons. One, I didn't want to disappoint or sadden my dad. I knew it would break his heart if I smoked pot. Two, I knew that I wasn't smart or talented enough for indulgences that could diminish my athletic and academic efforts. But mainly, I think I resisted drugs and alcohol for the same reason I resisted *Miami Vice*, Andrew Dice Clay, and football. I wanted no part of anything that was exalted by the worst of teenaged boy-dom.

Nevertheless, I teared up at all the typical moments. The father-and-daughter dance, the "Sunrise, Sunset" *Fiddler* track where Max and my mom danced. I'm a sucker for the sentimental. It was sad. Max would be moving into his in-laws' home until a school in Newton, Massachusetts, was finished being turned into a condo. I'd seen this before. I still saw my brother Rick occasionally after he got married, but I could never occupy as much of his mind as I once did. Until college, two falls away, it would be just me reading in my room, my mom two rooms away watching prime-time soaps too loud.

I muddled through the school year, showing occasional flashes of brilliance in school and on the basketball court, but, for the most part, I underperformed. Other than English, I got B's and C's, a significant divergence from the National Honor Society–meriting achievements of tenth grade. I couldn't find a girl who I liked who also liked me. I also think liking me had become a disqualifier.

I did have some good friends who shared my passion for stand-up comedy, and after one of them got his driver's license that spring, he took a group of four of us to a club called Nick's Comedy Stop in the theater/red-light district in Boston's Back Bay. It was there that I saw, up close, practitioners of a craft I dreamed of mastering.

We walked up two flights of stairs to this three-hundred-seat, smoke-clouded, low-ceilinged Valhalla of stand-up comedy. There were six-feet-high black-and-white photos of Boston comedy legends I'd heard Rick rave about: Don Gavin, Steve Sweeney, Jay Leno, who I'd seen guest-hosting for Carson. There was an excited din of chatter that amplified my anticipation. I wondered what the comedians were doing. Going over their jokes? Stretching? Warming up their voice? Were they nervous? I was nervous.

The comedians, all men, all in their mid-thirties, all chain-smokers, were confident, loud, effortless, streetwise, and hilarious. The sold-out crowd was rapt during every setup and exploded with laughter on every punch line. The stand-ups talked about having girlfriends and sex, so it also seemed that women found them attractive despite the fact that these were not handsome men. That was something that edified me.

We went back a couple of months later. The first time we went I was exhilarated by the jokes and performance. The second time, I watched the comedians make their way through the audience before they took the stage. How grand they were. How did they summon the courage to take that walk? What a feeling I had when they walked offstage and *right past me*. How did *they* feel?

I was in awe of them but also felt afraid for them. The same feeling I got when I was eleven and watched Andre the Giant stomp toward the ring at the Boston Garden.

I didn't decide to become a comedian that night, but I knew on the ride home that doing anything else would be a miserable compromise.

April 2018

It's April 2018, I have felt good, sometimes great, for almost six months. My mother is gathering clothes to bring to the Goodwill bin. I must give her credit, the closets in the house are no longer bursting with clothes and boxes like when I lived there growing up. She still uses the oven as a cupboard and hoards enough periodicals to stock a newsstand, but for the most part the house is orderly.

She asks if I want to keep my Peabody High School 1988 football jacket. I don't. I never got any joy from it. I can't even remember wearing the navy-blue coat with the capital *P* patch over the heart and "Gul-Man" sewed into the left shoulder. It never fit.

Twelfth

At 6:30 A.M. on June 23, 1988, on my first day of summer vacation, the red phone on the red shag rang. Who died?

I would have let it ring, but if it was for me, I wouldn't want my mother to answer it. I picked up.

"Hello."

"Gul Man! John Jetsyn calling."

"Hey!"

"The Gul Man will meet the Jetsyns at Universe Gym in Salem at seven A.M. and henceforth every weekday until the beginning of triples on August fourteenth."

"Triples" were the three-a-day practices that I had overheard every Peabody football player lament. They may have hated the practices, but they *loved* boasting about them. It was proof of their grit.

I laughed. "I'm sorry, John, I can't play football."

"Gul Man, what do you weigh?"

"Two hundred pounds. But I haven't eaten breakfast yet."

"Gul Man, train with the Jetsyns. By August, the Gul Man will be two hundred and forty pounds and ripped like Arnold."

I laughed . . . and pictured myself wearing rimless sunglasses and a leather jacket without a shirt on, and I laughed again.

"Thanks, man, but I can't. I'm not a football player. . . . You'll be disappointed. . . . I'll be humiliated. . . . Take my word for it, I'm not . . . I appreciate the offer but . . ."

"Just work out with the Jetsyns *today*."

"Just today? I don't know. . . ."

"Just today."

"Just today? At seven?"

"Seven."

I wrote down their phone number (740-4141) and directions to Universe Gym on the back of a letter I had received from the basketball coach at Bowdoin College. I knew on the drive over there that once these guys went out of their way for me, I wouldn't be able to get out of it. I always feel immediately indebted to anyone who helps me. It's a side effect of not feeling you deserve anything. I was pathologically grateful and solicitous of anyone who was generous to me. If you gave me a ride home from school and asked me to, I'd aid and abet your armed robbery.

I thought maybe this time, because the stakes were so high, I would change my pattern. But I knew better. By showing up at Universe Gym, I was signing a contract. At least it would all be over by Thanksgiving.

Five days a week we'd lift weights for a couple of hours in this dingy air-condition-less gym. The Jetsyns wore do-rags over their long wavy manes, no shirts, no shoes, no socks. They were as averse to clothing as they were to pronouns and contractions.

They'd root me on while I lifted weights.

"Two more, Gul Man. One more, Gul Man. Yeah, Gul Man. The Gul Man is getting *YOJ* [their pronunciation of huge]."

Then they'd take me out for breakfast at Red's diner and pump up my ego.

"You guys really think I'll get in a game?" I'd ask.

"*Shit* yeah." In unison. "Get in a game, Gul Man? With the

Jetsyns guiding the Gul Man? Preparing the Gul Man? Sculpting the Gul Man? By the time the season starts, the Gul Man will be starting *both* ways [offense and defense]. The Gul Man's biggest problem this year will be deciding which scholarship to accept and which young enchantress to take to the prom."

Six weeks later, the day before practice started, at the weigh-in, the scale bore out at least one of their predictions: I weighed 240 pounds. Some of their other forecasts would take more time to manifest.

Billy, my friend since fifth grade, went out for the team with me. The night before the first practice I was in a panic. While we watched *All in the Family* in his living room, I confided in him.

"I can't do this. I should've said something weeks ago. I'm going to call 'em and explain to 'em that I'm not up to this and I'm not going to play. I'll thank 'em for their time and that'll be the end of it. If I have to, I'll repay 'em for the breakfasts. They'll understand, right? They're not children. Right?"

Billy gave me good advice.

"Gary, they will *kill* you."

I was in the high school locker room at 7:00 A.M. the next day. I had slept for what felt like eight seconds.

In the foyer to the locker room, where the coach kept his refrigerator, Scotch-taped to the cinder block wall was a photocopied poem. The title was "Don't Quit."

I needed something to quell my anxiety, even if it was just some light reading. Because the title was so bland, I assumed it was some meathead Mike Ditka, Bill Parcells, horseshit.

I expected it to say, "Don't quit, Sally," and "Winners never quit because they're not p------ like you, you little wuss, fairy, baby. Now stop sniveling, take your thumb out of your ass, and hit someone, Mary."

The poetry was mostly prosaic bromides, but I found value in these sentences:

And he learned too late, when the night slipped down,
How close he was to the golden crown.

["Don't Quit" by Edgar A. Guest]

I read it every day before the first of the three-a-day practices and again at the end of the third.

I had met Peabody's head football coach over the summer. At the Jetsyns' insistence I drove to his home in August wearing a tank top they had given me to show off their work. I let him know I was going out for the team and had been training with "the twins" all summer. His name was Edward Nizwantowski, but everyone called him Niz, even his wife. Niz. Rhymes with Biz.

Niz had straight blond hair combed back and a ruddy, thick-skinned complexion. If I only knew the g-dlore surrounding the job of high school football coach, I would have drawn this man.

And if charged with inventing a name for the high school football coach I drew, I'd name him Edward Nizwantowski, but everyone would call him Niz, even his wife. To that drawing I would also add his sunglasses, his voice, his mannerisms, his immaculate black Chevy Suburban, his perfectly manicured emerald-green lawn surrounding his freshly painted home and leafless aboveground pool. I'd give my creation Niz's walk, too. He had a walk that said, *I'm me. I enjoy being me. Before you decide you don't want to be me, you should try being me.*

I talked to him just outside his front door. I was nervous and aware of every word I said, yet I can't really remember any of them. The only thing I remember from our meeting is that he told me to bring a lunch in the morning and keep it in the refrigerator outside the coaches' office so I wouldn't have to go home for lunch in between the first and second practice. I thought that was thoughtful of him, to give me some valuable, time-saving, nutritional advice. Also, letting me use his Frigidaire. The only other thing I remember him saying was, "Now, son, you're not going to change your mind, are you?"

Ha! Of course I will. Dozens of times between now and the first practice, but I'll never tell anyone, not after you just said "You're not going to change your mind" like that.

I resented people who looked like Niz, but I didn't resent Niz. Yes, I was afraid of him, I was afraid of all blond men, but I admired him. I had seen him lead the team to the state championship game when I was in tenth grade. I saw how it uplifted the school and the city—not me, though, I found "school spirit" insane. Nevertheless, he was good at this and *serious* about it. That counted with me. Sports was one of the few areas in life I had found the most fairness, a meritocracy that you couldn't bully, bullshit, or "my uncle owns the theater" your way into.

For the first couple of weeks, we practiced three times a day: eight to ten thirty, lunch, one to three thirty, dinner, then seven to nine under the lights. I was told that the third practice was a violation of the state's athletic rules, which made us all feel like outlaws.

I'd drive home relieved after the third practice, feeling very achy, bruised, and depleted, but proud. I'd fall asleep in seconds. The sleep was wrecked by dreams of practice, so it felt like I was at practice fourteen hours a day. I woke up every day feeling like I had been dropped on the sidewalk from a great height. And my neck hurt, not from any collisions but from the unusual activity of carrying around the helmet on my head.

A couple of weeks into practice Niz gave us a rundown of how the week was going to go and said our first scrimmage of the season would cap the week.

"And Friday night we do *battle*" was how he put it.

Do battle? What the *hell*? I never agreed to "do battle." I'm scared enough without this combat lingo. More unsettling was that the other kids seemed *excited* by the looming battle. They *cheered*. As much as I hated practice, at least the stakes were low.

Let's postpone the battle. Let's just keep practicing, I'm starting to get the hang of it.

Friday night came. A lot of the guys did battle. I watched the battle from a distance, relieved when the battle was whistled complete. Though it was exciting to watch from a safe distance, I told Billy on the ride home that if I could get into a real game at least once that season, it would make the whole thing worth the effort.

The next preseason game was identical for me. No action. I was relieved. It was okay with me if I was too green to take a chance on.

Five days later came the final preseason game. This was the one in which everyone was going to get a chance to play, "to earn some minutes." Halfway through the second quarter I saw the Jetsyns lobbying Niz for me.

"Put Gul Man in."

"Put Gul Man in."

Into my mouthpiece I repeated a different refrain.

"Please say no. Please say no."

I get it, Coach. What kind of message are we sending if a neophyte can go out for football his senior year and just walk on the field three weeks later? No hard feelings.

Then Niz beckoned me.

"Geary!" he yelled.

He put his arm over my shoulder pads and sent me in at right defensive end with these instructions: "Don't let *anyone* get *outside* you."

"Yes, Coach."

I was about to show the Jetsyns what I knew when they proposed this cockamamie idea nine months ago. *I'm not a football player. If they give me any crap for embarrassing them, I'll tell them how I predicted this. Then I'd flee the region.*

First down and ten to go for Beverly in their gorgeous orange-and-black uniforms. Their helmets had a Panther paw print. I'd have been more intimidated if it was a panther growling or even a panther silhouette. But a paw? Puh-leez. I imagined a panther cub having his little paw dipped in orange paint, then his handler gently pressing it on the helmets then sucking on a baby bottle. This calmed me.

Out on the lush green field I took my position on the right end of the defensive line. My "Please say no" mantra was replaced by "Please run left." The first play was a run to the side of the field I wasn't on. The prayer was working. I kept my promise to Niz, no one got outside of me. Second down, six yards to go.

On second down they ran to that other side again, gaining four more yards to make it third and two. I continued my "Please run left" chant.

I didn't realize that in football parlance I had been praying for them to run to my side. It's my *right* but if Beverly runs *left*, they'll be coming straight toward me. G-d must have known what I was praying for, or else He was just as unfamiliar with gridiron geography as me.

Hopefully Beverly will see no reason to test my side, for they are doing well attacking that other side. *Keep it up, Panther Cubs, you're doin' great.*

The ball carrier in the first two plays was a senior in high school named Dana something. He was their star. I can't remember his last name, but I remember it was a sharp, crisp name. No ethnic baggage. It was a name like Parker or Jones or West.

Peters. Dana *Peters.* Swoon. What a great name. That's a leg up from the cradle. When they issue the Dana Peterses of the world their birth certificates, I'll bet it comes with a two-car garage and a problem with high-end Scotch.

Third and two. If I can get through this play, I will exit holding my head high atop my unbroken spine.

The first day of football I had noticed that the bars making up the face mask laid a frame over the world. You saw everything play out on a display of sorts. As you moved forward there was also a Spielbergian zoom that was intensified by the fact that the subjects were racing toward you. It added a surreal detachment like you were watching it all happen to someone else. Were the perspective not so terrifying, it would've been riveting.

The Beverly quarterback hunched over. I was thinking, *Don't let anyone run around you*, but also *I should have let that red telephone ring. But then my mother would have picked up.*

"Who may I ask is speaking? . . . Judson? . . . Justin? Oh, *Jet*-syn? What is this regarding, honey? Gah! Gah! Gary! Pick up the phone, honey, it's Mr. Judson! I'm sorry, honey, Jetsyn! Gah, it's Mr. Jetsyn!"

Right now, I could be at home, on the couch, watching *The Bugs Bunny & Tweety Show*, bowl of cinnamon Life atop my belly. *That's* a Saturday. Though I never liked Tweety. I found his insipid baby voice cloying.

The center snapped the ball to the quarterback, who turned toward my side and started running . . . toward the sideline I had sworn to keep him from. Oh J-sus. He quickly shoveled the ball a yard or two behind him to Dana Peters, the steely-eyed hunk, who caught it in stride.

Peters wore eye black under each eye, that oily schmutz that reduces glare. It was also quite effective at psyching out novice pansies.

Then he sprinted straight *toward* me. What the hell was he doing? Why wasn't he trying to evade me? I was scared shitless.

Then, I felt something familiar in my tummy. That feeling I got when I raised my hand to answer a question no one else knew. And when I had an open shot within eighteen feet of a basketball hoop. And right before I said something funny. It was half glee, half *J-sus Chr-st, Gar, don't blow this.*

I'd only ever tackled anyone in drills where the guys were *required* to run right toward you. This felt like that. Too good to be true. One of us was underestimating the other. I closed in intensely but guardedly, like I was pursuing a loose neighborhood dog. A friendly neighborhood dog whose vaccinations were up to date. Adding drama was that all of this was playing out in that "lens" in the center of my helmet.

I had dreamed of this for weeks, awful dreams. Dreams where I was embarrassed and broke bones. *Maybe this is a dream, I'll pinch myself later*—in the meantime, we were about to collide.

At a trot, he ran in to me. Not *into* me. Rather, he ran in toward me, and then, *to* me. He entered my orbit. I allowed him to get into my chest and abdomen, then I engulfed him with my arms.

I didn't really tackle him as much as I *apprehended* him. I grabbed him around his shoulders with my arms and hands, lifted him off his feet, and wrestled him to the grass. We tumbled to the turf together. Some other kids piled on. I thought this would be much harder.

He lost three yards. Fourth down. I ran to the sideline, where the Jetsyns greeted me with great affection.

"Yeah, Gul Man. F—yeah, Gul Man. What did we tell you?"

Blood surged through my ears and temples. I had at least fifty-five pounds on Dana Peters, yet my rawness, familiarity with the Torah, and total lack of sex appeal made me feel like a David to his Goliath.

Our offense quickly gave the ball back to Beverly, and once again I was on the field.

On third down and six, the quarterback took the snap and galloped toward my side. When it became clear he couldn't find anyone downfield, he started to head back to the middle of the field. The Gul Man gave chase.

Oh dear, sweet, innocent Beverly. Will you ever learn? I stalked him, caught him, then wrapped my arms around him and took him to the grass. My first sack. Again, I ran to the sideline and the Jetsyns showered me with praise.

Then it was halftime. We were losing, and Niz was furious, blasting the team: "You guys are playing with no intensity. I don't care if you make mistakes but make 'em at full speed, with some fiya [fire]. You guys are playing soft, like you don't want to be out there, like you don't want to knock anyone on their ass. You don't wanna be here? You wanna be at the beach with your girlfriends? The only one out there really stickin' anyone is Geary Gulman, a kid who's only been playin' football for a couple-a weeks."

I remember he had always pronounced my name *Geary,* and it irked me, right until that moment. Now I loved being Geary. I looked down at the floor, bit my lip, struggling to stifle a grin. I wanted to stand on a bench and raise my hands over my head in victory.

"Yeah, you *sissies!* Geary Gulman is the only one stickin' people. Why can't you stick people? And stop going to the beach with your girlfriends. You think Geary Gulman goes to the beach with his girlfriends? He goes to the beach with his friend Billy and every now and again with his family, but no girlfriends!"

My uniform pants and my jersey had grass stains on them. My fingernails were dirty, I had bruises all over my arms. I had done battle. Mission accomplished. *I'm a man. Now, let me retire before I screw it up.*

This seemed too good to be real life, like I'd scripted it. I pinched my arm as hard as I could. Not a dream.

I started the second half on the field, at right defensive end. We quickly got the ball back and went on offense. On third down and sixish the Jetsyns, emboldened by the coach's halftime approbation of their Gul Man, pressed Niz to put me in as a receiver.

I was hoping he'd say no, but this time I wasn't praying for it. Niz put his arm around me and told me the play I should run in and deliver to the huddle. It was called the TED pass. TED was an acronym for tight end delay. When the ball was snapped, I'd pretend I was pass blocking, protecting the quarterback. Then I would leave the defender, run five yards toward the center of the field, and look for the ball.

The center snapped the ball on "hit." I blocked for a beat, then took off. The quarterback lobbed the ball high; I reached up on tiptoes and grabbed it over my right shoulder with my right hand and tucked it into my right side above my hip, exactly as the Jetsyns had taught me. Then I ran for my life.

I tried to be hard to tackle, but I was content with not instantly dropping the ball in terror. I gained an extra eight yards before a few teenaged boys grabbed me around each leg and ended my forward progress. I went down, satisfied. I had made it look like I wanted more than just to catch the ball and play dead. Pinch.

The next time we needed a first down, Niz put me in again. It was a different play call, but I essentially did the same thing. Run five yards. Reach up. One-hand grab. Tuck, run, fall, pinch.

I caught another ball, my third, and made two more sacks. One time after I was knocked to the ground by a blocker, the ball carrier came toward me and tried to hurdle me. The fool! While on my belly, I reached up with my right hand, grabbed him by the ankle, and pulled him to the lawn. On the sideline Niz said, "That was the play of a veteran, Geary."

The following Saturday we played against Salem High School; this was an annual opening game with our biggest rival, the Salem Witches. The game would count toward our record. This time, instead of coming off the bench, I would start at right defensive end and play tight end during every passing down. I emerged from this crucible in far better spirits than Peabody native John Proctor had 296 years prior. The Gul Man did the same things in that game as he had in the previous game, only this time there was a crowd, and cheerleaders, and as I'd soon find out, journalists.

The next night, a Sunday, on the wheat-yellow kitchen phone, I got a call from a newspaper reporter from the *Salem Evening News*. He wanted to do a story on me. It ran on Monday. The headline: "Mr. Raw Potential."

Niz was quoted saying, "If you write about him, he won't be our secret weapon anymore."

There were pictures of me in two other local newspapers. In one I was standing over three members of the Salem defensive backfield who clung to my ankles from the ground. The caption called me Gary "Gul-Man" Gulman. The size difference made me look more *Gulliver* than *Gulman*. I had to laugh. Partly out of glee, partly from the eeriness of the Jetsyns' prophecies.

Before a light practice on Monday Niz handed out stickers to recognize valued contributions by individuals and units. Our team was called the Tanners in homage to our once-booming leather industry. Instead of a boot or a suitcase we embraced a bovine theme, so the stickers were a bull's head. He gave everyone on defense a sticker for shutting out the Witches. I got two stickers for my two sacks and three stickers for gaining thirty yards in receiving. These were the first stickers I had collected since third grade. These stickers did not come with the shame they once had because they were stuck on football helmets rather than in an album alongside googly-eyed Big Birds.

That afternoon's practice was particularly satisfying because every Jewish kid on the team, me, Andy Freedman, Howie Morse, and Matt Bloom, were excused early for Rosh Hashanah services. I went with my dad. I had been to the temple since my bar mitzvah, but this felt like my first return to temple as a man, or at least a man's man.

I played well in the next two games, not as dominant but

still contributing. In the fourth game of the season we played in Quincy, Massachusetts, against the Quincy Presidents. We were undefeated and ranked in the top five in the state. It was a balmy Friday October night and a little foggy.

Early in the game we had the ball on Quincy's four-yard line, first and goal to go. I went in to execute the tight end delay. This was a chance for my first touchdown of the season. I'd never scored a touchdown. I was nervous.

The center snapped the ball on "hit, hit." I rose out of my three-point stance and jogged two yards toward the middle of the field, where I crouched into a strong, balanced stance. The quarterback lobbed a spiral toward me. I caught it between the eight and the two on my white road jersey. I tucked it and spun toward the end zone.

Oh my word. The end zone. It's within my reach. I can fall forward and reach the goal line even if they tackle me. Not dynamic, no, but it would count for six points and it's just my first.

The scene was dense. I was surrounded by small Presidents. My feet were around two yards from the end zone.

I should lunge toward the solid white line before they bring me down.

I knew very little about the rules of football, but I did know that your whole body didn't have to cross the line marking the beginning of the end zone. If any part of the ball were to "break the plane" of the end zone it would count for six points. My ascendant football skills were about to intersect with my love of euclidean geometry.

I reached out with the ball and aimed its tip at the plane. I dove toward the white stripe while stretching out my right arm.

Here we go. The Jetsyns are going to be so proud. I'm going to be so proud. My dad will go nuts when I tell him. Rick will be excited; Max might even be impressed. My mother, I'm not sure, I imagine she'll be concerned that this will eventually get me killed.

Spiking the ball is a penalty, so after I score, I will just hand the ball to the ref. Then I'll stand with my arms over my head and let our offense adore me. Then I'll sprint to the sideline and let those people adore me. It's going to be a very fun bus ride home to Peabody.

As I dove forward and aimed the point of the ball at the goal line, some sneaky little President slapped the ball out of my hand. Quincy recovered the fumble in their end zone. I still haven't recovered.

The Jetsyns consoled me saying, "Next time, the Gul Man will not timidly reach for the end zone. Next time, the Gul Man will put a shoulder down and attack the end zone with great fury."

I sure will. Next time.

I never played another down on offense. That night, the meringue foundation my football confidence was built on dissolved in the fog.

We won that game but would lose the next game to end our undefeated streak and knock us out of contention for a state championship. As the season wore on, I wore down. The diminishing sunlight diminished my will. I stumbled, never regaining my footing.

Our last game was on Thanksgiving. The stands were full on both sides. I had always found the cultural phenomenon of the Thanksgiving Day game baffling. It was too late in the fall to make anyone go outside. What kind of people wake up early on their day off to cheer for teenagers? Boo teenagers? Paint their faces for teenagers?

This was the first Thanksgiving Day game I'd ever been to. Preserving the remains of my commitment to this commitment was the only thing that could have gotten me out of bed before noon over Thanksgiving break.

We lost. I made no tackles. My most strenuous exertion that

morning was stifling my joy as I returned to the locker room. I read "Don't Quit" one last time.

> So stick to the fight when you're hardest hit.
> It's when things seem worst,
> You must not quit.

I sat down in front of my locker and wept. Tears of joy.

I indulged in some "To think I did all that . . ." ("My Way" Paul Anka) reverie.

This crying is great, I thought. *Everyone's gonna think I'm all broken up about losing the game. I'm not.*

I wanted to stand on the bench in front of the locker, screaming, "So long, suckiz! I'm freeeeeeeeeeeeee!"

I pulled my jersey and shoulder pads over my head. *Good job, Gar.* I'd qualified for my discharge papers: a letterman jacket with a chenille football sewn on. That coat would attest to my courage and be conferred by the great and powerful Niz in a case of serendipitous assonance.

Finally, this daily referendum on my manhood was over.

A volunteer assistant interrupted my musing to introduce me to a guy in an oversized forest-green windbreaker. He was an assistant football coach at Dartmouth College. He wanted me to visit the school and said they'd love to have me play there next year.

"Play football?" I said.

"Yes."

"Football?"

Laughing. "Yes, what else?"

Imitating Marty Feldman in *Young Frankenstein* I said, "You're puttin' me on."

Did you just watch me? I stink. You can ask any of the kids in this room. I started off with some promise, but a precipitous atrophy commenced five weeks ago.

He said he'd talk to Niz and set something up. Good. Niz would correct this mistake.

"Nice kid, that Geary Gulman. Terrific athlete. Good listener. Witty. Nice head of thick wavy hair. Not a football player. He tried. Leave him be."

The following week in school, I got pulled out of class once a day to meet college football coaches so they could tell me what a bright future I had. In addition to Dartmouth, I received men from Harvard, Holy Cross, UMass, University of New Hampshire, University of Maine, and others within a similar stratum of collegiate football distinction.

It was exciting, meeting with *men*. Football men. Gentile men. Upbeat men. Men with a bounce to their walk and strings on their sunglasses. Men who winked. Unshaven men who chewed tobacco, wore turf shoes, and had wives named Patti.

This outpouring of attention was because, some time over the past couple of months, Niz had mailed video copies of my first game to a bunch of schools.

I was interested. At the very least, it would allow me to get into a decent, maybe even a singular college. Also, if I didn't pan out, it wouldn't be that high of a fall. Nobody would care but me, and I wouldn't care very much.

Just before Christmas break, I got called down to Niz's office. Greeting me that day were a couple of men in maroon windbreakers and matching baseball caps. I recognized the color scheme of their apparel immediately. Boston College.

I'd seen them on TV, most recently at Penn State in front of 93,000 fans.

It was exciting, glamorous, manly. It felt like a validation of the pride I felt occasionally, for weeklong stretches. I was invited to meet their head coach, Jack Bicknell. I sat across from

Coach Bicknell, who I recognized from television, in his office overlooking BC's giant stadium, in front of his desk with a pipe carousel on it. I thought: *I* am *special. I* am *talented. I* am *a man.*

I must be. Right?

At one point, with a smile, Coach Bicknell looked over his desk at me and said, "Well, son, I'm gonna go ahead and offer ya [a scholarship]. This is a one-year renewable contract, but I'll tell you right up front that unless you murder someone, we will renew it every year until you graduate, even if you get injured."

This sounded great, as long as I got injured. I accepted in February. I was going to be a big-time college football player.

How would I pull this off? Maybe I'd outgrow Mister Rogers. Maybe I won't cry every time I hear John Denver's "Sunshine on My Shoulders." Maybe someday I won't run to the TV when I hear the first few xylophone notes of the *Sesame Street* theme. Maybe someday I won't need to sleep with the light on after watching *Ghostbusters* or *Gremlins*. Maybe I'll look back someday and wonder, *Whatever happened to my blanky?*

Oh Gary, what are you doing? Just suppressing every iota of my personality.

This was a dream come true. Just not my dream.

I'd continue to fumble that school year. I fumbled the end of my high school basketball career. With our team down just a few points, late in the second half of game eighteen out of twenty, Coach Bitter benched me with no explanation. I was furious, and with just two games left to complete three varsity seasons with some distinction and goodwill, I stood up from the flaking cobalt-blue wooden bench, pulled my jersey over my head, and flung it over my shoulder. I started eighteen games and didn't even appear in the team picture in the yearbook.

I fumbled academically. In the first two quarters of the year

I failed an honors physics class taught by Mr. DeCourcy, the same outstanding teacher I had for honors chemistry in tenth. He came to me one day and said that he had looked up my tenth-grade chem grades and that I had been a straight-A student. That he had to look it up broke my heart. I had assumed he would have remembered what a diligent, well-behaved student I was. Physics built on ideas and formulas as it progressed, and once I was behind, it felt overwhelming to try to catch up. I was living that nightmare where you're late for a final and you can't remember your locker combination and where your classroom is and what's the point because you haven't studied and why did I leave the house without pants?

I withdrew, receiving no credits, and had to take an Intro to Psychology class to stay on track to graduate in June. In psychology class I learned Maslow's hierarchy of needs but not why I had stopped wearing my seat belt and looking both ways when I crossed the street. I learned about my id, ego, and superego but not why I felt covered by a veil that muted colors and disharmonized music; why food tasted bland or why I was numb to touch; why my sense of smell worked but I was often brought to tears by the scent of baby powder, Hallmark stores, and burning leaves. I learned the term "self-esteem" but not what to do if yours felt like a bicycle tire with a slow leak.

I didn't know anything was wrong. I hadn't been alive long enough or around enough healthy people to understand how broken my worldview was. I would think, *Gary, you feel bad because you haven't done anything great. Do something great and* then *you'll feel good. Until* then, *try to feel good about the struggling and suffering. I lived for* then. "What doesn't kill you makes you stronger." "Sweat is liquid gold." "Winners never quit, and quitters never win."

Sometimes it would motivate me. Sometimes it would make

me resent the winners. Sometimes despair would overtake my resolve and my mental soundtrack would break it down.

Gary, you're what they call a loser. There may be some summers of prosperity but never forget, winter is lurking. The fish will die. The girl will break your heart. You'll miss the layup. You'll flunk the challenging class. You'll gain some ground in the spring and feel hopeful . . .

Then you'll fumble on the goal line.

To close out my high school dating career there was a fumble more comical but no less disconcerting than my football blunder. A football teammate had told me about a girl in our class who liked me and that "if you play your cards right you could get laid."

I got dizzy the same way I had when the paperboy explained the bases to me in sixth grade.

"If you play your cards right."

I don't play cards. I tell people it's because I don't gamble, the truth is: I don't *shuffle*. I can't execute that flamboyant cascading-bridge move expected of all adult dealers. I've tried to learn it. I practiced as a kid. I know what would happen the night of the poker game. I'd practice all day for it and get comfortable but when it was my turn to deal, I'd choke under the scrutiny and the cards would fly hither and/or yon. I knew sex was a long shot, but maybe I'd have a date to the senior prom?

We went out on a few dates, and then one afternoon with her parents at work, we kissed on her living room couch. She wore corduroys and a sweater. I had on Girbaud khakis, and the aquamarine-and-white-striped Ralph Lauren rugby shirt handed down years earlier by handsome Max. I had also donned my cleanest pair of white Fruit of the Loom briefs, just in case.

She was lying on top of me and we were kissing with vigor, and *tongue*. I never believed the French had any right to claim provenance for an act of love that certainly predated government. I'm sure humanoids were using that versatile organ to kiss long before they were using it to speak. Nevertheless, to my Gallic friends, let me say: tres *bien*.

The novel presentation of this most stimulating of smooches, along with the adjacency and contact of our bodies and the infrequency of this type of intimacy . . . well, friends, for Gary Gulman at eighteen years old, that was all it took.

I rushed home, making up an excuse about a ride to work I had promised Billy and then disappeared my favorite jockeys and hand-washed my good pants in the bathroom sink (I didn't know how to use the washer/dryer).

I was so embarrassed, and as ridiculous as this sounds: I was concerned that a single layer of corduroy was not a reliable contraceptive. I know it's crazy, to be as timid as I was but believe my offspring could fight through chinos *and* corduroy, but I just kept circling this thought: *If she got pregnant, I'd have to forego college and get a job to support us. I'd never stop regretting it.* I still had nightmares about a fumble months before. I was so shaken that I avoided the girl in school, and when she confronted me, I told her I just wanted to be friends.

No sex. No date for the prom.

Another thing I regret dropping during my senior year was my comedy practice. Those guys who I went to comedy clubs with junior year had graduated, so I didn't go to a comedy show again until college. Also, I was around a lot of boys who thought laughing was weakness, and as the Jetsyns put it, "The Gul Man's humor is a little highbrow for these brutes. Football locker rooms are a shit, piss, and fart crowd, Gul Man."

I tried to be funny on the field a couple of times. When an assistant coach gave a rambling pep talk about aggressiveness that included "You gotta be ready to run over your own mother to get to the ball," I said from the back of a huddle, "Now that's unreasonable." No laughs. Many glares.

Another gaffe was during a September warm-up drill. We were in the middle of an exercise called karaoke in which we would run sideways and loosen our trunks and groins by crossing and uncrossing our legs while swiveling our hips. It was graceful and looked choreographed, like a bizarre audition for a repertory dance troupe. It always felt like a light moment, so an opportune time to croon: "'I'm gonna wash that man right outta my hair.'"

No laughter, a smattering of "Gulman, you f—in' dork." I don't know how you can call something *karaoke* and be surprised when someone breaks into song.

The one thing I was able to hold on to senior year was my friends. Even though Billy was busy working and dating we were able to maintain a routine where we played a lot of backyard Wiffle ball and ate a lot of take-out roast beef sandwiches. At least once a week we sat side by side on his living room couch rewatching videotapes of *The Naked Gun* and *Young Frankenstein*. He'd regale me with tales of his dating exploits, and we'd laugh and reminisce. Sometimes Lori joined us.

Lori was like a sister, family, but without the guilt and criticism. I was my most comfortable around her. I remember during one of the many troughs of high school, we saw *Planes, Trains and Automobiles* together, just the two of us. At the end of the film, while we laughed our way up the aisle of the Sack Six Cinema (formerly Sack Three) in Danvers, I had a fleeting feeling of peace. It was uplifting to be around someone who knew me at my loneliest, my gawkiest, my socially ineptest. Someone who never cared whether I was athletic or popular. We liked the same type of joke, the same type of people, and we didn't keep kosher. That was enough. It felt like maybe with friends like Lori and Bill I had the ingredients to make for an imperfect but worthwhile life.

That night at the movies was a ray of contentment that momentarily penetrated the smog of my melancholy.

Of course, I couldn't grasp the meaning then. My conclusion at the time was, *Maybe if you're funny in college, you will fill a slot for a group, and they will overlook your nose and your offbeat personality.*

I saw Joanie a few times during senior year. She helped my mom tame the house before all the visits from the college coaches. She had become a grandmother, and she was great at it, even mastering Nintendo's *The Legend of Zelda* to keep up with her grandkids. She also came over to help me pack for college and made no judgments when I put my blanky in with the bag of bedding. I'd miss her the most.

I graduated on a cloudless Sunday in June. My physics F knocked me out of the National Honor Society, so instead of sitting in the group of high achievers with gold tassels, I sat with kids whose last name started with *G*. It was hot out, and I was miserable in that polyester navy gown. Have they figured out yet how to make apparel for graduates that doesn't cause heatstroke? Hasn't the cloak outlived its charm?

There are no pictures from that day. Nobody who came that day, both my parents, my brothers and their wives, thought this was worth commemorating on film. Not one picture. It pleased me that they didn't bring a camera because I wouldn't have wanted to take any pictures. It would also confirm my belief that I had been raised by wolves. No, that's not fair. Wolves would have brought a camera, except of course for the notoriously ill-tempered Mackenzie Valley Wolf.

Who cares, I was never going to look back at that day.

My family wanted to take me to a nice restaurant, TGI Fridays. I didn't feel I deserved it. What are we celebrating, that I got out of bed on 180 days? I didn't make honor roll even one marking period senior year. I should have scored every touchdown and made every tackle. I was bigger and faster than everyone who I faced, and just like in school and basketball, I had frittered away my potential. I had limped over the finish line, and you want me to eat potato skins to celebrate it?

I got in an argument with my mother over whether I'd go out to eat.

"Well, *we're* going, with or without you."

I hadn't been given an ultimatum like this since I was six, when I didn't want to leave the beach.

"Bye, Gah, we're leaving."

This time I didn't come running.

I did make one request.

"Can you make me a tuna sandwich on toast?"

She made it, then headed out the door.

"Last chance . . ."

"I'm not goin'."

"You're so *odd*," she snapped.

On my graduation day, at my request, they left me behind and went to TGI Fridays. I stayed home alone.

New York City, 2023

Sadé and I moved back in together in New York City on May 26, 2018. Eleven months after we locked the steel rollup door of the Queens storage unit, we rolled it back up. Greeting us was a canvas painting of Robert Indiana's iconic LOVE sculpture that Sadé had strategically placed at eye level to greet us when (IF!) we returned together.

By that time, I was touring again with a collection of jokes and anecdotes associated with my illness, hospitalization, and developing recovery. My manager and I had an idea for a documentary/comedy special about my past year and a filmmaker was interested in hearing about it. I was hopeful but realistic: if something came of the meeting, that would be great, but, for the first time I can remember, I wasn't relying on it to bolster my self-worth.

My depresh will have been in remish for six years when this book is published. I feel safe tempting fate because the foundation my recovery is built on is *strong,* and my doctor told me it's highly unlikely for someone to relapse after a recovery so robust. I'm dedicated to my mental health the same way I was to my jump shot, my strength and conditioning, and my joke writing. Because the bottom was so deep, because the recovery was so hard-fought, I am more vigilant about my mental health than I've ever been.

I remember Graduation Day 1989: after my family left for Fridays I drove to Universe Gym to lift weights for two hours. Once more I was embracing the strategy that doomed Gatsby.

The Great Gatsby famously ends with this striking and poetic paragraph:

> *Gatsby believed in the green light, the orgastic future that year by year recedes before us. It eluded us then, but that's no matter— tomorrow we will run faster, stretch out our arms farther. . . . And one fine morning—*
>
> *So we beat on, boats against the current, borne back ceaselessly into the past.*

From childhood through age forty-seven I believed the remedy for my melancholy was to run faster and stretch out my arms farther. I was still chasing the green light at the end of the dock. And there were some fine mornings, but they were fleeting, and it was killing me.

What would I say to that kid from thirty years (almost exactly) in his future?

"GET OUT OF THE BOAT!"

Whenever I am driving behind little kids in a school bus, they wave. I wave back, and they get so excited, and it always makes me happy. It's bittersweet because I know what's in store for some of them. If I could tell the misfits something to make the journey through school and beyond more comfortable, it would be this:

> You will always be the same person the bus driver was so happy to see on the first day of school.

Never stop noticing things like a bus driver opening and closing a door from way past her reach.

Don't worry too much about show-and-tell. Toys and lunch boxes don't make you happy, and some people are fibbing.

Just try to get some laughs.

If you're scared about something you've never done before like reading, or multiplication, or dating? Say this: "I'll figure it out." Then remind yourself of everything you've figured out so far.

It's okay if it takes you a while to make friends; you'll better appreciate what a friend is worth.

As you grow, so will your world, and the bigger your world, the more people will hear your story and say, "I know how you feel."

In the meantime, hold on tight to your Joanies, Billys, Finns, Loris, and Sadés, and never forget this: all the great laughs come from the minds of misfits.

Acknowledgments

To the people who come to my shows and/or watch me on TV and/or read and/or hear this book, thank you for making a weird little boy's big dream come true. You've saved my life so many times.

In 2015 Jacqueline Novak, the ridiculously talented actress, author (*How to Weep in Public*), comedian (*Get on Your Knees*), and podcaster (*Poog*) urged me to write a book and then held my hand while I wrote a book proposal. Thank you, Jacqueline, for being so generous and encouraging and kind.

Thank you to my agent, Suzanne Gluck, for taking me on as a client with just a dusty proposal. Thanks to my agents at APA for so beautifully setting up my book tour.

Thank you to my manager, Brian (a.k.a. Cliff, a.k.a. B-Swift) Stern. As Adam Yauch (MCA RIP) said about Michael Diamond: "You're an idea man, not a yes man." Also at AGI, thanks to Ken Slotnick and former assistants, Chris Burns, Andrew Bloom, and the magnificent Alex Brizel, for doing so much to make our lives easier.

To Mom, Rick and Max, and Dad in heaven, thank you for bringing me everywhere with you when I was a kid and indulging my precocity.

Thank you to all the members of that noblest of professions, teaching. Especially: Mrs. Carol Robbins; Mrs. Judy Burns; Mr. George Hennessey (RIP); Mrs. Jan Anderson; Herr Victor Passacantilli; Mrs. Elaine Marshall; Mr. John Marshall; Mr. David Sinclair; Mr. Earl S. Nason III; Mr. Jack Oleks; Mr. Edward "Niz" Nizwantowski; Mr. Bill Story (RIP); Mr. Bob Danish; Professor John McCarthy (RIP); Professor John McAleer (RIP); Father Richard McGowan, SJ; Kevin Lyons.

To Ellie the kindergarten bus driver, wherever you are, thanks for being so happy to see me every morning.

To my extended family from Peabody and beyond, with special thanks to:

John and Joe "Jetsyn" Taché; the Siegels; the Graffs; the Duponts; the Burnses; the Fitzgeralds; the Marmions; the Hollands; Drew Freedman; Will Marmion; Lori Kremer; Ken Kocher; Darren Kepnes; Bob Kelly; Colin Quinn; DJ Nash; Griffin Nash; Chris Calogero; Jennifer Eldridge; Gail Falkoff; Lori Greenberg; Howard Greenberg; Howard Morse; Tom Ryan; Frank Waterman; Ryan Hamilton; Amy Schumer; Chris Fischer; Brian Gordon; Diane Deminski; Sean Fitzgerald; Jimmy and Kristina Panettiere; Erica Sandstrom; Mike and Minh Power; J. P. Buck; Seth Meyers; Kevin and Laura McGlaughlin; Adam Roeser; Paul D'Angelo; Chris Fleming; Nikki Glaser; Rick Jenkins; Dr. Melissa Remis-Zinavoy; Don Gavin; Jeff Garlin; Pete Holmes; Aunt Jan McNutt; Kevin Lomasney; Jack Lomasney; Chris Elliott; Adam Resnick; Zach Bornstein; Dan Smith; Ira Glass; Elna Baker; Maria Bamford; Bad Robot's JJ and Hannah; Patton Oswalt; John Moe; Steven Himmelfarb; Phil Murphy; Mike Murphy; Nina Rosenstein; Aaron Spina; Stuart, Sam, Isaac, and Danya Briefer; Elon Gold; Mark "Flanny" Flanagan; Julia Whitehead and the Kurt Vonnegut Museum; Chris Bowers; Brian Kiley; Alonzo Bodden; Liz and Lew Schneider; Conan

O'Brien; the Madoff-Nicholases; Livie and Judy Hollander; Max Boehme; Keith Stubbs; Harry Hildebrand; Shatona Sanders; Shaianne Allen; Tiahna Spencer; Andy Frasco; Cousin Emily Abedon; Josh Church; Cookie Washington; Steve Macone; Neilsy, Pammy, and Risa (RIP).

Jon Gulman, thanks for that kind breakfast talk during the depresh.

To Dr. Tom McGuinness, Dr. Richard Friedman, and Alan Lefkowitz, and all the psych ward nurses and doctors: thanks for fixing my brain.

Chris and Steve Mazzilli, thanks for being there for me so many times.

Adrian Nicole Leblanc and Dr. Stuart Lewis, thanks for your love and for sharing Valentine's Day with us, especially the one where they frisked you.

Todd Glass, you're a great friend and an inspiration and the funniest person I know.

Judd Apatow, thanks for your wisdom and for encouraging me to write a book and then touting it, allowing me to further monetize my mental illness.

Mike Bonfiglio, what a miracle to find you at forty-seven! Thank you for reading every draft of this book and giving enthusiastic and honest feedback and encouragement. Sorry for not including your blurb, but I was told "He doesn't sell books."

Amy, Anna, Brian, and Sammy Koppelman, thanks for taking in this stray and nourishing me with food and love.

"Joans" Noyes, thank you for making my childhood delightful for eight hours every ten days.

Jason Hurwitz, you're the best best friend in the world. Thanks for all the unconditional love, the Schmys, and the punch lines to the thirty-eight-year setups.

At Flatiron, thank you to Bob Miller, Megan Lynch, and

Sam Zukergood. Will Schwalbe, my editor, thank you for your guidance, encouragement, patience, instruction, generosity, wisdom, and expertise. You gave me a master's course in memoir, a million times thank you.

And Sadé, you never gave up on us. If I knew as a boy I'd wind up with you as my wife, I'd have had no worries. As Kurt Vonnegut's uncle said: "If this isn't nice, I don't know what is."

About the Author

Gary Gulman is one of the most popular touring comics, selling out theaters nationwide including Carnegie Hall. He has been a guest on every major late-night comedy program. Gulman's four comedy specials include HBO's *The Great Depresh*, a highly acclaimed look at mental illness. In 2019 he appeared in the international blockbuster *Joker*. He has a recurring role on the Hulu comedy series *Life & Beth*. A product of Boston, Gulman was previously a scholarship college football player, an accountant, and a high school teacher. *Misfit* is his first book.

garygulman.com